Planning by Consent

Planning, History and the Environment Series

Editor:
Professor Dennis Hardy, Middlesex University, UK

Editorial Board:
Professor Arturo Almandoz, Universidad Simón Bolivar, Caracas, Venezuela
Professor Nezar AlSayyad, University of California, Berkeley, USA
Professor Eugenie L. Birch, University of Pennsylvania, Philadelphia, USA
Professor Robert Bruegmann, University of Illinois at Chicago, USA
Professor Jeffrey W. Cody, Chinese University of Hong Kong, Hong Kong
Professor Robert Freestone, University of New South Wales, Sydney, Australia
Professor David Gordon, Queen's University, Kingston, Ontario, Canada
Professor Sir Peter Hall, University College London, UK
Dr Peter Larkham, University of Central England, Birmingham, UK
Professor Anthony Sutcliffe, Nottingham University, UK

Technical Editor
Ann Rudkin, Alexandrine Press, Oxford, UK

Published titles

The Rise of Modern Urban Planning, 1800–1914 edited by Anthony Sutcliffe

Shaping an Urban World: Planning in the twentieth century edited by Gordon E. Cherry

Planning for Conservation: An international perspective edited by Roger Kain

Metropolis 1980–1940 edited by Anthony Sutcliffe

Arcadia for All: The legacy of a makeshift landscape by Dennis Hardy and Colin Ward

Planning and Urban Growth in Southern Europe edited by Martin Ward

Thomas Adams and the Modern Planning Movement: Britain, Canada and the United States by Michael Simpson

Holford: A study in architecture, planning and civic design by Gordon E. Cherry and Leith Penny

Goodnight Campers! The history of the British holiday camp by Colin Ward and Dennis Hardy

Model Housing: From the Great Exhibition to the Festival of Britain by S. Martin Gaskell

Two Centuries of American Planning edited by Daniel Schaffer

Planning and Urban Growth in the Nordic Countries edited by Thomas Hall

From Garden Cities to New Towns: Campaigning for town and country planning, 1899–1946 by Dennis Hardy

From New Towns to Green Politics: Campaigning for town and country planning 1946–1990 by Dennis Hardy

The Garden City: Past, present and future edited by Stephen V. Ward

The Place of Home: English domestic environments by Alison Ravetz with Richard Turkington

Prefabs: A history of the UK temporary housing programme by Brenda Vale

Planning the Great Metropolis: The 1929 Regional Plan of New York and Its Environs by David A. Johnson

Rural Change and Planning: England and Wales in the twentieth century by Gordon E. Cherry and Alan Rogers

Of Planting and Planning: The making of British colonial cities by Robert Home

Planning Europe's Capital Cities: Aspects of nineteenth-century urban development by Thomas Hall

Politics and Preservation: A policy history of the built heritage, 1882–1996 by John Delafons

Selling Places: The marketing and promotion of towns and cities, 1850–2000 by Stephen V. Ward

Changing Suburbs: Foundation, form and function edited by Richard Harris and Peter Larkham

The Australian Metropolis: A planning history edited by Stephen Hamnett and Robert Freestone

Utopian England: Community experiments 1900–1945 by Dennis Hardy

Urban Planning in a Changing World: The twentieth experience edited by Robert Freestone

Twentieth-Century Suburbs: A morphological approach by J.W.R. Whitehand and C.M.H. Carr

Council Housing and Culture: The history of a social experiment by Alison Ravetz

Title published in 2002

Planning Latin America's Capital Cities, 1850–1950 edited by Arturo Almandoz

Titles published in 2003

Exporting American Architecture, 1870–2000 by Jeffrey W. Cody

Planning by Consent: the Origins and Nature of British Development Control by Philip Booth

Planning by Consent

the Origins and Nature of British Developmental Control

Philip Booth

Routledge
Taylor & Francis Group

LONDON AND NEW YORK

First published 2003 by Routledge,
11 New Fetter Lane,
London EC4P 4EE

Simultaneously published in the USA and Canada
by Routledge
29 West 35th Street, New York, NY 10001

Routledge is an imprint of the Taylor & Francis Group

Typeset in Palatino and Humanist by PNR Design, Didcot
Printed and bound in Great Britain by TJ International Ltd, Padstow, Cornwall

This book was commissioned and edited by Alexandrine Press, Oxford

British Library Cataloguing in Publication Data

A catalogue record for this book is available from the British Library

Library of Congress Cataloging in Publication Data

Booth, Philip, 1946–
    Planning by consent : the origins and nature of British development
control / Philip Booth.
        p. cm. — (Planning, history, and the environment series)
Includes bibliographical references and index.
    ISBN 0–419–24410–7 (alk. paper)
    1. City planning—Great Britain. 2. Regional planning—Great Britain.
3. City planning and redevelopment law—Great Britain. 4. Land use—
Law and legislation—Great Britain. I. Title. II. Series.
    HT169.G7 B583 2003
    307.1'216'0941—dc21

                                                      2002154395

Contents

Preface

The genesis of this book lies in the work on Britain in my earlier book, *Controlling Development*, which presented a comparison of the French and British planning systems. There, in order to be able to explain the essential characteristics of British development control I thought it was necessary to devote some space to the evolution of the system. This enabled me to set the British system against the very different evolution of the French approach to the control of urban development; the ultimate purpose was to contrast the treatment of the fundamental problems of uncertainty and discretionary power. Although at the time I was unaware of Stephen Crow's article *Development Control: the Child that Grew up in the Cold* (Crow, 1996), I became convinced that there was a great deal more to be said about history of the development control system in Britain that would offer more insight into the present disarray in the system and – perhaps – help identify ways forward.

The past 25 years has not been short of histories of the planning system in this country and indeed elsewhere in Europe. From Ashworth's (1954) pioneering study in the 1950s, the task of explaining the way in which planning had developed was taken up by the late Gordon Cherry and continued by Anthony Sutcliffe, Stephen Ward and others. In this respect, the setting up of the International Planning History Society under Cherry's and Sutcliffe's leadership was formative in making planning history a distinct sphere of study within the more general field of urban history. Most of this work has, however, focused on plans and policies, and if the implementation of those plans and policies through mechanisms for approving projects has not gone entirely unremarked, it has seldom taken pride of place. I believed there was a case for exploring the history of British planning through the control of development, not the preparation of plans.

The very fact that I could consider – as indeed does the profession as a whole – that the development control system is a distinct entity with a history to be explored already says a good deal about the nature of development control in Britain. Nowhere else would the process of determining applications for development projects be considered a 'system' in quite this way. Yet that perception sits oddly alongside Crow's portrayal of development control as an expedient device grafted onto a system of plans. This suggested that the expedient device was drawing upon an older tradition of decision-making. There was clearly a case for looking at the antecedents of development control under the planning acts.

Indeed, part of my initial thesis was that explanations for the current state of things in development control were to be found as much in distant as in recent history. Of the many peculiarities of urban development in Britain is the fact that for two centuries control was privatized under the leasehold system which, at its best, was highly effective. On the basis of work done years ago on seventeenth century development in London, I came to the view that leasehold control was a formative influence on building bylaws under the public health Acts in the nineteenth century – themselves very much a proto-planning control – and in turn on the planning system itself from 1909. What I had not anticipated at the outset was that the Middle Ages would also offer important explanations of the characteristics of planning control in the twentieth century. The way in which the law of property had developed in the feudal era seems to have been at the heart of conceptualizations implicit in current planning legislation.

This book does, therefore, offer a long – not a short – view of the way in which development control has evolved in this country. It presents a chronological account of control from the thirteenth century onwards and uses case study material to illuminate generalities of historical description. It identifies key periods in the evolution and unifies the narrative by reference to a number of recurrent themes. It concludes prospectively by trying to identify the questions to be addressed if planning control is to continue to serve a useful function. In taking so long a view the book almost inevitably deals with at least aspects of development control in a rather more cursory fashion than perhaps it should. But my essential purpose here was to find explanations for the idiosyncratic nature of British development control at the beginning of the twenty-first century in the belief that historical explanations were at least as important as those derived from current practice. It is also my hope that insight offered by historical explanation may serve to stimulate the much needed intellectual debate about what development control needs to be in the future.

In unravelling this history, I have been given assistance from various quarters. Anthony Sutcliffe's, Ann Rudkin's, John Punter's and John Delafons's initial enthusiasm for the project encouraged me to think it was worth doing. I was lucky enough to receive a grant from the British Academy under their Small Personal Research Grants Scheme that enabled me to undertake the necessary fieldwork and, above all, to spend a month in London to research the archives held at the Public Record Office, mainly for Chapters 3, 4 and 5. I was given sabbatical leave for the Spring Semester 1999 during which I completed a great deal of both the research and the writing, and I am grateful to my colleagues for covering some of my duties during that period. Lyn Davies lent me material from his work for the

Expenditure Committee review of development control in the 1970s and Robert Marshall some useful texts from the 1950s. I also received a good deal of assistance from staff at Sheffield City Archives and the Sheffield Local Studies Library and from the Archivist at King's College, Cambridge. At Hart District Council and Thurrock Borough Council, members of the planning departments looked out relevant case files and found me space to study them on their premises at my leisure. SPISE kindly invited me to attend the tenth anniversary of the burning of an effigy of Nicholas Ridley at a low point in the history of the proposal for Bramshill Plantation. Finally, Ian Burgess, Christine Goacher, Melanie Holdsworth and Dale Shaw typed the manuscript in the odd moments between a host of other duties and Christine administered the British Academy grant. To all of these go my thanks.

Philip Booth
Sheffield
January 2003

ACKNOWLEDGEMENTS

Figure 2.3 appears by courtesy of the St Louis, Missouri, Museum of Art. Figure 2.5 appears by kind permission of the Head of Leisure Services at Sheffield City Council. Figures 3.2, 3.3 and 3.6 appear by kind permission of the Provost and Fellows of King's College, Cambridge. Figures 3.1 and 3.4 appear with the consent of the Public Record Office. Figure 6.3 is reproduced by courtesy of the *Reading Evening Post*.

Chapter One

The Glory of the British Planning System

The heart of British planning is the permitting system, strengthened by the government ownership of the development potential of land. This is one of the glories of the British system, but it also generates deep discontent – because the flexibility the planners prize in the system is viewed by the developers as too prone to arbitrary decision making and surprise rulings on proposed projects.

(Haar, 1984, p. 204)

To describe a process as banal as the filling out of an application form or the issuing a permit as a *glory* may seem far-fetched. For, at its most basic, development control is no more than that: the stuff of countless different administrative procedures designed to regulate aspects of our daily lives. But if the process is banal, its content need not necessarily be so: this routine bureaucratic procedure brings the public at large into contact with the nature of land-use change with a directness that almost nothing else achieves. It does so through the resolutely trivial, as in the proposal to build a back extension, as much as through the major project that may significantly alter a neighbourhood, a town or a region.

As a process, it does not get a good press. Planners are all too ready to permit some outrage to common decency in the environment; they take an inordinate time to make up their minds; their decisions are arbitrary, wilful or, worse, motivated by political dogma or financial gain. The process is seen as negative and reactive, bureaucratic and time wasting. It is overwhelmingly concerned with trivia. The planners themselves see it as a thankless task and one which they are happy to escape in favour of the seemingly more glamorous and intellectually challenging work of policy-making and evaluation. Neither the public nor the developers nor the planning profession itself appear to like development control very much even if no one has quite dared to suggest its outright abolition. We are emphatically not used to seeing it described as a 'glory'.

Why then does Haar, an American lawyer, view British development control in such a favourable light? At the simplest level, the system of applying for a permit each time a land-use change is proposed is in no way unique to Britain. During the twentieth century all the developed countries of the world found comparable ways of controlling development, and all were founded on some general idea of a public good that would be served by such systems of control. In fact closer examination suggests that the superficial similarities – the making of applications, the issuing of permits – conceal significant differences of approach and underlying rationale. These differences are both of process and of content. Systems for controlling the urban environment do not necessarily share the same objectives. The process by which applications are dealt with and the way in which decisions are taken vary very markedly and reveal wide divergences in understanding about the nature of authority and accountability. Exploration of systems of control in these terms begins to reveal a British system which is clearly distinctive when compared with those in other parts of Europe or indeed in the rest of the world.

The essentials of the system are simply described. The Town and Country Planning Act passed in 1947, and not fundamentally altered since, sets out a definition of development that would cover all forms of land-use change. Anyone carrying out development, so defined, would need a valid planning permission before doing so. Finally, local authorities were given the task of determining planning applications. In carrying out their task, they were obliged to consider planning policy as set out in the development plans, which they were also required to prepare, as well as other circumstances that might bear upon the acceptability of the proposal. Not all development would require local authority consent. The legislation also allowed for consent to be given by order of the Minister responsible for planning. But the major interest in the system has always lain in the way in which local authorities have used their powers.

Put in these terms, the process hardly appears very remarkable. The oddness of the system by comparison with forms of control in other parts of the world only becomes fully apparent if we study the detailed wording of the Act itself. Two key sections of the current legislation have remained little changed from those of the 1947 Act. The first, Section 55, contains the definition of development. Development is defined not only as physical change, expressed in the phrase 'building, engineering, mining or other operations in, on, over or under land' but also 'any material change of use of buildings or other land'. Several features of the wording are noteworthy: the apparent quaintness of the term 'operations'; the reference to engineering and mining as well as to building; the inclusion of 'material change of use' without any further elaboration of what distinguishes a material change from any other. The all-embracing nature of the control is clear, as is the ability to conceive of an abstract quality – land use – as a concrete reality. No other planning system proposes a definition of this kind as a preliminary to control and no definition is as wide-ranging as that in British legislation.

Section 70, which sets out the criteria for determining applications for planning permission, is the second key part of the Act. Local authorities are required 'to have regard to the development plan, insofar as it is material to the application, and to any other material considerations'. Though the originality of this wording has often been remarked upon, its effects are nevertheless worth rehearsing. First, it deliberately weakens the connection between the plan and the decision on a particular project. The Act specifically recognizes that a plan may not be pertinent to the decision to be taken. Equally, other factors may be as, or more, significant than the plan in determining the outcome of a planning application. No other planning system creates quite this kind of partial divorce between policy and control; most others derive their legitimacy from a pre-ordained set of regulations or some kind of zoning that spells out what is permissible to the developer and on what grounds the controlling authority must base its decision.

Secondly, the wording of Section 70 explicitly confers discretionary power on the local authority. It is for the authority to decide whether the plan is in fact material to the decision, and what other material considerations need to be taken into account. No other system offers quite this kind of discretionary freedom.

The wording of the Act was of course an expression of the preoccupations of politicians and administrators during the 1940s. Pressure had developed for a system that would be universal in its application. It had to include all forms of development and it had to apply regardless of the state of planning policy. The desire for universal control was summed up in the idea that legislation should nationalize the rights to future development of land. Although the legitimacy of State involvement in the control of development is shared by any system in which private activity is subject to public control, the particular formulation of the concept is idiosyncratically British. The British legal profession has always made great play with the right of the owner to 'enjoy' his or her property. We can note the way in which the 1947 Act divided the current 'enjoyment' of land (in other words, land in its current state) from its future development and so gave concrete existence to another essentially abstract concept.

Pressure had also built up for a system that would be flexible, hence the desire to loosen the absolute link between the plan and the development control decision. It was part of a pragmatic administrative tradition that rejected minutely prescribed limits in favour of a case-by-case approach that favoured precedent and procedural rules over substantive regulation. Finally, the wording confirms the role of local authorities in the control process. In general terms, British development control is not so very different from systems elsewhere. But the implication of Section 70 is that local authorities are not merely acting as agents of the State in controlling development, they are being given the freedom to determine their own destiny. The activity is not purely administrative, it becomes explicitly political. And, by further implication, the Act gives them freedom to negotiate the best solution to a given problem of development.

Underlying these general implications of the legislation are two longstanding and interlinked traditions. The first is that of common law with its heavy reliance on judge-made law. Other systems of law also use the judgements of the courts to inform the intentions of the legislation, but in common law judgements on individual cases have a central role (Waldron, 1990). Moreover statute law is framed in such a way that often allows judges to interpret general legislative intentions in the light of circumstance. Case law has remained highly significant for the understanding of the way in which the law may be used. The apparently unfettered freedoms contained in sections of the Town and Country Planning Act have in practice been subject to judicial scrutiny and the limits to discretionary behaviour have been set. But the way in which judges have behaved, in referring to legal precedent, in balancing competing interests and in applying generalized tests to particular cases, has come to inform administrative practice, too.

The other tradition which underlies the discretionary powers of the Act is that of procedural fairness. The power to decide is legitimated, not by reference to regulation carrying the force of law, but by the way in which the decision is taken. It implies a trust in the behaviour of those appointed or elected to take decisions. It also requires a judicial scrutiny of the way in which decisions are taken. Significant among the legal tests that judges will apply to administrative behaviour is whether the decision-maker acted *ultra vires* – beyond the powers accorded by law. Yet within those powers, those who take decisions must also show that they did so fairly and reasonably.

Other Systems of Control

In all of this the contrast with planning systems in most other parts of Europe is striking. The contrast is most marked when Britain is compared with those countries that form part of the Napoleonic inheritance. In France, for example, the very different terms in which planning is discussed gives a clue to the divergence of Britain and its European neighbours. In Britain, much of the discussion about planning in general and development control in particular has centred on the need for flexibility, and on how that flexibility might be achieved. In France on the other hand, the discourse has focused on the terms *sécurité* and *certitude* – (legal) security and certainty – as tests of good planning. Where in Britain we have been content with a pragmatic vagueness in our planning legislation, the French look for clarity and precision.

The reasons for this emphasis on precision and definition are bound up with the way in which the legal system has been used to define rights and duties. Property rights in France could not in theory or in practice be divided in the way that they were in Britain after the 1947 Act. Future use and development of land were as much part of the right to property protected by the constitution as was current enjoyment. This did not mean the State had no right to interfere in property rights, however. French lawyers could conceptualize the power of the State in terms of the Roman law principle of *imperium*, the overarching control by the State of its citizens, within which *dominium*, the right to private property, had to be couched (Gaudemet, 1995). The effect of conceptualizing property in this way was to place great emphasis on the need to identify precisely what the rights guaranteed by the constitution actually amounted to. Codified law could spell out in immense detail what the rights and duties of citizens and government alike would be. The citizen would know what he or she was expected to do, and what might be expected of the administration. In theory, nothing would be left to chance.

This insistence on certainty and on rights and obligations finds a clear expression in the French planning system. Like most French administrative law, the legislation for town planning is codified but the code, quite apart from setting out processes and procedures, also covers matters of what in Britain would be called policy and not law. Indeed, the distinction between law and policy which is highly significant in Britain is largely absent in France. The detailed land-use plans created under the town planning code are not thought of as a general statement of land-use policy in the way that their British counterparts would be. *Plans d'occupation des sols* (local land-use plans)[1] create zones for every part of the territory they cover, and for every zone there are precise instructions expressed as regulations carrying the force of law. These regulations are written under 15 headings prescribed by the code itself. In this way, the plan becomes a substitute for the code. It identifies precisely how property owners may exercise their rights to *dominium* and what the grounds for decision-making by public authorities will be. As with codified law in general, in theory nothing is left to chance and rights and obligations are clearly specified (see Booth, 1996).

France, no less than Britain, has a system of permits, the *permis de construire,* authorizing specific projects. But although the making and determination of applications bears a superficial resemblance to British practice, the legitimacy of the process has very different foundations. The working of the code gives some indication of this difference. Where the part of the British Town and Country Planning Act dealing with development control begins with the all-embracing definition of development, in the French code the starting point is an obligation:

Whosoever desires to undertake or establish a construction, whether for residential purposes or not and whether or not on foundations, must first obtain a permission to build . . . (Article L.421-1)

Quite apart from the duty that is imposed by this article of the code, we may note that the main thrust of the requirement is in relation to physical development not, as in the British case, to land use.

Where a *plan d'occupation des sols* is in force, a decision must be taken by reference to the plan, and in theory at least, the person making an application will have a very good idea about the acceptability of proposal before the permission is granted. Indeed, a proposal which conforms in every detail to the plan and its regulations must be approved. In this light, the way in which the application is dealt with is by a process distinctly different from that in Britain. The primary concern is to know whether the project is legal in that it conforms to the regulations in force, not whether it is appropriate for the place and the circumstance. Unlike the partial divorce of plan and development control decision in Britain, the relationship in the French case is absolute and binding. As if to emphasize the point, until 1983 decisions were taken by the local mayor acting not in a political capacity as an elected representative but as an agent of the State. Although that is no longer true for much of the country, the mayor's duty is everywhere to uphold the law as much as to further the interests of his or her commune.

Just as with the insistence on flexibility in the British system, the creation of a system that places a premium on certainty has created as many problems as it has solved. The practice of development control in France displays a great deal of discretionary behaviour and political decision-making. Fixed regulations turn out to be considerably less fixed that they at first appear. But there is a significant difference between the discretion offered by British legislation and the discretionary behaviour of French officials. In Britain, in general, discretionary freedom is formally conferred on local authorities by the wording of the Act. In France, the possibilities for exercising discretion are often not explicit. Where there is explicit choice offered by the law, it is confined to the way in which a particular regulation in the code or in the plan is applied. Cumulatively, this may amount to very considerable discretionary leverage on the development proposal to be determined. That in turn has given rise to renewed call for clarity and certainty within the system.

So the legitimacy of the French system of development control depends upon a tradition of law quite unlike that of the common law system of Britain. But though the characteristics of British development control are in part due to the nature of common law, it does not follow that other countries whose legal systems depend on common law have adopted the same approach to planning as Britain. In the United States, for example, the existence of a written constitution and the emphasis placed on the individual's right to own property led some to question whether the State had any right to intervene in the development process at all. For Americans, the key concept is that of the 'taking' (that is an unlawful denial of the property owner's rights to his or her land) and the question that judges are at pains to determine is whether any form of State action amounts to an unwarranted interference with the rights and liberties of the individual guaranteed by the constitution.

That question was successfully resolved for zoning ordinances in the 1920s by the *Ambler Realty v. The Village of Euclid* case following which zoning became an acceptable part of American way of life. The justification of the Euclid case was that zoning could be equated with other forms of 'police' powers which the State legitimately exercised to ensure the rights of everyone. At the time, Euclid was seen as a famous victory for planning, but as Haar (1989) has pointed out, the reason that zoning so quickly established itself in the United States was because developers saw a considerable advantage in a system that introduced a degree of order into an otherwise chaotic land market. And of course for residents too zoning had its distinct attractions. Put grandly, it was the means by which their constitutional rights as owners and occupiers could be guaranteed. In more cynical terms, zoning would become the means by which the physical and social character, and particularly the latter, could be protected from unwarranted invasion.

In theory, zoning ordinances were the detailed expression of policy set out in land-use plans. In practice, zoning ordinances appear to have developed a life of their own existing as often as not in isolation as the only planning document that applies in many urban areas. Even more than French *plans d'occupation des sols*, zoning ordinances all too often appear to freeze a *status quo*, and offer nothing in terms of a prospective vision. Zoning has also fuelled American litigiousness.

The narrow constraints of zoning ordinances, far from deterring unwanted development, seem merely to have encouraged the legal ingenuity of developers. Overcoming these constraints has led to battles to be fought out in court, the 'zoning game' eloquently evoked by Babcock (1966) and Babcock and Siemon (1990). In this context, the flexibility of the British development control system begins to look enviably attractive, not least because it only rarely involves the courts.

The rigidities of American zoning have elicited ingenuity in the planning profession, too. Cullingworth (1993) and Wakeford (1990) have noted the various devices that some American zoning ordinances have used to create flexibility and choice and to allow for negotiated development. The critical reaction to these devices is not all negative. Wakeford wondered whether the 'special interest' zoning used in San Francisco, which allowed the city authorities to protect areas of a particular mixed-use character from market forces, might not be useful in Britain. Far more doubtful has been the technique of 'incentive zoning', first introduced in the New York zoning ordinance of 1961. The zoning allowed, but did not require, the provision of a plaza in exchange for an increase in floor area ratio, as a means of encouraging developers to provide public open space. The policy worked to the extent that downtown New York has acquired a large number of such plazas and the device has been used to secure other ends in cities across the United States. Yet as Cullingworth (1993) points out, the utility of providing downtown Manhattan with so many plazas is far from clear and the cost of doing so has been great. Above all, the benefit is not tied to a coherent planning policy. In the search for flexibility, zoning had moved away from a simple declaration of development rights and constraints.

The conclusions that we can draw from such comparisons are not that one system of development control is necessarily better than any other. More to the point is the fact that all systems of planning face inherent problems: how to contain future uncertainty; how to allow for appropriate response to the unforeseen circumstance; how to ensure that discretionary behaviour is exercised responsibly. The response to such problems is of course the product of the political, administrative and legal culture of particular countries. The unwanted effects of these diverse responses are equally diverse. Emphasize certainty as the key attribute of a system of control and you find that the subterfuges used to surmount constraints threatens the very legitimacy of the system. Elevate flexibility as the touchstone of the effective planning system and you may find yourself enmeshed in impenetrable ambiguities which do not serve anyone very well (for a further discussion of these ideas see Booth, 1996). But all systems have struggled with problems that have been central to debates in Britain. What should the connection be between the decision taken on individual projects and longerterm policy contained in plans? How do you ensure that policy is respected in the determination of planning applications? What do you do if policy no longer seems relevant to the decision to be taken? These are questions that have to be addressed if development control in whatever guise is to work at all.

The Objects of Control

The discussion so far has focused on development control as a process, but rather begs the question of what we want to control development for. What becomes clear from both the origins and the current practice of development control in Britain, as well as from the systems of control in other countries, is the diversity of objectives. Such objectives are both explicit and implicit, to be teased out of statements of intent and arguments that are used to justify decisions taken. The very earliest forms of control over urban development appear to have been generated, not by some vision of a public interest distinct from the private rights of individuals, but specifically as a means of protecting and defining the rights of individuals to be defended from their neighbours' activities. The doctrine of nuisance, conceived first of all in terms of protection from physical inconvenience caused by faulty gutters or privies or defective party walls, allowed the legal system to intervene in neighbour disputes and set out rules by which individual behaviour might be measured and property rights defended. What at first applied to the fabric of cities came in time to apply to the activities which took place on land and in buildings. Well before the beginnings of modern town planning in the twentieth century, a whole series of uses were identified as nuisances and a landowner or a lessee could hope for protection from the likes of tallow chandlers and iron founders.

The way in which apparently private interests should nevertheless have come to be resolved in a public arena gives rise to two further considerations. One is the implied belief that private disputes did in fact impinge on public good order. The other is the evident assumption that the State had a role in creating and defending private property rights. The distinction that successive governments have tried to maintain since the passing of the 1947 Town and Country Planning Act between matters of public interest, which the Act was designed to address, and private disputes, which were outside remit, looks flawed in relation to the historical origins of control.

Questions of a public interest which lay over and beyond the interest of private property owners do also inform early attempts to control urban form, however. Fear of fire and later the desire to control development in the interests of public health have an important pedigree in the origins of the modern development control system. Such control meant limitations had to be imposed on building materials and building form, and also more generally on layout and spacing. Layout was also controlled to protect another acknowledged public interest, the maintenance of the King's Highway and of back lanes and alleys. The way in which such control was exercised was by the imposition of building lines, so that no individual property encroached on the right of free passage.

From the relatively limited concern with fire, health and highways the scope widened in the twentieth century to cover a whole series of functional criteria. To the desire to protect a building line, never lost, have been added other physical criteria for the layout of roads. To spacing of buildings has been added the concern to ensure adequate private and public open space and sufficient privacy. The underlying intention has been that the environment should *work* for its users, even if the ways in which functionality is expressed imply professional and public values that are not always fully articulated.

A second area of public interest which became the object of control from the seventeenth century onwards is the control of appearance. Aesthetic control has been highly contentious from the very beginning and has tended to pit conceptions of public interest against a belief in individual liberty of action. Quite what public interest is expressed through aesthetic control is open to debate. It is clearly not a case of art for art's sake, even if a concern for visual delight is also present in the rationale for controlling design. Images of public order and of the good life all appear to be contained in this rationale. Appearance may also signify social status and in this way control of design may become a proxy for control of the social, as well as means of securing the aesthetic, character of an area. Yet appearance clearly matters deeply to people and fights over aesthetic control today are themselves probably witness to the fact.

Control over the social character has always been a major concern. In Britain, government policy has insisted that planning has to do with use and development of land and that the character of the user is irrelevant to the decisions to be taken. Yet there is reason to doubt that existing residents and owners have constrained their thinking in this way. Fears that new development would not merely spoil the view but bring the wrong sort of people seem to have been prevalent, not only in class-ridden Britain but elsewhere, too. In the United States, the problem of 'exclusionary zoning', ordinances specifically designed to keep out undesirables, has remained a topic of debate. The trouble is that control intended to deal with a land use and the physical environment can all too easily be manipulated to protect social character. It is usually quite possible to find a justification that sits squarely within the framework of planning law for attempts to influence the kind of people who move into an area.

Finally, in Britain, control over land use as opposed to physical development has come to be seen as having a public, not simply a private, dimension. What began by being defined as a nuisance that impinged on a person's private rights came to be interpreted as having a generalized effect. The right to be protected from the harmful effects of polluting industry or from excessive noise, or the right to the quiet enjoyment of one's own surroundings came to be seen as collective, not private and personal. In these circumstances, individual owners should no longer have to rely on private initiatives to ensure that right: for the State to intervene to promote the general welfare through the control of land use was entirely appropriate.

Development control has, therefore, been concerned to promote a bundle of different ends which are not always consistent. If there is any kind of overall consistency it is that the disparate ends all involve visions of a good life in which harmony in the built environment reflects, and is sometimes used to mould, social harmony and public order. The problem is that the visions of the good life that may be expressed in the development control process may themselves be in conflict. What starts as the will to promote living conditions that create opportunity for everyone can lapse all too easily into a desire to protect an ideal environment for a chosen few.

Development control is conceived as having a clear public interest justification, even if that justification is muddied by the diversity of ends and the difficulty of defining the boundary between public and private interest. Development control is further complicated by having both tactical and strategic elements. Much of the control function is reactive in character and is about securing tactical improvements in projects whose general acceptability is not in question. Many of the functional controls have been of this type. If housing development is to go ahead, then at least the development control process can ensure that road widths and the spacing of houses are adequate. Much aesthetic control is of this order, too: bricks should match the neighbouring development; design detail should reflect the local vernacular. The implied argument is that small but significant gains may be achieved by these means. But universal control of development was introduced in 1947 with the clear understanding that there were strategic as well as tactical objectives to be met in controlling individual proposals. The intention behind controlling land use came to include not only a desire to offset the immediate impact of noise and pollution but also the need to achieve a proper distribution of activities locally, regionally and nationally. In this way, the control of land use became the means of implementing a long-term strategy, not just something to secure gains in the short term. It required, in principle at least, a committed and coherent policy laid out in a plan.

The final point to consider is the way in which public interest is expressed and applied to individual decisions. Here, once again, there are significant differences between the British development control system and those of other parts of the world. In France, for example, the desire to establish legal certainty results in criteria that take the form of fixed regulations, often expressed as measurable standards. Both the planning code and even more the regulations of the *plan d'occupation des sols* set out what developers may or may not do in precise terms. Plot ratios and building envelope controls have proliferated (see Evenson, 1980). In theory nothing is left to chance and the French have exercised very considerable control over the urban design characteristics of their cities. A system that requires local authorities to reflect on the material considerations of a case is clearly not one that envisages fixed regulations as the means by which policy is expressed, nor was it intended to be. Rather, the justification for decisions was expressed as criteria more or less highly elaborated. Where a French mayor will issue a decision notice (which is in fact a legal document) in which a decision is justified by reference to articles of the code or of the plan in force, the British district council's notice, justified only when the application is refused or a permission is subject to conditions, may make reference only to broad principles. British development control has always relied on ambiguous concepts like amenity to justify decisions, concepts which, however poorly they may be articulated, are nonetheless laden with value and meaning.

The policy base for development control in Britain does not just depend upon broad principles or statements of criteria. In the best traditions of case law, local authorities have tried to evolve their own rules of behaviour which help to limit the open-ended nature of their duties. In this, the role of precedent begins to assume some importance: formulae for dealing with applications are derived from experience and become part of the routine. Local authorities have tended to develop a whole series of supplementary statements and informal policy documents as a way of expressing to themselves and to applicants how they intend to behave. Lists of standard conditions have helped ease the burden that discretionary power places on decision-making, and also lessen the possibility of legal challenge. Local authorities have not only relied on self-generated rules and procedural behaviour, however. Although the law specifically invites an approach based on criteria and not on regulation as a means of breaking the stranglehold of bylaw control introduced in the nineteenth century, the 50 years of universal control have nevertheless been marked by the use of measurable standards as well as by open-ended statements of policy. Dimensional norms, for dwelling densities or road layout or the spacing of buildings or the provision of open space, have all been relied upon. Paradoxically, in a system which was premised on the need for flexibility their use has led to accusations of rigidity. Why the system should have resorted – retreated, perhaps? – to the kind of constraining standards that it was explicitly set up to get away from requires some explanation. It points both to some of the difficulties of a system which implies wide discretion in decision-making and to some important historical continuities. Indeed until the twentieth century, control was to a very large extent applied through measurable standards, and we may argue that the approach had become deeply ingrained in both central and local government thinking. The use of measurable standards can also be seen as a way of giving some order to an otherwise overwhelming freedom of action. And for central government, to advocate the application of such standards is a way of ensuring that local authorities behave themselves (Booth, 1996).

The problem with all these forms of justification is that they leave so much unsaid. Lurking behind terms like 'amenity' is a whole range of professional and public values that may or may not be shared. The same is true of the apparently objective use of measurable standards. What, we might enquire, makes so many dwellings to the hectare or so many hectares of open space per 1000 inhabitants sacrosanct? There must be a strong supposition that they, too, serve as proxies for values which are not fully articulated.

British development control is, therefore, characterized by both its process and its content. The process is one which, in the name of flexibility, has severed the absolute link between the plan and the development control decision and explicitly conferred wide discretion on local authorities. It is a process that has absorbed the pragmatism of the English case-law tradition, to place a heavy emphasis on dealing with cases 'on their merits' and give due weight to precedent. It is a process within which local authorities have developed procedural strategies to manage the complexities of decision-making. As for the objects of control by this process, the system has gathered together a series of different ends under the general rubric of public interest. The diversity of content, and of its means of expression, suggest the presence of values that are not explicit, but endure either because they are widely shared or because the ambiguity of expression allows a useful breadth of interpretation. But underlying both the idiosyncrasies of process and content lie another set of assumptions. The first we have already explored and is that it is possible to define a public interest in the control of future development that justifies State intervention. The second is that local authorities are the appropriate trustees of that interest and that they can be relied upon to act impartially on behalf of the public. The third is that the justification for that trusteeship relies on the principle of due process and procedural fairness rather than on the legality of decisions taken.

Such an overview sketches out the character of the British development control system and what sets it apart from other systems of urban control. Inevitably, some suggestion of the precursors of the present system emerges in a discussion of the current system's form and content. But the explanations for British development control evolving in its idiosyncratic way are more elusive. Why did the system place flexibility at the very heart of its concerns? Why did it formally confer discretionary freedom on decision-makers? Why did the system not adopt a pattern of zoning and regulation which has by and large become the standard elsewhere in the world? These are some of the questions which this book attempts to answer by looking at the evolution of urban control under the planning Acts since the first Act of 1909 and by considering the forms of control that preceded the planning legislation.

The search for answers to these questions is not simply of academic interest. For much of its existence development control has been disparaged for its bureaucracy and its inefficiency. It has been seen as inhibiting both useful economic development and innovative architectural design. On the other hand, planners have been accused of being too closely involved with developers and of allowing development to take place that has been to the disbenefit of the public at large. None of these accusations is without some grounding in experience. But the argument of this book is that the real problem with development control does not lie in these kinds of accusation, but rather in the responses to them. Much of the attack on development control's time wasting and negativity has been resolutely managerialist. What was required, the argument has run, was a far more efficient management of the system, with sanctions and penalties for those local authorities that failed to reach targets. In practice, penalizing time-wasting local authorities has been difficult, but that has not lessened the emphasis on efficiency within both central and local government. A second tendency, particularly during the last 25 years, has been the increasing weight given to the negotiating of planning gain. Here arguments have been both for and against. Agreements were either an unfair burden on developers or a means of enabling necessary development.

What both sets of arguments have tended to overlook is what we actually wanted development control to achieve. There is little point in having an efficient system if it delivers goods of trivial import. And negotiating planning gain, or allowing developers to offer 'obligations' on the provision of infrastructure as part of their proposals (as has become an established part of current practice) may have a distorting effect on the ends that development control might legitimately serve. So the exploration of the historical origins of development control is also a way of returning to first principles. What is the nature of the interest that the State controls? To what ends might that control be put?

A History of British Development Control

We have already noted how the 1947 Town and Country Planning Act introduced the requirement that all development needed a valid permission before it could proceed. We have noted, too, the wide-ranging definition of development which forms a key part of the legislation. But development control did not spring fully armed like Mars from the minds of the legislators in 1947. The argument of this book is that there are also historical explanations for the current state of development control, which are to be found in both a recent and a distant past. These explanations are necessary not only for a full understanding of the current disarray in development control, but also to point the way forward. They do so by reminding us of the origins of the modern system, and of how its purposes have been understood. The historical antecedents of the system also give us insight into the formative influences from the wider fields of law, administration and politics.

If 1947 is accepted as the foundation of the modern system, we are apt to forget that the 1947 Act was preceded by a system of 'interim control' whose scope had been considerably extended by the 1932 Town and Country Planning Act. This interim control bore many of the hallmarks of the system that we now operate. Certainly, this control did not apply everywhere – the local authority had to have passed a resolution to prepare a plan – and it ceased to have effect after the plan had been approved. Crow (1996) has already traced this history from its source; for him development control was something which from negligible beginnings came gradually to occupy a central place in planning. However, in homing in on a memorandum from the Town Planning Institute as the *real* starting date for development control, Crow does not acknowledge that the system of control under the planning Acts has an important precursor in regulatory control in the late nineteenth century. For the nature of planning control, both in planning schemes and in the system of interim control before plans were approved, was both influenced by, and a reaction to, building bylaw control under the public health Acts which goes back to 1848.

The building bylaws were by and large regulatory and normative and had a profound impact not only on building construction but also on the layout of towns. By the passing of the first planning legislation almost every urban area had had at least 25 years of experience in applying bylaws, and in some towns a great deal more. And that experience had been mixed. More progressive local authorities, anxious to experiment with new forms of housing layout, found the normative standards of the model bylaws unnecessarily restrictive and were calling for greater 'elasticity'. The fact that they were doing so suggests a certain maturity in the decision-making process. Perhaps a true starting date for development control is not 1947 but 1858, when central government first issued model bylaws for the control of new development which local authorities were encouraged, but not obliged, to adopt.

But once again, on closer inspection, 1858 seems a less definite date the closer we get to it. In fact the public health Acts were but the tail end of a history of the public control of urban form that has a much longer pedigree. For instance, the 1774 London Building Act had been a thoroughgoing attempt to develop measurable standards for new building that would be applied by a band of public service officials, the district surveyors. Though this Act was by far the most detailed legislation that had existed to that point, it follows in a direct line of succession to the London Rebuilding Act of a century before which had laid down standards for the way in which the City of London was to be rebuilt after the Great Fire of 1666. And the 1667 Rebuilding Act followed closely the increasingly detailed royal proclamations issued by Elizabeth I, James I and Charles I ostensibly proscribing all new building but in practice prescribing building materials and design details. In these terms, 1580 looks a more plausible starting date than 1848.

Yet even here, a starting date is problematic: the royal proclamations did not just emerge unheralded. Venture back yet further and we discover that, before the early modern period, regulations had existed to control building form and layout and that these regulations had been applied in London by the mayor and aldermen, in turn advised by paid experts, the city viewers. These regulations were built upon an understanding of the concept of nuisance and were very largely about resolving disputes between neighbouring landowners. To understand development control in the twenty-first century, we need to return to the feudal era.

Peeling off the layers of history to reveal deeper and yet deeper origins for modern practice may have an antiquarian interest but does not in itself quite make the case for a historical explanation for current dilemmas. Indeed, presenting history in this linear fashion runs the risk of trivializing a complicated and intriguing story. For one thing, it implies *progression*: a humble beginning pointing inexorably towards a glorious present. If, Haar notwithstanding, we doubt the glory, the idea of progression looks flawed. Secondly, this linear presentation makes the fallacious assumption that the phenomenon and process of control remain relatively constant. Urban control, we can all too readily suppose, has always been about public authorities acting in the public interest to restrain the activities of private individuals. The changes that occur are about increasing sophistication and refinement, not fundamentals. Reference to the Middle Ages already begins to give the lie to this kind of understanding. As we have noted, medieval control did not directly depend on an understanding of a greater public good: it was concerned with the regulation of something that we would regard as not being wholly within the public domain. The distinction between private and public and the understanding of a collective interest are not merely not constant, they hardly exist in recognizable form at the beginning of this linear history.

Seen in terms of these fundamental understandings, the history of development control not only becomes more interesting, it becomes considerably more relevant to the twenty-first century. It becomes more relevant because it challenges our assumptions about – for example – the notion of public and private interest. It helps us to see why development control in Britain is so distinctly different from most other systems in Europe and elsewhere. It explains the nature of our current system in a way that allows us to see both the possibilities for, and the constraints on, future change.

There is, then, a thematic element in this history of development control that a linear presentation could obscure. Principal among these themes is this distinction between public and private domains. A mature system of public control, we may argue, depends for its legitimacy on a well developed understanding of the nature and limits of private property. And the linear history of the public control over development does indeed run in parallel with a developing sense of the property rights of individuals. At the beginning of the twenty-first century, anyone who is a freeholder has more or less absolute rights, at least to the current enjoyment of the land which they own. Certainly those rights are hedged about by constraints imposed by statute of which planning is only one, but the nature of ownership is such as to imply that there is a core of rights in ownership which are entirely personal and exclusive. Yet that understanding, which in any case represents only a partial truth, is in direct contrast to a medieval understanding of property. What is striking is how far in medieval England ownership as expressed by the term tenure, so far from being absolute, was precarious and contingent. Moreover, coming into an estate which might or might not include the acquisition of landed property, was essentially bound up with entering into a position in society, such as to make modern distinctions between public and private domains more or less meaningless.

But, again, the presentation of this history as a smooth linear progression from a feudal to a modern conception of property represents only a partial truth. It does not reflect some of the interesting survivals of an older order that have been, the argument of this book runs, a formative element in creating the British planning system in the twenty-first century. Nor does it do justice to the complexities of the story. How, for example, are we to regard the landed estates, whose contribution to the control of urban development was highly significant in the eighteenth and nineteenth centuries? Are they a throwback to the feudal period? But the feudal hierarchy, with the king as the ultimate temporal authority, had gone. Do they prefigure modern attitudes to property by representing an absolute ownership that Perkin (1989) argues was established by the end of the seventeenth century? Yet dynastic succession was still of great significance. Then, too, it ignores the element of trusteeship present in ownership of land which was to inform municipal attitudes in the nineteenth century. In the last analysis, we can see this history of private property rights and public control in terms of the legal concept of interest. The question that recurs is whether there can be a collective interest that can coexist with a private interest in the use in development of land.

A second theme is that of the appropriate mechanism for ensuring the effective control of development. From surprisingly early, there were attempts to create a network of officials who would ensure that controls were respected. In the first instance, it was the mayor and aldermen of London who took responsibility directly for resolving disputes about nuisances. Soon, perhaps from the very beginning, they were assisted by 'sworn viewers' who visited and measured and made depositions before the assizes, and who came to wield considerable power. They represent an early form of public service. From the seventeenth century onwards their place was taken by surveyors who might be as much involved in the laying out of new development as they were in controlling work by others. And while until the mid-nineteenth century these surveyors were mainly working for private landlords in the exercise of control, there is the gradual establishment of a public service, particularly in London after the 1774 Building Act, which established by statute the office of district surveyor. It was logical, perhaps inevitable, that after the 1835 Municipal Corporations Act the new municipal corporations should begin to retain the services of their own surveyors, paid for from the public purse.

The role of these expert surveyors is clearly considerable in the story of control. But we need to be wary of making a direct comparison between the modern development control officer and surveyors 200 years before. First, the clear distinction between public and private service that now obtains was not fully present until the end of the nineteenth century. District surveyors in London were paid a fee for each house they surveyed and were expected to retain a private practice; much the same was true for the city viewers three centuries earlier, who were not beyond acting on behalf of clients in a way that conflicted with their public duties. And even in the nineteenth century municipal surveyors might well retain a private practice as well as their public office, without any apparent concern for conflict of interest.

The second point is that while there might be expert advice available, ensuring a proper decision-making authority was rather more difficult. The medieval evidence suggests that there were lines of accountability that linked the city viewers to the mayor and aldermen acting in a judicial capacity. The flaw in the 1774 London Building Act was that the district surveyors were answerable in a fairly attenuated way, in the City to the Common Council, but in the suburbs to magistrates of the counties of Middlesex and Surrey. It was the same problem that had bedevilled the attempts by the earlier Stuart monarchy to control London's growth. Only the creation of municipal boroughs after the 1835 Municipal Corporations Act led to a much higher degree of accountability and much more rigorous application of controls. The experts' responsibility was by now far more clearly defined.

Interestingly, the question of accountability was not just one that affected public authorities. So, for example, we find the Grosvenor estate attempting from the early nineteenth century to make its decision-making rather less dependent on the personal whim of the Duke of Westminster himself by establishing a board for the approval of plans. And by the beginning of the twentieth century, the board of trustees of Dulwich College were operating to all intents and purposes like a local authority development control committee.

A third theme is that of the criteria for decision-making. Throughout the whole period presented here there is a very strong element of wanting to impose normative regulations for new development which would take the form of measurable standards. From the outset, the desire seems to have been to create objective criteria for the resolution of disputes, but in time they came to embody received wisdom on propriety and healthfulness. Indeed, we have already noted that these measurable standards whose form remains remarkably consistent over seven centuries seem to have quite distinct objectives which nevertheless overlapped. One objective was to establish the rights of freeholders and the extent of protection they might expect from the activities of others. Another had to do with constructional performance and the reduction of fire risk. A third objective, present from the mid-nineteenth century, was the prevention of disease. Finally there was an aesthetic objective. At various stages, conspicuously in the early seventeenth and twentieth centuries, standards have been used to promote beauty as well as health.

But there has also been a dissatisfaction with measurable standards. The experience of the building bylaws under the public health legislation was that measurable standards were in the end too constraining. In particular, in delivering a sanitary objective, they failed to achieve an aesthetic one. Much the same criticism had been levelled by the mid-Victorians against the products of the 1774 Act: Georgian terraces were castigated for their monotony in much the same way as the bylaw terraces were to be 50 years later. The call, then, was for 'elasticity' so that standards could be tailored to meet the particular circumstance and respond to an only partly articulated concern for a new aesthetic order. Yet the very people who argued against the standards in the bylaws produced their own: Raymond Unwin was deeply critical of public health bylaws, but insisted on density and spacing standards which, by the 1950s, came to be seen as the new tyranny.

In fact control in the twentieth century was caught in the horns of a dilemma. The glory of planning control has been its flexibility and responsiveness to change. The requirement to consider 'other material considerations' imposed by the 1947 Town and Country Planning Act is the response to the call for elasticity at the beginning of the century. But by what criteria were those considerations to be judged? Over the course of the century it became quite clear that a bundle of sometimes conflicting values informs the decisions taken on planning applications. In such circumstances, it has been easier on occasions to revert to measurable standards to lessen the inevitable stress caused by having to determine each case 'on its merits'. The trouble, once again, was that these standards were often acting as proxy for values that were still not fully assimilated. They might be easy to apply, but they did not remove the dilemma.

Quite apart from the problem with standards, there has been a question of the duality of purpose, to achieve on the one hand a physical, and on the other, a social, order. In practice these two objectives were never fully separate, nor indeed could they be. Medieval controls were about maintaining social harmony by preventing neighbour disputes. Tudor and Stuart controls aimed to reduce the potential for civil unrest by preventing new building. However, by allowing some new building providing it conformed to a rigorous aesthetic code, they were also attempting to encourage residence in London by the gentry and the aristocracy. In more recent times, the idea of promoting a certain kind of development, ostensibly for aesthetic reasons, may well be as much about social as architectural proprieties. Once again, all too often, values have not been properly articulated to the point at which it is no longer clear why decisions are taken in certain ways.

The fourth theme has to do with the development of discretionary power. In an earlier book, I dealt with the concept of discretion in a comparative context (Booth, 1996). There, I attempted to explain some of the causes of the explicit grant of discretionary power on local authorities and some of the impacts that the use of discretion had on the process of control, as it affects both the controller and the controlled. At least part of that story had to do with the trust we place in those who take decisions, and the level of accountability of decision-makers. The growing maturity of local authorities in the late nineteenth century led to their seeking to shake off the narrow constraints of bylaws. But the desire of local authorities to take decisions on their own behalf as they saw fit calls into question the role of the central power to direct policy implementation; in this, one lot of discretionary freedoms comes up against another. Urban development has frequently been the cause around which conflicts between local and central government have coalesced. It was contributory to the constitutional crisis of the early seventeenth century. It was equally the focus of tension between central and local government in the 1980s.

These themes are woven into the chronological sequence around which the book is structured. For in spite of the strictures about the limitations of presenting a linear sequence, the history recounted here is presented in a continuous narrative from the Middle Ages to the present day. Continuous it may be, but it is not unstructured: for within the sequence there are moments of greater significance which require particular attention and certain key dates which appear to mark decisive changes in the course of this history. Key dates are not hard to find, and most of them relate to legislative change. The Assize of Nuisance of 1275 with its detailed regulations for party walls, gutters and windows in effect marks the start of the narrative as a whole. 1580, the date of Elizabeth I's first proclamation against new building, might be a second. The 1667 London Rebuilding Act and the 1774 London Building Act, in codifying standards for buildings and administering control, also appear to be significant landmarks. The Local Government Act of 1858, under which the first model bylaws were produced, seems to mark a turning point in municipal control in the interests of public health. The coming of the first planning legislation in 1909 is clearly important, while the 1947 Town and Country Planning Act with its imposition of universal control and its nationalization of development rights is crucial.

On closer inspection, these key dates look less significant, however. Almost all turn out to have had important antecedents, or significant subsequent elaboration that reduced the impact of the legislation itself. The 1275 Assize for example is almost certainly a compilation from earlier sources which do not survive. The 1580 proclamation is the start of something new in the involvement of the Crown in seeking to control urban development, but the proclamations issued by James I are considerably more important in defining the scope of control of new construction.

The 1667 London Rebuilding Act might have had greater impact if its scope had extended beyond the immediate task of rebuilding the city. The 1774 London Building Act was even more problematic. It was by far the most detailed legislation of its kind to date, and made significant changes to the administration of control. But to what extent did it simply codify current best practice? And how far did the changes that took place in the form of urban development in the late eighteenth and early nineteenth century reflect changes in the building industry and the real estate market rather than changes in the legislation?

Much the same goes for the dates identified in the twentieth century. The direct impact of the 1909 Housing, Town Planning etc. Act on the history of development control (as opposed to development plans) is limited although we shall note the importance of discretionary clauses in the early planning schemes. In many ways the rather less well known 1932 Town and Country Planning Act had more impact on development control with its substantial formalization of interim control and might carry more weight in the search for key dates. And the 1947 Act, conceptually significant though it clearly was, had been so long anticipated in discussion and had in practice done no more than to extend an existing activity, that it ceases to be quite the frontier that it at first appears to be.

If key dates look suspect as an explanation for important change, the idea of significant episodes or phases is a good deal more promising. These key phases are points in the history of development control in which there appears to have been a more or less intense working through of the themes that we have developed above. The first such stage is the most ill-defined in terms of time and covers the whole of the later Middle Ages. Its significance is not primarily in terms of the introduction of regulatory control, important though that was. The more fundamental significance of this phase lay in defining the nature of tenure in landed property and the degree of protection the law could offer to those who had tenure. The formalizing of a feudal concept of property which recognized the coexistence of interests in one piece of land was to have a formative influence not only on the capacity to carry out urban development but, later, on the planning system itself.

The second key phase straddles the turn of the seventeenth century. There are several dimensions to the significance of this period. The laying down of standards for new building that conformed to a new aesthetic canon but also addressed the risk of fire and the availability of materials is often seen as the most important aspect of the period. But the period is perhaps more important for its growing assumption that there might be a larger common interest in controlling development that went beyond the regulation of disputes between adjoining freeholders. It is also significant for the direct involvement of central powers, and the growing tension between the Crown and the City of London that resulted. Indeed the abuse of the royal prerogative in the period before the Civil War can be seen as a root cause of a remarkable phenomenon in the later seventeenth century: the privatization of the control through the activities of the great landed estates who assured a remarkably effective level of oversight of urban development in a period when control of any kind by public authorities was notably deficient.

The third key phase comes in the mid-nineteenth century. It is in this period we see the re-establishment of public control over new development as a direct consequence of the failure of private landlords to act effectively in the prevention of slum conditions. The newly created municipal boroughs were anxious to assume responsibility for the development of their areas and began to forge a new understanding of public interest in their desire to improve conditions. It was also a period of experimentation with collective decision-making and with the criteria on which decisions could be based. It was of paramount importance in establishing a *process*, in which councils of elected representatives, acting in the public interest, exercised statutory control corporately.

The fourth key phase comes with the introduction of statutory land-use planning in 1909. But it is not the Act itself which is critical here. The period is much more significant for the increasing dissatisfaction with the rigid limits of bylaw regulation and the attempt to find new forms of 'elastic' control in the wording of the new planning schemes. In this we see local authorities such as Ruislip-Northwood Urban District whose planning scheme forms part of that narrative, taking specific powers to approve or refuse development on the grounds of its appearance even if in general terms the development conformed to the requirements of the plan.

The fifth phase is that of the 1940s. This remarkable period has already been charted by Cullingworth (1975, 1980) and involved an intense reflection on the nature of land-use planning. In particular, it saw the realization of the logic that seemed to be driving planning control, from something that was partial in scope and conceived of as marginal to the true purpose of plan making to something that was central to the planning system and universal in its application. The logic was to find expression in the desire to nationalize future development rights.

The final phase is the 1970s which presents a stark contrast to the optimism of 30 years before. It starts with a crisis of numbers with planning applications increasing nationally by more than 50 per cent in a 3-year period. It ends with a crisis of interpretation. For the impact of the crisis of numbers was to focus attention on the question of delay to the exclusion of almost everything else. The two major reviews of development control in the period that might have widened the debate served only to narrow it. The impact of this period was to ensure that development control was discussed almost entirely in terms of managerial efficiency for the remainder of the century. It left the system with inadequate intellectual resources to meet the sustained attack of the following decade.

In the end, the glory of the system is in the process. American lawyers (see Haar, 1984) praised the system for its responsiveness to change and its relative lack of legal complexity. However, the trouble with an emphasis on process is that it may obscure the ends which the process is designed to achieve. Controlling urban development is not, we have already noted, a single phenomenon and the objectives of control have varied widely over the course of the history that this book covers. Modern development control is a palimpsest of attitudes to the urban environment, an accumulation of ideas and practices which are value laden, but which have often not been fully articulated. We have often given the appearance of not knowing what we want development control *for*. No wonder, perhaps, that the debate has centred on performance at the expense of anything else. On the other hand, what you can do depends in part on how you can do it. The nature of the process is important and there have been significant shifts of process as the objectives of control have changed. So this history explores both ends and means and looks at the interaction between the two.

Earlier we rejected the idea of the history of development control as a smooth, linear process or as a collection of key dates, in favour of a series of formative phases in which key relationships were worked out. Running across these phases then are a series of recurrent themes which could serve to unify this account. Inevitably, the main focus of the book is on the twentieth century; the penultimate chapter deals with the debates of the past decade. However, the next chapter attempts to tease out those aspects of urban control before 1900 that were formative of control under the planning Acts in the twentieth century. It identifies the origins of control under the planning Acts. It looks at the way in which the core concerns for the control of development in Britain were established. It shows what the planning Acts were designed to react against.

The book also uses case studies to exemplify the central arguments. Some of the material comes from other published sources, particularly for the eighteenth and nineteenth centuries. Some of the material has been assembled for this book. Material from Sheffield has been used both for the nineteenth and twentieth centuries, not because Sheffield was particularly remarkable, indeed rather the opposite. Sheffield is the ordinary, rather than the exceptional, case of urban development control, a touchstone of how a process was experienced on the ground, a counterpoint to official thinking at the centre. In a way, the history of development control is a history of experiment, of adventure almost, a quest to find how conditions in cities can be adapted to best effect. It is time to begin the account of that experiment.

Note

1. New legislation in 2000 changed the title of these plans, but not their fundamental character as regulatory documents (see p. 182).

Chapter Two

Property, Contract and Regulation: Urban Control before Planning

The form of development control which emerged, originally as an administrative expedient during the first half of the twentieth century, is distinctly different from the forms of control that preceded it and from the regulatory systems of continental Europe. Yet it was in no sense a system without precedent. The insistence on flexibility and the desire for discretionary power was a reaction to the forms of regulation that had developed in the second half of the nineteenth century. At the same time, there appear to be significant continuities with practice as it had developed before 1900. Measured standards and the application of rules to common problems continue in the development control system and had a clear parentage in the sanitary regulation, in control through leasehold agreements, and in the law of equity. The concern both for physical form and for land-use activity had already been the subject of leasehold agreements. The search for appropriate means of applying and enforcing policies for new development had been a preoccupation long before the establishment of town planning committees and development control sections within town halls. The fact that development control could take off so rapidly in the 1920s and 1930s as a major aspect of British town planning was due to the extensive foundations that had already been laid.

There are indeed four ways in which development control in the twentieth century depended on earlier forms of control and on the way problems had been resolved in earlier centuries. The first of these concerns the attempts to define and articulate the objectives of control. The earliest forms of control were very largely about the regulation of disputes between neighbours and this kind of dispute resolution finds recognizable echoes in the practice, if not the principle, of development control in the twentieth century. The will to control public space and the desire to promote order and delight in the built environment have almost as long a pedigree and are just as much present in the modern development control system. Control may also have a strategic aspect. Much of the development control system in the twentieth century had been concerned with matters of detail and of detailed impact, as were its predecessors. But the idea of control in the interests of long-term, large-scale strategy is not solely a creature of the twentieth century. Already under Elizabeth I, as we shall see, public authorities were attempting the control of new development with the explicit aim of preventing further growth of the City of London and in this way maintaining civil order. The fact that this strategic objective was lost between the seventeenth century and the twentieth century is very largely due to the constitutional settlement that ensured that the Crown would not be involved in local matters.

The second has to do with the search for ways of securing compliance with, and the enforcement of, predetermined standards. From the very earlier stages of urban control, paid officials existed to inspect and measure as part of the process of ensuring that regulations were honoured and that the extent of a grievance against those who had apparently flouted the regulations could be established. One of the difficulties was the way in which these viewers and surveyors, paid by fee for particular tasks, might find their work for private clients in conflict with their public duties. This was a tension that was only resolved in the nineteenth century when a salaried service of building surveyors wholly answerable to the newly created municipal councils replaced the employment of surveyors in private practice paid by fee to undertake work as and when necessary. By the twentieth century the technical capacity to control development was already available.

The third way is in the development of appropriate fora for decision-making. Early control of the urban environment was largely autocratic with a heavy emphasis on adjudication in the event of dispute. Even in the Middle Ages, however, the beginnings of a corporate approach to control are evident with the mayor and alderman of the City of London holding a responsibility for applying regulations. And much later, we see some of the large landowners in the nineteenth century creating boards who would take responsibility for the terms in which leases would be renewed as a way of introducing consistency and objectivity in the decisionmaking process. Such behaviour clearly foreshadows that of municipal councils and provides the point of departure for the way in which planning committees were to behave in the twentieth century.

The final way in which development control in the twentieth century depended on older thinking has to do with the question of interests in property. Development control is underpinned by the understanding that there is a public interest which is distinct from private interests of individual landowners. There is an argument for saying that a mature system for the control of development in the public interest depends on a mature understanding also of the nature and limits of private property. In that light modern development control is the fruit of a continuing search for the nature of rights that those who have interests in land could be said to enjoy. At the same time there appears to be a growing awareness that some alleged nuisances might have an impact on more than just immediate neighbours. The legal concept of the common nuisance was a useful way of articulating the problem and gave a new legitimacy to public authorities of whatever stamp to intervene in the process of development.

Nuisance and Tenure: The Medieval Origins of Development Control

The beginnings of the desire to control urban development and to find a rationale for doing so go back at least to the Middle Ages. For it is in the medieval period that we can already find forms of regulatory control which suggest some of the problems that the modern development control system has to deal with. The period also seems to be the source of some of the conceptual foundations of the modern system which drive not from regulatory control but from the theorizing about the nature of property ownership.

The beginnings of regulatory control are to be found very early. To begin with, this control was largely conceived of as a means of regulating disputes between adjoining owners and defining the nature of nuisance to which neighbours might reasonably object. It was, in other words, an extension of the proprietary rights that a freeholder might be said to enjoy. There is evidence that already by 1300 several boroughs in England had developed customs in relation to nuisance (Chew and Kellaway, 1973). Tradition dates the earliest attempts at creating such regulations in London to the end of the twelfth century under the mayorality of Hugh fitz Ailwin. Certainly fitz Ailwin did produce a series of regulations in 1212 following a disastrous fire, and these regulations 'were directly concerned with fire prevention and rebuilding after fire' (ibid., p. ix).

The first firm evidence for regulatory control in London does not come until nearly a century later, however. An Assize of Nuisance, in effect a series of regulations controlling building form, was said to have been drawn up in 1275, almost certainly a compilation of even earlier regulations. These regulations of the Assize covered walls, gutters, windows, pavements and privies. Regulations on party walls were particularly detailed and required freeholders to give 1½ feet of land and to share the cost of building a wall 3 feet wide and 15 feet high. Relieving arches set into the wall had to be no more than 1 foot deep in order to allow for at least 1 foot of solid wall between adjoining properties. The Assize also made it possible for freeholders to construct a wall on his or her neighbour's land if the neighbour was unwilling or unable to pay for it. Only freeholders could bring actions to court and the nuisance complained about must have caused damage. The nuisance had to be of a kind covered by the regulations in the Assize. Finally, the tenement in question had to be inspected. Actions under the Assize were mainly heard at a congregation of the mayor and alderman acting in a judicial role, or more rarely before a court of law presided by a judge. The first evidence of the Assize being applied comes from cases from 1301 onwards. In essence this Assize of Nuisance and its application were primarily about the resolution of private disputes and derived from the need to establish the rights and limits of freehold tenure. The origins of the Assize lie in attempts to give protection to those who occupied land as freeholders which came to be seen as a protection from the abusive activities of adjoining freeholders.

From a very early stage, and certainly from the beginning of the fourteenth century, the mayor and alderman were helped in the task of inspection of nuisances. Two masons and two carpenters who later became known as City Viewers were sworn in to measure the fabric of buildings subject to complaint. Viewers continued to be appointed until the beginning of the eighteenth century when record of their existence ends (Loengard, 1989). Their significance lies in their role as precursors of modern paid officials. But it is important to recognize that the viewers were not yet public servants in a modern sense. Though they were sworn in, they continued to carry out work for private clients. In that respect, inspections for the mayor and alderman were for them an activity like any other, particularly since so much hinged on questions of private dispute. Indeed, Loengard (1989) makes clear that even in the sixteenth century the boundary between public and private activity was still muddied. Private commissions might flow from work for public authorities and records of mysterious rewards and payments to viewers for food and drink do not, as Loengard puts it, 'make for unbounded confidence in the system' (*ibid.*, p. xxviii).

If this early period of control is largely characterized by the resolution of private disputes and the poor definition of public service, even at the beginning there is evidence of some sense of public interest. The problems of ruinous buildings or defective paving or the stopping up of paths, lanes or ditches were not covered by the Assize of Nuisance. But they could involve action by the wardmote, the council of aldermen that existed in each of the City of London's wards. A rather larger problem of common interest was that of encroachment on the King's Highway. In 1246 there was an inquest into such encroachments and freeholders might in the simplest cases be required to demolish porches or extensions that encroached upon a street line. As often as not, rather than demolishing the offending structure, the freeholder might be required to pay an annual fine to the king proportional to the size of the structure (Chew and Weinbaum, 1970). Such behaviour revealed a curious ambivalence between the desire to protect the environment in the public interest and a quite different interest in adding to royal revenues. Whether in the Middle Ages such ambivalence was the subject of comment is not clear; it certainly became so by the seventeenth century.

The other aspect of medieval attitudes to property has to do with theory as much as with practice. The feudal system of land tenure had been developed in continental Europe and was based on the principle that land was occupied in return for service to a feudal superior. However, nowhere was it applied more single-mindedly than in England after the Norman Conquest, where the sovereign took possession of the conquered territory and offered tenancies to his nobles who became tenants-in-chief to the Crown. In their turn, tenants-in-chief offered tenancies to others who might actually occupy and work the land so acquired. In principle, and sometimes in practice, there could be an extended hierarchy of people with an interest in one particular piece of land. But at whatever level, the principle was the same: the land was held in return for service. That service might be military, or could involve domestic duties. It could also involve the saying or prayers or masses. By far the most common form of feudal tenure was the grant of land in return for agricultural produce. All these so-called free tenures could be bequeathed at will by tenants to their direct male descendants, but they had their limitations. Free tenure depended on the willingness of the feudal lord to recognize an inheritor of the tenure, or on the feudal lord's own successor recognizing a tenant's title to the land. Another kind of agricultural tenure designated as unfree offered even more limited rights to the tenant who was entirely dependent on the goodwill of the lord of the manor and was not able to bequeath his tenancy even to his own direct descendants. The important point about all forms of feudal tenure was that they ensured that there could be no absolute proprietor of land other than the king. To everyone else landownership depended on the goodwill of their immediate superior in a hierarchy of status.

In practice, this 'pure' feudal system was modified from an early stage. By the thirteenth century service was almost entirely commuted into money payments. From the end of the thirteenth century, law forbade the creation of further feudal tenures. Gradually another form of tenure, the leasehold, became increasingly

prominent. Whereas most feudal tenures were held at least for the lifetime of
the tenant, the lease was granted for a specified term of years after which the
land reverted to the landowner. From the point of view of the landowner, leases
offered considerable flexibility and gave greater control over the land lease[1] than
did other forms of tenure. For the lessee, the lease conferred an interest which was
apparently even more provisional than the rights afforded by free tenure. There
was no possibility of inheritance and no guarantee that a lease could be renewed.
Yet in time the flexibility of the lease came to be seen as an advantage for lessees,
too. It was for long regarded as being personal property and did not at first benefit
from the legal protection offered to other tenures. But as personal property it
could be far more easily disposed of and was to become a major instrument for
the control of urban development in the eighteenth and nineteenth centuries
(Holdsworth, 1927).

The feudal tenant would appear to have had a precarious foothold in such a
system of property. In practice much was done in the Middle Ages to protect what
few rights a tenant actually had. One problem was that for any parcel of land
there might be several people who could claim a legitimate interest. Another was
that even with free tenure there were limited possibilities for disposing of land
or bequeathing it at will. Two significant developments in legal doctrine helped
to surmount these difficulties. The first was the doctrine of estates. In modern
parlance, the word estate has come to signify a physical object – the country estate,
the housing estate – but at its outset it was designed to give concrete existence to
the abstract concept of an interest in land. Such a doctrine recognized that there
could be concurrent interests and allowed judges to weigh the merits of one estate
in land against another in cases of dispute. Further, it made possible the definition
of interests by time. In this way it became possible for a tenant to occupy for his
or her lifetime land on which someone else might have the right to the tenancy in
reversion, that is, at the point at which the first tenant had died. But the second
tenant was held to have an estate in that parcel of land from the point at which he
or she was granted the tenancy in reversion, not from the moment of possession
(Gray and Symes, 1981).

The second way in which legal doctrine sought to overcome the limitations of
feudal tenure was through the development of the trust. In order to allow a tenant
greater freedom in passing lands to others, the practice developed of assigning
land to someone who was charged with managing it on behalf of – 'to the use
of' – a third party. The beneficiary would not hold the title to the land but would
have the right to benefit from it. The trustee's duty was to the beneficiary. In the
Middle Ages the practice developed in which the trustee might in fact be fictitious,

no more than a legal device to transfer land to a third party. When the practice of nominating a fictitious trustee was finally stopped in the sixteenth century, the concept of the trust did not disappear. Instead it re-emerged in the seventeenth and eighteenth centuries with the emphasis placed upon the trustees rather than upon the 'use' in the land that it created. The general effect was the same, however: in a trust relationship the administration of property has become separated from its enjoyment and the trustee carries a moral responsibility on behalf of someone else (Gray and Symes, 1981).

The courts of common law acted to protect the interests of tenants and give substance to their apparently precarious tenures. To start with, the major concern was to be able to detect who was in possession of land and to ensure that anyone who dispossessed the person with the right to the possession of land was punished. Common law did not, however, recognize the rights of a beneficiary of a trust, since in common law the trustee held the title to land, not the beneficiary. From the thirteenth century the Chancellor's Court (Chancery) began to find ways of redressing this balance in a body of rules that became known as *equity*. The law of equity allowed the beneficiary of a trust to ensure that the terms of the trust were complied with. In a more general way, the law of equity dealt with all the problems of competing interests in land. Equitable remedies were discretionary and not mandatory, unlike those available in common law. Judgements based on the law of equity, perhaps even more than in common law, depended on the evaluation of the specifics of a given case. These could then be set against a developing body of judge made rules. The case-by-case approach which characterizes modern development control has its origins in the approach to defending property rights adopted by medieval courts.

The significance of the Middle Ages for modern development control is essentially two-fold. It is a period in which the beginnings of regulatory control are to be found with the recognition that not all questions of nuisance were connected solely with disputes between neighbours. It is also the period in which an understanding of private property developed which was not based upon the absolute control of a parcel of land by single landowner but upon the possibility of multiple interests which could each be defended at law. The idea that there could be future interests in land to be distinguished from its current enjoyment seems to point to the possibility realized in the 1947 Town and Country Planning Act that future development rights could be taken by the State without the rights to current enjoyment by a private landowner being affected. Medieval property law had laid the conceptual foundations for modern town planning (for a further discussion of this point, see Booth, 2002).

From Royal Decrees to Leasehold Agreements: The Privatization of Control

If the medieval period contains the beginnings of the approach to the control of urban development, it is not until the end of the sixteenth century that we see the emergence of control by public authorities which has a clear strategic objective. This beginning of strategic control in which public good order is paramount coincides with the very marked increase in the population of England's biggest city, London. The direct involvement of the monarchy in urban control from the end of the sixteenth century was an attempt to limit and shape the apparently inexorable growth of the city and by so doing to stem its destabilizing affects. The period from 1580 to 1774 which begins with the royal decree and ends with a major piece of legislation is also the period in which London moved from being a huddled medieval settlement rather on the fringe of Europe to becoming a primate city. But alongside the physical transformation was experimentation with forms of control and types of administration. The control of urban development was closely associated with constitutional arrangements during the Stuart monarchy.

The estimates of the population of London in the period are inevitably imprecise, but there seems to be agreement that its population grew by at least four times between 1550 and 1700, from 120,000 to between 500,000 and 650,000 in 1700 (McKellar, 1999). By the first census of 1801, the population had reached more than 900,000. In the face of this apparently unstoppable growth the attempts of Elizabeth I and her Stuart successors to stop the growth looked laughably ineffectual. Yet the story is a great deal more complicated than one of an unequal struggle between an ineffective administration and massive demographic forces.

Elizabeth I's proclamations and the Act of Parliament of 1593 simply forbade buildings on new foundations in the cities of London and Westminster and in an area 3 miles beyond their gates and also prevented the subdivision of houses to accommodate new households. These proclamations and the Act relied for their implementation on the mayor and alderman in the City of London and in Middlesex and Surrey on the justices of the peace, who were to remain the prime source of civil authority in much of the country until 1835. The scale of the problem almost certainly defeated their capacity to enforce the proclamations and there is no record of any action being taken until 1590, 10 years after the first proclamation had been issued. Thereafter a special commission was set up by the Privy Council, and offenders were dealt with (Barnes, 1971).

The proclamations by James I and Charles I represent a significant development beyond a simple restriction on new building which is nevertheless repeated.

Already in 1605, a proclamation declared that new building must be wholly in brick or stone and that 'the forefront thereof shall be uniforme in order and forme' (Larkin and Hughes, 1973, no. 51). This relatively modest statement of intent was followed by the much more grandiloquent proclamation 10 years later in which James I declared:

. . . that it was said by the first Emperor of Rome that, he had found the City of Rome of Bricke, and left it of marble, So that Wee whom God hath honoured to be the first King of Great Britain, might be able to say in some proportion, That Wee have found our Citie and Suburbs of London of Stickes and left them of Bricke being a Materiall farre more durable, safe from fire, beautifull and magnificent. (Larkin and Hughes, 1973, no. 152)

This in turn was followed in 1618 by yet another proclamation which set out for the first time detailed construction standards and explicit guidance on the proportion and detailing of the street elevations of buildings.

The rationale for these proclamations was partly the growing shortage of timber and the desire to reduce the risk of fire; so much is clear from the wording of the proclamations themselves. But the proclamations also have an aesthetic as well as a utilitarian purpose. A fascination with the architecture of the Italian renaissance and the desire to emulate the cities of continental Europe seemed to have been at work. To this end, James I was very largely assisted by Inigo Jones. Jones had travelled twice to Italy, at the end of the sixteenth century and again in 1613–1614 and had therefore seen Italian renaissance architecture at first hand. Jones was appointed Royal Surveyor in 1615 and is likely to have been responsible for the content of the 1618 proclamation, although there is no direct proof (Summerson, 1966; Harris and Higgott, 1989). What James I had started was continued by Charles I. Jones was retained as Royal Surveyor and two further proclamations were issued which refined the advice given in the 1618 proclamation. In particular, the second of the two in 1630 makes explicit reference to a revitalized Commission for Buildings of which Jones was to be a member and whose remit was to be the enforcement of the ban on new buildings and the application of the new constructional standards (Larkin and Hughes, 1983).

The influence Jones exerted over architectural design over the next two centuries is well known and need not concern us here. His impact on urban development comes, apart from the royal proclamations already referred to, through his probable involvement in the celebrated scheme for Covent Garden. The Russell family, ennobled as the Earls and later Dukes, of Bedford, in the sixteenth century had acquired land north of the Strand which included a walled enclosure which had originally belonged to a convent. The Russells had allowed building to take place on part of the land, along Long Acre running parallel to the Strand to the north and on Bedfordbury to the west. All this building had taken place in contravention of the successive royal proclamations. On his accession, Francis Russell, 4th Earl of Bedford, realizing that to proceed with further development was to risk punishment, applied to the King for a licence to develop the walled, central portion of the site. The licence was granted in 1630 and after

Figure 2.1. London: Lindsey House, Lincoln's Inn Fields. These houses, roughly contemporary with the scheme for Covent Garden, demonstrate the influence of Inigo Jones and the Commission for Buildings in imposing an aesthetic ideal through the control of all new buildings.

the payment of a fine of £2,000 the Earl of Bedford was effectively pardoned for the illegal development already carried out. The license did not directly require the involvement of Jones or the Commission for Buildings. But the Earl of Bedford must have submitted plans to the Commission for approval which would make Jones's involvement likely (Sheppard, 1970).

Certainly the plan for Covent Garden was as revolutionary as Jones's designs for individual buildings. Its central square was without precedent in England although it was clearly related to continental prototypes. The regular treatment of the façades of the houses facing the square and the use of classical detailing may have been suggested by the standards in royal proclamations, but this was the first built example. Covent Garden led to innumerable layouts over the next two centuries of regular housing arranged round a square. But we need to recognize that Covent Garden represents an important shift in the objectives of control. The case of Covent Garden demonstrates that Charles I was not opposed to all development, providing it was of the right sort. It had to conform to an aesthetic canon which would make London the equal of its continental rivals. It also had to be for the right sort of people. Covent Garden was explicitly aimed at residents who were members of the gentry and aristocracy.

Something else was at work in this control of building, however. The Stuart monarchs saw the fining of offenders against the royal proclamations as a convenient source of revenue that did not require the approval of Parliament (Barnes, 1971). The City rightly objected that simply fining offenders instead of demolishing the buildings negated the intention of the proclamations. Particularly insidious in this view was the habit of 'compounding' with offenders, that is to say, agreeing what proportion of the fine should be paid and over what period. Control of urban development was beginning to be used with explicit aesthetic and social objectives. At the same time, the public authority, in this case the Crown, was to some large extent compromised by the desire for financial gain.

If there was some justice in the City's objections to the King's failure to stop new development, its arguments were also informed by self-interest. Unbridled growth in the suburbs led to the emergence of a workforce which was outside the control of the City Livery Companies and which therefore threatened the particular rights and privileges of the City. For much the same reason, the City opposed Charles I's proposal to incorporate the suburbs into four wards which would be independent of the City (Pearl, 1961). Such a proposal would have laid the basis for a rational administration of the growing metropolis and a more consistent approach to the control of new development. In the event such reform had to wait for another 250 years. Control of urban development was heavily implicated in the struggle between the City and the Crown as to how authority should be exercised and by whom.

There was a larger dilemma that attached to the use of authoritarian power in royal proclamations which was to know how they related to common and to statutory law. In the seventeenth century, one theory held that a proclamation could not create an offence that was not already an offence under the law. The other, expounded by Lord Chancellor Ellesmere, declared that the King 'could restreyne the libertie of his subjects that are ageynste the commonweale', and specifically cited the proclamations against buildings as an example (quoted by Barnes 1971, pp. 87, 88). Whichever interpretation was correct, the general impact was the same and led to an extension of the private law of nuisance to the public realm. The development of a legal doctrine of 'common nuisance' may not have required, as Barnes observed, a major leap of imagination. But it was an important step towards establishing a principle of public interest that was distinguishable from private property interests. Another of the conceptual foundations of modern development control had been laid.

The era of royal proclamations whose ostensible purpose was to restrict urban development petered out in the later seventeenth century. This retreat from control of overall growth was in part due to the fierce resistance to the use of the royal prerogative that had been a major cause of complaint of the Parliamentarians in the Civil War. Charles II made two attempts to control development that echoed the intentions of Charles I's proclamations and represents something of a throwback to an absolutist form of government. But the Restoration of the Monarchy was, according to Morrill (1993), 'predicated on a massive decentralization of power' and the seventeenth century saw a 'decline of the hands-on central executive control of local administration' (p. 405) which was confirmed by the Settlement with William III in 1689. A final attempt to control London's growth was contained in a Bill introduced into Parliament in 1709 under Queen Anne, but it was vigorously opposed and then withdrawn. No further attempt to control London's growth, as opposed to the form of buildings, was made until the imposition of the metropolitan green belt in the mid-twentieth century.

What replaced the royal proclamations was a series of Acts of Parliament whose intentions were solely to control the form of new development, not to prevent it. The major impetus to this process was the Great Fire of 1666 which destroyed almost all the medieval city. In the immediate aftermath Sir Christopher Wren and others proposed plans which would have radically restructured the plan of the City. This approach was rejected, in favour of regulations that allowed for rebuilding on more or less the existing street pattern with strict controls over the form of buildings fronting the street. The regulations for the construction of new buildings follow directly from the proclamations before the Civil War and Summerson (1945) asserts that they did no more than codify what was already best practice. Two things set the Rebuilding Act of 1667 apart from its predecessors, however. One was the control of the heights of buildings according to the width of the streets which they fronted. The other was the appointment of surveyors who would stake out streets and plots and the setting-up of a Fire Court to handle disputes. The old reliance on the mayor and aldermen and on the city viewers was replaced by something approaching a modern administration.

The failure to implement Wren's plan was, on the face of it, a lost opportunity. In fact the swiftness with which the legislative means for rebuilding the city were put in place and the work put in hand is astonishing. By the mid-1670s building was substantially complete even if some public buildings, most notably St. Paul's Cathedral, took much longer. It is important to recognize, however, that the effects of the Rebuilding Act were limited to the City and that once building was complete, the Fire Court was disbanded and the work of the surveyors came to an end. The West End was not subject to comparable legislation until the beginning of the eighteenth century when two short Acts were passed aimed primarily at controlling the spread of fire and minimizing the risk of decay. Party walls had to be extended 18 inches above roof level, timber cornices were banned from street elevations and windows had to be recessed behind the façade. This was nowhere near as comprehensive as the Rebuilding Act. But it did apply to a defined territory that included not only the whole of the Cities of London and Westminster but also twelve suburban parishes in Surrey and Middlesex to which were added under George I St. Marylebone, Paddington, St. Pancras and St. Luke's, Chelsea (Brett-James, 1935). This was the area which was required to make annual returns of deaths and was in turn to become the administrative unit for the control of development under later legislation.

It was not until more than 100 years after the Rebuilding Act of 1667 that the next major piece of legislation to control urban development was given royal assent. The London Building Act of 1774 was essentially a building construction code, not an instrument for land-use planning control. It did not seek to impose limits on new development as the Stuart proclamations had done, nor did it offer the kind of controls over the heights of buildings in relation to streets as the Rebuilding Act required. It was a minutely drafted code of construction, whose impact on Georgian terraced housing has been noted by Rasmussen (1967), Summerson (1945) and others. But it dealt with far more than housing. It made provision for what it termed seven 'rates' of buildings, the first few of which included, but were

Figure 2.2. London: Rugby Estate, Great Ormond Street. Houses of the 1720s, displaying the recessed windows required by the early 18th century legislation.

not restricted to, terraced housing. These 'rates of building' were identified by value for non-residential buildings and by floor area for housing. Section 60 of the Act specified that any infringement of the regulations would be held to be a 'common nuisance' with the possibility of jail for the offenders. The Act applied to the same area as its predecessors and was to endure unaltered for 70 years.

Leaving aside the extensive drafting of building standards and the unequivocal identification of their infringement as being a matter of public, not individual, concern, the major innovation of the Act was to provide for a comprehensive and enduring form of administration. Under Section 62, the mayor and aldermen of the City and the justices of the peace were required to appoint surveyors who would be sworn to take responsibility for defining districts within the area covered by the Act. A particular novelty was that surveyors were to indemnify builders against prosecution by certifying that the builders were in accordance with the standard laid out in the Act. Surveyors' fees were specified and provision was made for punishment in the event of surveyor's 'misbehaviour' (Section 68). There was, nevertheless, a weakness in the administrative framework set in place in the Act. The Act may have set in train the appointment of surveyors to identify infringements and to certify new buildings, but they were not backed by a structure of local government that was adequate to enforce the regulations. In the last resort, it was still the mayor and aldermen in the City and the justices of peace outside who still had to ensure that the law was respected. Although Mingay (1963) concludes that in the main the justices of the peace did their duty conscientiously and humanely, the possibilities for collusion over building in and around London were high. As Clarke (1992) shows in her study of Somers Town, justices of the peace might themselves be directly involved in building and so be perfectly willing to turn a blind eye to illegal building practice. Moreover, surveyors by charging those they certified a fee rather than being paid from the public purse, and by not being able to sustain a livelihood from their building Act work alone, were as susceptible to corruption as the medieval city viewers had been.

The Privatization of Control

Important though the 1774 Act was, it nevertheless represents something of a retreat from the attempts to regulate urban development in the previous century. In part, this retreat represents the reaction to an autocratic style of government that had set the Crown against its subjects. Strategic land-use control was therefore too heavily identified with an unacceptable form of government. But it was also to do with the effectiveness of private landowners and builders in the allocation and release of land for new development through the issuing of building leases. Leasehold tenure, as we have seen, was already used in the medieval period as a way of overcoming some of the limitations of feudal tenure. It was used particularly to prevent the conversion of arable land to pasture. It began to find a new application with the demographic growth of London which made urban rather than agricultural development the most profitable use.

Leasehold tenure had a particular advantage for owners of settled estates. Settled estates were those in which the freehold was settled on the second-generation inheritor. In this way the immediate successor of a landowner only acquired a life interest in the land and could not dispose of it outright. Legal limitations were such that this process of settling the estate had to be repeated every generation, but it was an effective means of ensuring dynastic succession and was much used by the major landowning families. The current occupier of such settled estates may have been unable to sell the land outright, but could nevertheless issue leases to builders as a way of generating income. There was an added advantage in that when the lease expired both the land and the buildings upon it reverted to the landowner who thus benefited not only from the annual ground rent but also the improved capital value of the land at the end of the lease.

Leases on settled estates had been restricted to 25 years, or 40 years for religious institutions, under Elizabeth I, but landowners came to realize that 25 years was too short a period to satisfy builders and could leave owners with only a life interest in the land with an awkward problem when the lease expired of buildings that could neither be demolished nor improved. From the end of the seventeenth century large landowners began to apply to Parliament for Acts which would give them the right to offer much longer leases to builders. The way was clear for the large-scale development of London which took place during the eighteenth and nineteenth centuries on the aristocratic estates, particularly in London's West End. Both the allocation and the release of land for development and the control over the form of building and the uses to which buildings were put were achieved by the contractual agreements attached to the building leases. The application and enforcement of control was therefore very largely in private hands.

The way in which the largest estates managed their property is well known. In Bloomsbury, the activities of the Dukes of Bedford, whose predecessors had developed Covent Garden, have been fully explored by Olsen (1982) while the Survey of London has contributed a detailed study of the Grosvenor estate in Mayfair (Sheppard, 1977). The results have been celebrated by Rasmussen (1967) and by Summerson (1945). The development of Bloomsbury as a series of squares and parallel streets in the late eighteenth and early nineteenth centuries is very largely due to the energy of John Russell, 6th Duke of Bedford, and his successor Francis, combined with the equally dedicated work of their surveyors and agents. The Bedford estate employed full-time salaried staff: an agent for the whole of the Bedford landholdings which included agricultural as well as urban land, and a steward for each estate. By the early nineteenth century the Bedford estate was

Figure 2.3. John Russell, 6th Duke of Bedford, by Ingres. He was responsible for much of the development of Bloomsbury. (*Source*: St Louis, Missouri, Museum of Art)

clearly being run as a well managed business (Olsen, 1982). The fact that so much of Bloomsbury still remains as it was built is a witness of the care which the estate exercised in issuing leases and in managing the development once it was built.

But the process was far from being effortless. The Grosvenor estate in Mayfair which was developed from the early eighteenth century begins to illustrate some of the difficulties. In the early years building agreements issued by the Grosvenors which preceded the granting of leases were conspicuous for 'their lack of precision, even by the relatively lax standards of the day . . . much seems to have been left to the good sense of builders and future tenants' (Sheppard 1977, p. 15). Neither building agreements nor leases followed a standard pattern and leases for adjacent plots were not drawn up to terminate in the same year. There was, moreover, little attempt at creating an architectural unity on the estate, although in this the Grosvenor estate was not exceptional in the early eighteenth century. On the other hand, the leases did make specific references to the way in which buildings could be used. Trades such as butcher, tallow chandler, soap maker, brewer, victualler, coffee house proprietor, working brazier and blacksmith, among others were not prohibited outright but were subject to a premium on the ground rent which varied according to location. The intention was probably to deter such uses rather than to increase the estate's income, but it does indicate a clear willingness to manage land use as well as building form. The process continued in the nineteenth century when the use of deterrent rents gave way to a list of uses that were prohibited outright. Tight control was not easy, nevertheless. Market pressures, together with the laxity of earlier leases, might make some uses difficult to resist or control. And financial interests might override a desire to protect residents from nuisance. Public houses were given leases throughout the estate in both centuries in return for the payment of a substantial premium.

The difficulties created by the relatively haphazard approach to the granting of leases in the early years began to become apparent when those leases came to an end. Because leases expired at different dates, means were devised to ensure that new leases of uniform length were granted from the same starting date so allowing the estate to manage the redevelopment of the estate in a coordinated way at the end of the nineteenth century. Mayfair, which at one stage looked as though it might lose its status as one of London's most fashionable districts in favour of newer developments to the west, was effectively rescued by the renewed desire to take control. The difficulties in managing the estate coincided with the family's financial difficulties at the end of the eighteenth century. The Mayfair estate was transferred to a trust which managed the estate on behalf of the Grosvenors. Although the trust itself was wound up by 1807, the financial difficulties having been resolved, its method of working, through a board composed of the Grosvenors' legal advisors, their estates surveyor and estate agent, did not change. The process of land-use management and control was becoming a corporate activity, albeit one that was wholly within the private sector.

Perhaps the most conspicuous example of successful leasehold control is the laying out and management of Eastbourne by the Duke of Devonshire. Here, spurred on by the craze for sea-bathing in the early nineteenth century, the Devonshire family in conjunction with the Gilbert family, the other major landowner in the area, set about creating what they intended to be a high class resort. This was not simply done through prohibitions on individual leases. There was a deliberate policy to exclude industry and to make clear distinctions between classes of housing. In the end, the Devonshires had to accept that some service industry would be necessary to serve the needs of Eastbourne's residents and, by the same token, that some working-class housing would have to be built. But both were kept well away from the best residential areas in the south west of the town. It was, in Cannadine's words, 'the classic, ideal form of nineteenth century resort zoning' (Cannadine 1980, p. 258). It was matched in Britain only by Folkestone, but finds an echo in the planning of colonial cities, of which the zoning of ethnic groups in Raffles's Singapore is roughly contemporary with the beginnings of Eastbourne (Cangi, 1993).

The Bedford and Grosvenor estates represent the leasehold system at its best. It did not always work so well. Clarke's study of Somers Town (1992) north of the Euston Road between Kings Cross and Euston stations, and therefore immediately to the north of the Bedford estate in Bloomsbury, is a good example of what might go wrong in the control of new development and its subsequent management. Lord Somers, the landowner, appears to have been less interested in the long-term capital value of the estate than increasing ground rents in the short term. Rather than issuing leases and building agreements he leased land in blocks to Jacob Leroux who became responsible for the laying out of roads and sewers and for conveying subleases to builders. Although Lord Somers's lease to Leroux specified the value of houses to be built, he relied on Leroux's agreements with builders for the implementation of these terms. Leroux, as a lessee, had of course less interest than Lord Somers in maintaining the long-term value of the estate. As Clarke (1992) puts it:

The leasehold system depended on a consistent improvement in value through supervision and maintenance. For Somers Town, however, Leroux and not Lord Somers was responsible for the repair of the premises, buildings and all ways and passages as well as paying a portion of the expense of rebuilding walls and roads. As Leroux failed to conform to the original intentions of the scheme and the reversionary value was anyway not his, he had more interest in trying to pass his responsibilities of maintaining the value of the estate onto his sub-tenants . . . (p. 183)

Figure 2.4. London: Seven Dials. The column is a replica of the one erected by Thomas Neale at the junction of the seven streets when the area was first laid out. Few if any of the original houses remain.

Lord Somers did make one attempt to recover control of the estate by buying back the leases in 1811, but by that time it was too late: the pattern of sub-leasing was too complicated. When Leroux died the deterioration of the estate accelerated, and by the end of the nineteenth century Somers Town was a textbook example of the evils of the leasehold system.

Somers Town was not an isolated case. Throughout the period from the mid-seventeenth century to the end of the nineteenth century there were examples of development in which a desire to create a revenue from rents in the short term and a lack of management led to slum conditions. In the 1690s, for example, Thomas Neale laid out the development of Seven Dials immediately to the north of Covent Garden. With its column (replaced in replica since 1988–89) and its radiating pattern of streets it was, if briefly, remarkable. But Neale's interest appears to have been in making an immediate speculative capital gain by raising ground rents rather than in maintaining its long-term value. He appears to have sold his interest in Seven Dials by 1695, and the estate was not maintained as an entity (Booth, 1980). Like Somers Town, it rapidly became a by-word for bad housing conditions and social depravity. Dyos paints a very similar picture in the development of Camberwell in the nineteenth century. There, at the end of the eighteenth century, the largest landlord failed to anticipate the pressure for development and leased land in ways that allowed sub-lessees to build with minimal control (Dyos, 1961). Even landlords of well managed estates were not immune from problems. Cannadine (1980) describes the sedulous care with which the Calthorpe family developed and maintained the Edgbaston estate in Birmingham. Building form was carefully controlled and undesirable uses excluded. But on their London estates the story was rather different. At Grays Inn Road, the quality of the development was only assured because the Calthorpes were fortunate enough to have the resourceful builder, Thomas Cubitt, as their lessee. On their City Road holdings, leaving development to a lessee had very much the same effect at Somers Town, and the area became a slum.

The message in every case was the same. For the leasehold system to work effectively, the desire for short-term return had to be tempered by a long-term interest in the improvement of capital values and there needed to be a capacity to manage the development through the lifetime of the lease. Even when the management of the estate was competent, other forces were at work to undermine the effectiveness of the leasehold agreement as a means of controlling urban development. Clarke (1992), for example, argues that the move towards the more tightly organized building industry which relied on the fixed price contract and waged labour rather than the output of artisan builders working on their own account, not only increased production but led to an increased commodification of housing. The sale price or rental value of the houses became the dominant concern and immediate profits began to dominate the traditional interest in long-term value. If a builder was now always concerned to minimize production costs, control might have to take a rather different form.

We have already seen the negative impact of an interest in short-term profit on a badly managed estate in the case of Somers Town. In the nineteenth century, it equally began to affect attitudes to the control of urban development where intentions were rather better. The case of the Sharrow estate in Sheffield owned by the cutler, George Wostenholm, is a case in point. Wostenholm was not exactly a self-made man, but from relatively modest beginnings made a notable success of his father's cutlery firm through the energy with which he developed trade particularly with the United States. As so many successful businessmen were to do in the nineteenth century he bought land at Sharrow, then just outside the built-up area of Sheffield, to create a country seat and park for himself. Further purchases

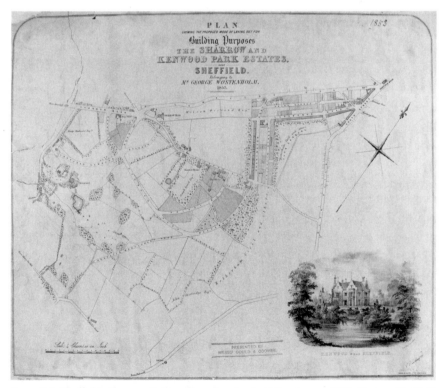

Figure 2.5. Sheffield: Sharrow Estate. Plan showing building leases, 1853. (*Source*: Sheffield Local Studies Library, S(22) 1 M)

of land in the 1840s and 1850s allowed him to propose the development of an exclusive residential suburb (Bexfield, 1945; Stainton, 1924).

Wostenholm's intentions were certainly on a grand scale. He commissioned a well-known landscape architect to prepare a site layout and then issued building leases for villas along the roads which Wostenholm himself laid out and planted with avenues of trees. So much was entirely consistent with the model provided by the aristocratic estates we have already discussed. From an early stage Wostenholm began selling the freehold of the land he had bought, however. Some of these sales were to a local builder, Thomas Steade, who was in the end responsible for much of the housing built on the estate, but the freehold of individual plots was also sold. The result was that the estate that Wostenholm's widow inherited on his death was no longer a coherent whole. Much of the central part of the estate was no longer in Wostenholm's ownership at all and parts of the more modest housing were let on 800-year leases, which meant that the ground landlord had little effective control over, or interest in, its long-term management.[1] Though the sale of freehold may have been prompted by Wostenholm's relative lack of success in getting the development of the Sharrow estate going, he was also evidently treating the land as a saleable commodity. In spite of the initial vision to create an exclusive suburb, Wostenholm showed less interest in the long-term management of the estate than he did in the profits to be made from sales.

Developing legal doctrine may also serve to explain why the traditional form of control through leasehold agreements was weakening. Restrictive covenants could be, and were, applied to leasehold agreements and formed a contract between landlord and lessee. It was, in theory at least, easy for the landlord to enforce such contracts. Restrictive covenants could also, of course, be attached to freehold sale agreements and Wostenholm had, for example, placed stringent requirements on Thomas Steade. But their long-term legal effects were less clear. To what extent did they bind successive owners of the freehold?

The key case here was *Tulk v. Moxhay (1848)*. Moxhay had bought the land of Leicester Square in London in the knowledge that the vendor had entered into an agreement with the original owner not to build on the gardens of the square itself. The courts ruled that although Moxhay did not have a contract with the original owner of the square, he was nevertheless still bound by the original covenant. Grant presents the Tulk v. Moxhay case as a major step forward towards modern land-use control because it confirmed that restrictive covenants were enduring and did not just bind those who had entered into the covenant in the first place. Just because there was no 'contractual nexus' between Moxhay and the original owner did not mean that Moxhay was free to break the covenant and build on the gardens (Grant, 1982; McAuslan, 1975). Though subsequent cases imposed limitations on the right to enforce covenants, the judgement did have two very significant consequences. First, it provided the conceptual foundation for control that 'ran with the land' and in this way bound successive owners of the particular piece of land, even if they had no contractual relationship with the original owner who had imposed the restrictive covenant. This idea that covenants attached to the land and not to just to the contract between the original owner and a particular purchaser provided the basis on which planning legislation was later to depend. Secondly, we may argue that by strengthening the legal power of covenants, it reduced the need for landowners to use the classic leasehold agreement as a way of maintaining the force of restrictive covenants. But by removing the reliance on leasehold tenure, the capacity for long-term management of both the fabric and land uses was attenuated.

Another area in which doctrine was developing was in the law of nuisance. We have already seen how the concept of nuisance had been used in the regulation of disputes between adjoining owners in the Middle Ages. By the nineteenth century it was possible for individuals to defend themselves against a long list of nuisances which already by the end of eighteenth century had been codified by, for example, Viner's *Abridgement* (1791). Common law was by and large supportive of an individual's right to seek protection from nuisance. With the Industrial Revolution, judges found themselves faced with arguments about the public utility of an offending use and about the extent and impact of nuisance caused by industry. The result was to force judges to enter an arena of public policy-making for which they were probably ill-suited (McLaren, 1983).

So as the law developed in both the application of restrictive covenants and in the control of nuisance, the limitations of private sector control of urban development became increasingly apparent. Indeed the problems arose as much with land use as they did with the physical fabric of cities. Problems of disease and poor housing in the nineteenth century led directly to a realization that renewed public intervention in the control of urban development was necessary.

Municipal Corporations and Sanitary Control

The 1774 London Buildings Act remained unchanged for 70 years in London. However, within that period changes were taking place in the country as a whole which were to have a very considerable impact on the capacity to control urban development. Not only did cities like Bristol and Liverpool push to acquire their own legislation to control new buildings (Harper, 1985), the 1835 Municipal Corporations

Act led to the creation of a capacity to control through the introduction of elected corporations in 178 boroughs and cities (Cherry, 1996). Though only those with property were eligible to vote, the Act nevertheless represented a defeat by the newly emerging industrial middle classes over the older landowning gentry and aristocracy who were over-represented among the county justices of the peace. The administrative framework was in place onto which controls imposed by statute could now be grafted.

The middle years of the nineteenth century did indeed witness a series of Acts of Parliament intended to ensure that new development did not replicate the insanitary and overcrowded conditions that had proliferated in the previous 50 years. Of this legislation the most significant were the 1858 Local Government Act and the 1875 Public Health Act. These Acts specifically allowed municipal councils to make bylaws for the control of new development, and were in theory intended to be a decentralizing measure, to give municipal councils greater control over their own destiny. The 1858 Act did, however, also set up the Local Government Act Office at central government level, which had specific, if discretionary, powers related to town development. One of the early tasks of the office was to issue model bylaws in 1858 and then again in a more detailed form in 1877 following the 1875 Public Health Act. These bylaws could control structure, the space around buildings and their drainage and the dimensions of streets (Gaskell, 1983) and did so by imposing dimensional standards for all new development. To that extent the bylaws were within a mainstream of regulation that had been initiated two centuries before. Only the sanitary objective was new; for the rest, they had the same intentions and rather the same limitations of earlier legislation. The Office had perhaps imagined that its work in the control of building might stop with the drafting of the model bylaws. But in practice, as Lambert (1962) notes, the Office came to wield considerable influence, not least because municipal corporations turned to it for advice. In this way the Local Government Act Office established a role for central government in the control of urban development that was not overtly coercive but rather more subtly persuasive. This role was one which capitalized on local authorities' ignorance and the technical skills available within the Office itself. It was to set the pattern for relationships between central and local government for the next 100 years.

According to Muthesius (1982), 'all major towns issued bylaws according to the 1848 and 1858 Acts' and the 1877 Model Bylaws were adopted almost everywhere (p. 35). The fact that the Model Bylaws should have been so widely adopted from the outset suggests a strong latent desire for control in the country as a whole. Certainly Sheffield was no exception in adopting building bylaws in October

1864 and appointing a surveyor to ensure that the bylaws were applied. At first, the post of surveyor was part-time and the first appointee maintained a private office, just as the district surveyors and the surveyors to the great estates had done in London. By 1878 the post had become full-time and the borough surveyor had several assistants. The Council itself set up a Highways Committee and the first applications for bylaw approval were considered in January 1865 the era of public control of development had begun.[2]

The Sheffield bylaws did not depart from the general terms of the Model Bylaws of 1858. They contain constructional standards for new streets and there are eight sections on drainage. The bylaws also spelled out the requirements to submit plans and to have work in progress inspected. Fines for non-compliance were included. The regulations were almost entirely aimed at new housing but one brief clause dealt with the ventilation of public buildings. Two points are worthy of comment. First, the Council gave itself the power to modify the position of a new street 'for the purpose of causing it to communicate in a direct line with any other street adjoining or leading thereto, or for the purpose of making the same communicate therewith at a more convenient level' (Section 1). This was a small but significant step to the Council acquiring prospective rather than simply reactive control powers.

Figure 2.6. Sheffield: South View Road, 1995. The impact of Sheffield's building bylaws on housing.

Secondly, the regulations were drafted to confer considerable discretionary power on the Council and details of construction such as the thickness of walls were left to the undefined approval of the Council. Where there were fixed limits, the Council gave itself the freedom to make variations according to circumstance. The bylaws were, however, amplified by guidance notes issued by the surveyor which supplied a good deal of detail on the dimensional and constructional standards that were omitted from the bylaws themselves.

The records of the Highways Committee meetings show that the Council entered into its responsibilities with gusto. In the first ten months the Committee considered 321 plans for housing and rejected nearly a third. The workload appears to have increased steadily and although most applications were for housing, a substantial minority were for buildings for other uses, from schools and chapels to slaughterhouses, bakeries and even billiard and photographic rooms. Throughout 1865 and 1866 there is regular reference to proceedings being taken against builders who completed buildings contrary to approved plans or who failed to submit plans at all. Thereafter, the number of cases recorded diminished somewhat, which may reflect a growing acceptance by builders of the need to seek advance approval and greater understanding of bylaw requirements rather than a slackening of the council's watchfulness.[3] Sheffield was not unique in the seriousness with which it took the task of bylaw control. Muthesius (1982) argued that not only were bylaws widely adopted by councils but also that they were in general applied rigorously. Municipal corporations were taking over the mantle of the private landlord and assuming a trusteeship of the urban development in their area.

The apparent effortlessness of the transition to the public control of urban development through the use of bylaws is remarkable. It suggests that the ground had already been well prepared and that for local authorities to act in this way was by the second half of the nineteenth century something which came naturally to them. The use of public health bylaws appears to be the summation of a process that had started long before. But in fact it was no more than a beginning and one which fairly soon came to be seen as too limited by half. It was out of the perceived failure of the public health legislation that land-use planning in the twentieth century was born. What had been achieved was to establish a process and to create an understanding. The process was one in which individual proposals for urban development were scrutinized and evaluated against criteria set by a controlling authority. The understanding was that there was an important area of public interest in the control of development which stood apart from the private interests of landowners, builders and householders, for which the local authority was an appropriate trustee.

Conclusion: The Origins of Modern Development Control

Out of this rapid review of its history extending back some 600 years before the first town planning legislation, three categories of experience have a bearing on the evolution of development control in the twentieth century. First, are those elements which created the conceptual framework for a certain way of controlling urban development. This framework is derived partly from theorizing about the nature of land and development themselves and partly from the constitutional arrangements for taking decisions and legitimating action. Secondly, there are the objects of the control of urban development. Both of these reflect important continuities from the period before 1900 to development control under the planning Acts. But the third category of experience was largely negative. For modern development control also represented a reaction to what had preceded it while at the same time drawing very heavily upon past experience.

Some of the conceptual foundations of modern development control lie in the Middle Ages. The doctrine of estates which gave substance to the possibility of overlapping interests in land made it easy for the state to consider nationalizing future development rights. The argument is that the 'interest' represented by using the land in its current conditions could be divided from the 'interest' in the future development of that land. For the state to nationalize future development rights did not the need all land to be taken into public ownership. In this way the State was able to take an essentially radical step in the 1947 Town and Country Planning Act and disguise it as part of the continuum of property rights. It resulted in a State involvement in the control of development which was distinctly different from that in continental Europe. An equally significant concept was that of a trust which, as we have seen, emerged as a device to get round some of the limitations of feudal tenure. The trust established in the Middle Ages, with its often fictitious trustees, was certainly of a different order from those that were developed from the eighteenth century onwards. But the principle involved in those medieval trusts was to endure. In a trust, those who managed land – the trustees – did not occupy it but carried a moral responsibility for those who did: the trustees were *obliged* to act in the best interests of the beneficiaries who were the occupiers. The Grosvenor estate had already set up such a trust to manage land at the end of the eighteenth century. Again it was conceptually easy for the new municipal corporations to see themselves as trustees for their electorate in the management of land.

A second part of the conceptual framework was the development of common law and the law of equity. The emphasis placed on detailed inspection of the individual circumstances of each case and the evolution of judge-made rules for dealing with the particularities of cases were gradually transferred from the judicial to the administrative realm. The fact that the law of equity dealt specifically with property interests made the general approach particularly relevant to the control and management of land use which had to reconcile competing interests, albeit of a rather different order. In a more general way, the fact that justices of the peace were responsible for local administration in much of the country until the later nineteenth century made the transfer of the case law approach to administrative problems natural. Dealing with problems case by case also inevitably places an emphasis on the decision-makers' discretion to decide. Certainly the exercise of discretionary power, and the push for greater freedom to act is already evident by the nineteenth century.

A third part of this framework was the gradual development of the distinction between the private interests of those with tenure and the common interest of the population at large. The first glimmerings of this distinction are already present in the Middle Ages with the concern for encroachments on highways. But it is with the seventeenth and eighteenth centuries that legal doctrine begins to elaborate the concept, first as a way of making sense of the royal proclamations and then in statute law, such that by the nineteenth century the control of urban development could be seen as something which transcended private interests. By implication, the Tulk v. Moxhay judgement also pointed to an overarching interest in the way in which land was used: a restrictive covenant would no longer simply bind those who had originally made the contract.

The final part of the framework for development control in the twentieth century comes with the thinking about appropriate forms of local administration for control. The partial failure of the royal proclamations to restrict growth must have been the absence of a proper mechanism for ensuring the proclamations could be applied. The Commission for Buildings was only intermittently effective. On the other hand the surveyors appointed to deal with the rebuilding of London after the Great Fire clearly were effective. The only problem was that they, and the Fire Court set up to adjudicate in the event of dispute, ceased to exist when the rebuilding was complete. Nevertheless the establishment, from 1774, of a permanent body of surveyors who could certify that buildings conformed to the London Building Act was to create a much stronger precedent for the development of a public service than anything that had preceded it. What was lacking was a way of making these surveyors properly accountable for their work. The creation of the municipal corporations after 1835 in the major provincial towns provided a complete alternative to major landowners as the ultimate authority on the way in which development took place. The other kind of conceptualization was about the correct relationship between central and local authority. The Stuart monarchs' desire to impose their will on matters of urban development in London led to a radical rejection of central interference in local affairs. The activities of the great estates confirmed the capacity of the private sector to take a lead in development. But just as in time municipal corporations provided increasingly effective public leadership at the local level, so too, central government began to re-assert its authority. It did so by stealth, however. The Local Government Act Office came to exert considerable influence over the activities of local government, in spite of protestations that the government would not interfere with local authority responsibilities. Such a pattern would be repeated in the twentieth century.

So the conceptual foundations for development control under the planning Acts long pre-date the planning Acts themselves. So, too, do the objectives that have been set for development control. A frequently cited objective has been aesthetic. The Stuart monarchs before the Civil War tried explicitly to impose a canon of taste on new development and succeeded in that objective – perhaps fortuitously – rather better than in the absolute restrictions which they imposed by proclamation. Aesthetic preoccupations also continued to surface in the period in which control by landlords was paramount. Sometimes this had to do with overall form and layout, as in the Bedford estate, but it might equally have to do with matters of detail as records of the Grosvenor estate demonstrate. Though aesthetics were clearly not a consideration in the application of bylaw control, the reaction to bylaw control was, as we shall see, couched partly in aesthetic terms.

The control of urban development has also been justified in the interest of creating a safe and sanitary environment as well one which was aesthetically pleasing. Fear of fire and disease surface at all periods up to 1900, and as fire has ceased to be a preoccupation, the desire to create a healthy environment which responds to residents' needs has continued to inform attitudes to the control of development. It is true that the major problems as they were perceived in the eighteenth and nineteenth centuries have largely been conquered, but a rather more diffuse understanding of physical well-being which embraces problems of pollution and the need for healthy recreation, amongst other things, remains present in the general concern for environmental control.

A third objective has been the desire to control uses and activities as well as building form. We have noted that the explicit reference to material change of use in the Town and Country Planning Act 1947 is one of the things that set British development apart from other systems. Again, this preoccupation long pre-dates the planning Acts. Concern with activities which caused a nuisance had found routine expression in leasehold agreements by the beginning of the nineteenth century, and such concern was rooted in a well-developed common law tradition. The desire to gain control over material change of use is in no sense a product of thinking in the 1930s and 1940s; the planning Acts gave statutory force to what had hitherto lain in the realm of common law and private agreements. There is another aspect of this desire to control land use. Government policy in the past 50 years has emphasized that town planning controls the use of land and should not be concerned with the character of the user. Yet the desire to maintain social exclusiveness, often explicitly present in methods of control used before 1900, remains an undercurrent in present practice. The Stuarts did not only offer licenses in order to increase royal revenues. They were as much concerned that the potentially lawless were excluded from the capital and that new development attracted people of appropriate rank. The same concern is present in the activities of the great landlords in the eighteenth century and in the restrictions placed on development of villa estates in the nineteenth century. And what had initially been imposed from above rapidly came to be self-policing as residents themselves sought to maintain social exclusiveness.

The final aspect of continuity concerns the use of measurable standards for development. From the Assize of Nuisance onwards, regulations were put in place that identified dimensional norms for new development, whether these were expressed in terms of constructional detail or site layout. Instrumental in this process were surveyors who took over from the city viewers as a chief source of technical expertise and whose influence continued into the twentieth century. By the first town planning Acts these dimensional standards had crystallized into the use of building lines, the siting of buildings, and the imposition of dwelling densities. Though the standards used in the twentieth century did change, the underlying impulse was the same: to find objective measures of quality against which new developments could be evaluated. The early town planning schemes after 1909 were to be strikingly like the surveyors' plans attached to deeds of sale and leasehold agreements in the century before.

If development control in the twentieth century has significant continuities with the past we need also to remember that the development control system under the planning Acts represents a deliberate reaction to forms of control that had existed before 1900. The first reaction was against a system that relied heavily on private landlords and leasehold agreements. The leasehold agreement was widely perceived as perpetuating bad housing conditions (see Acland, 1914) even if Offer (1981) argues that the number of buildings nearing the end of their leases, and hence likely to be in a poor state of repair, were probably comparatively few. Private landlords were increasingly seen as concerned only with their own gain and the premiums they levied on the renewal of leases were anathematized as the 'unearned increment'. The control of urban development was too important to be left to the private sector.

A second reaction was against the rigid standards of the bylaws. Here there is a paradox. The public health bylaws were, as we have seen, applied in most of the country by the end of the nineteenth century. There is little doubt that they had a major impact on reducing disease. But the results they produced soon came to be criticized for their monotony. Local authorities saw themselves – and indeed were – bound by the standards imposed by the bylaws. Though they certainly attempted to stretch the limits of bylaw controls, the only real answer was to find a mode of control that escaped the bylaws altogether. Yet under the planning Acts as we have already noted, local authorities continued to impose dimensional norms on new development.

Part of the reason for the paradox of local authorities perpetuating the very form of control against which they had campaigned lies in a third reaction. The trouble with bylaw control, as with the 1774 London Building Act, was that it was essentially reactive. Decisions on where new development would take place and how it would relate to existing development were beyond its scope. Local authorities, having cut their teeth on bylaw control, now wanted to extend their activities to embrace strategic decisions and prospective policy-making. Yet they had at their disposal only the tools with which they were familiar.

Notes

1. Sheffield Archives. SC1017 Trust deed dated 18 August 1882.
2. Sheffield City Council, Minutes, 13 July 1864, 7 September 1864; Highways Committee, 6 January 1865.
3. Sheffield City Council, New Works and Plans Sub-Committee, 27 September 1867.

Chapter Three

The Search for Flexibility

By the beginning of the twentieth century the traditional mechanisms for the control of urban development were coming under sustained attack. The private landed interest which had been responsible for much of the finest domestic architecture of the eighteenth and nineteenth centuries was increasingly seen as making money at the expense of the middle classes and the industrious working classes. The Liberal Land Enquiry Committee, reporting in 1914, listed six objections to the leasehold system by leaseholders. These included the fact that improvements were appropriated by the landlord at the end of the lease, that renewals were difficult except on exorbitant and 'unjust terms', and that lessees were subject to controls and charges that were often perceived as unreasonable. In addition there were objections on public grounds. These concerned the difficulties of structural deterioration towards the end of the lease, the problems of 'fag-end' leases and the effects on rental levels of landlords' exaction (Acland, 1914, pp. 408–409). These points do, of course, do no more than reiterate criticisms which had been growing in the later nineteenth century. But what is striking in general is the way in which these criticisms reveal a loss of any belief that landlords might be acting in a general long-term public interest as well as to their own advantage.

In part, these criticisms sprang from a much wider power struggle between an older, landed aristocracy and a newer industrial and professional middle class. We also noted in the previous chapter the way in which the structure of landownership was changing. The great estates might have survived and were still controlling development in the areas of which they retained the freehold, but there were also more and more ground landlords whose main interest was in securing income and profit through the sale of buildings in the short term rather than in the management of an estate in perpetuity. This growing commodification of housing

– as against the management of the land which was the aristocratic landlord's main interest – together with the growth in numbers of freehold owner-occupiers was to have a significant impact on property relations in general, and clearly allowed a much sharper distinction between public and private interest. Moreover, where estates did still practice such strict control, they did so overwhelmingly to retain the exclusivity of the area, because maintaining middle-class respectability was consistent with the landlords' desire to improve the value of the land.

The nature of public control was also being questioned. The building bylaws which had become more or less universal by the end of the nineteenth century were in a direct line of succession to the controls imposed from the seventeenth century onwards. They identified clear constructional standards which builders were required to follow, and successive attempts to reformulate standards had led to an ever-increasing precision. What had changed was the capacity of the administration. By 1900 there was a properly constituted and unified system of local government that acted in the belief that it, too, had an interest in the way in which development took place. In the closing decades of the nineteenth century local authorities established an effective system for ensuring that standards were met.

The Limitations of the Public Health Act

But by 1900 the building bylaws were also beginning to come under sustained attack. There were three major reasons for the frustration. The first was aesthetic and sanitary. There seemed to be a growing belief that in spite of bylaw regulation builders were still perpetrating the practices that had led to slums in the past. The argument is succinctly summarized by Aldridge (1915):

But valuable as the new order and method were as compared with the chaos of development preceding the Bye-law period, the sanitary reformers of the Victorian era left undone the most important part of the task. They desired to secure order and achieved monotony. They rendered impossible the development of the old *cul-de-sac*, alley and court, but they brought into existence a street of a type which has been called, not without justice, a 'new slum'. They secured the provision of sanitary houses, but as a result of the limitation of their regulations, these sanitary houses were placed together in what the President of the Local Government Board . . . called in a picturesque phrase 'long rows of brick boxes with slate lids. (p. 143)

Although the Liberal Land Enquiry offered examples of considerable over-crowding in new terraced housing, these references to the creation of new slums were more concerned with aesthetics than sanitation. And in this, housing reformers such as Aldridge had been encouraged by the growing experimentation in housing that dates from the end of the nineteenth century. The low densities and the informal cottage architecture of Bournville and Port Sunlight and then, from 1900, of the work of Barry Parker and Raymond Unwin stood in marked contrast to the serried ranks of bylaw houses being built at very much the same time. The model bylaws effectively prevented garden city layouts, and indeed, at Hampstead Garden Suburb in 1906, Hendon bylaws had to be set aside by a private Act of Parliament to allow Unwin and Parker to create the *culs-de-sac* that were an integral part of the concept (Unwin, 1909).

The second reason for the frustration felt by housing reformers was that bylaws imposed unnecessary costs on buildings and so made housing more expensive than it need have been. J.S. Nettlefold, one of the great protagonists of the early town planning movement, was clear that a prime objective in ensuring good housing conditions must be to avoid unnecessary expense; bylaws had signally failed, in his view, to achieve 'better housing at reasonable rents' (Nettlefold, 1914, p.74). Much of the unnecessary expenditure was on roads that were built in excess of need. Unwin and Parker were similarly forthright about the unnecessary costs of bylaw construction and their model estate at New Earswick was deliberately developed with a layout and a style of cottage architecture which reduced costs with the aim of allowing affordable rents.

The third main reason for the frustration is perhaps the most significant of them all. Local authorities now believed they had a legitimate interest in controlling development but were persistently hampered in their ability to express that interest to the full. There are two strands to this argument. A report by three Lancashire Urban Districts reproduced in Aldridge's book summarizes the position neatly:

. . . landowners can each lay out their land to suit their own interest, irrespective of the public convenience, and without considering the effect on adjacent land. Builders can develop small areas of land as they like, provided they comply with the Local Bye-laws. They can crowd houses up to forty or fifty per acre. The unscrupulous builder can erect houses of the cheapest and commonest character amongst the best residential property, and thus greatly depreciate the neighbourhood. (cited by Aldridge, 1915, p. 187)

Local authorities were now wanting to exercise the powers that had traditionally been held by ground landlords. The search was on for a real increase in public control.

The other strand to the argument was the desire for increased 'elasticity' in the bylaws which is common to much of the writing of the period. This call for greater elasticity presented the protagonists of reform with more difficulties. The history of the control of urban development in the nineteenth century had, after all, been one of increasing precision in the way in which regulations were drafted in order to exclude the laxity that led to slum conditions. This had been as true of the private sector as of public statute. The trouble with precisely defined dimensional norms was that they provided a straitjacket which allowed neither experimentation in better quality layouts, nor cost reduction to ensure cheap rents.

To give voice to local authorities' frustration at their inability to exercise control as fully as they wished, in 1906 the National Housing Reform Council (later the National Housing and Town Planning Council) led a deputation to the Prime Minister, Henry Campbell-Bannerman. Canon Moore Ede, a member of the deputation, put the case in this way:

We ask that the bye-laws may be re-modelled, so as to give such elasticity as will, without lowering standards of house building or sanitary requirement, encourage variety in planning of areas and houses and greater choice in the materials employed. (cited by Aldridge, 1915, p. 175)

The point was made: to achieve the aesthetic quality and the economies now being sought, elasticity was needed. Campbell-Bannerman's reply sums up the dilemma that the call for elasticity suggested:

. . . again it is said 'Let the building bye-laws be made more elastic'. On the other hand, if they are to be useful they must be strict, and some people insist, with good reason, that they should be made more strict. (ibid, p. 181)

The dilemma was understandable: if the bylaws were made 'elastic' would not the process of control be thereby weakened?

At least the argument about elasticity was about more control not less. Local authorities were asking for greater discretion to control as they saw fit. The trouble with dimensional norms, which had been the substance of all legislation to control urban development until the beginning of the twentieth century, was the way in which the decision-maker was constrained. Much of the elasticity that existed in the system before the mid-nineteenth century was the product of inefficient or corrupt administration. Although corruption and inefficient administration would continue to be part of the reformed local government system, there seems to have been much greater public intolerance of both in the nineteenth century, perhaps because the awareness of a distinct public interest naturally gave rise to the desire for greater public accountability. Central government's growing role was in defining what the proper scope of control under the Public Health Act should be.

Local authorities, on the other hand, were testing in a more formal way the limits of their powers. According to the then Cambridge Borough Surveyor, the Local Government Board did not let local authorities include a clause in their bylaws which allowed the bylaws to be waived under given circumstances. At the same time the courts had refused to allow local authorities to depart from their own bylaws, but did take the view that bylaws 'should contain a dispensing power' (Julian, 1914, p. 63). And Julian also notes how the bylaws might in any case convey a discretionary power by using words like 'proper', 'adequate and 'suitable' without further qualification. Local authorities wanted, and to some extent achieved, 'elasticity' to exert greater control over what they saw as their legitimate interest. But discretionary clauses in the bylaws were not of themselves anything like enough.

The First Planning Legislation

The passage of the 1909 Housing, Town Planning etc. Act has been fully described by others (see Minett, 1974; Cherry, 1974; Sutcliffe, 1981). Its origins lie partly in the emerging desire to decongest industrial cities and to discover a new form of settlement layout of the kind that characterized the Garden City movement. Such a desire was fuelled by an interest in, and knowledge of, the experience of Germany in creating town extension plans, which was used as a lever on the government to enact legislation which would give British local authorities the same kind of powers (Sutcliffe, 1981). The creation of Hampstead Garden Suburb from 1906 gave a working example to MPs that was within easy reach of Westminster. The National Housing Reform Council had also specifically asked for the creation of a National Town Extension Commission in the course of their deputation to the Prime Minister in 1906. The Local Government Board was clearly unenthusiastic about this idea as indeed it was to the first town planning Bill as a whole in 1906.[1]

In the end, the legislation that was finally given royal assent was a considerable disappointment to its promoters (Herbert-Young, 1998). The town planning provisions allowed local authorities to prepare town planning schemes 'with the general object of securing proper sanitary conditions, amenity and convenience in connection with the laying out and use of land and any neighbouring land'. This wording was to allow for a significant discretionary element in schemes, and famously introduced the all-embracing term 'amenity' which, however poorly defined, was to become a point of reference for town planners thereafter. The scope of the Act was, therefore, potentially very wide and gave local authorities an all-embracing interest in the development land. The disappointment lay in the fact that the legislation was permissive not mandatory: town planning schemes created under the Act could only apply to 'any land in course of development or likely to be used for building purposes' (Section 5). Built up areas were specifically excluded. There may have been a growing body of opinion that favoured increasing local authority control over urban development, but there was still a strong legacy of the belief in the rights of landowners and the efficacy of private initiative. The argument centred very largely on the power (or lack of it) to make *plans*, not on the power to *control*. The two were seen as essentially indissoluble.

The Housing, Town Planning etc. Act allowed for the creation of town planning schemes which would set out a strategy for the future land use and lay down the road pattern of the area which the scheme covered. The scheme would consist of a plan together with a set of regulations which would spell out how the scheme was to be applied. What the Act did not do was to set up a procedure for control based upon the scheme: there was no equivalent of the planning permission that was to be the staple requirement of the 1947 legislation. Developers would be obliged to follow the provisions of the scheme once it had been approved, and the need for bylaw approval would continue to apply.

The sanction against buildings which did not conform to the scheme was demolition, or at least modification. But the approval required by the bylaws for construction implied that local authorities would in fact have a measure of oversight of individual decisions to develop before building began, even if the powers to approve or disapprove could only really be based upon the bylaws. This power of oversight was, as we shall see, something that local authorities sought to develop in their early planning schemes.

More significant than the intentions and limitations of the Act were the ways in which local authorities and the Local Government Board chose to use it. The number of schemes approved by the outbreak of World War I when activity on planning stopped were very few indeed: by 1919, 172 schemes had been started but only thirteen schemes had even been submitted for approval and of these five were in Birmingham (Cherry, 1974). The root causes of this poor record are fairly clear. One was procedural: the Local Government Board had to give consent to a local authority to proceed with the scheme and to the area to which it applied. All landowners had to be consulted before the scheme could commence and this process of registration was onerous and time consuming. Later discussions over the content of the scheme would then take place between the local authority and the Local Government Board which would culminate in a hearing before the Board's planning inspector. Only then would the Board grant approval for the scheme.

The other cause of delay was uncertainty on the part of both local and central government. The Local Government Board had power under Section 55 to make general regulations for the content of planning schemes and the scope of those general provisions were classified under nineteen headings in the fourth schedule to the Act. Thomas Adams thought that 'these provisions will very probably be in the form of an amplification of the bylaws' but saw their great virtue as being to distinguish between areas of different character, unlike the bylaws themselves (Culpin, 1909). No general provisions were in fact made before the outbreak of the war. The Board seems to have wanted to draw upon the experience of early schemes before doing so. J.A.E. Dickinson in evidence to the Departmental Committee on building bylaws in 1914 could comment somewhat complacently that he thought that 'local authorities are recognizing that we have rendered a great deal of assistance to them in connection with the form of schemes, and in that sense we are now engaged in settling the general provision of the future'.[2] But much of the credit for innovation in clauses must go to the local authorities themselves. An exchange of letters between the Board and E.R. Abbott, Clerk to Ruislip-Northwood Urban District Council, in 1911 made clear both the district's desire for the guidance of general provisions and the absence of any intention on the Board's part to prepare such provisions 'at an early date'.[3] A letter a month earlier from the Town Clerk of Birmingham made exactly the same request.[4] Perhaps official uncertainty at the Board was a reflection of their lack of enthusiasm for the legislation in the first place.

Although only a very few schemes might have been finalized under the 1909 legislation and only three actually received formal approval by the outbreak of war,[5] there was perhaps rather more enthusiasm at the local level than these figures suggest. Sheffield, for example, had by 1913 made considerable headway in defining areas for town planning schemes and had received authorization for schemes on 6000 acres (2500 hectares), approximately half the land available for development within the city. Wike, the City Surveyor, was clear why planning schemes were needed:

The advantage of possessing legislation will at once be realised when it is stated that, in cases where several estates adjoin each other, there is nothing to prevent an owner laying out his estate irrespective of any other owner. In Sheffield, this has resulted in many cases in the formation of narrow cul-de-sacs which by a little re-arrangement or a give-and-take principle might have become good through roads . . . In future . . . the lines of all main and secondary roads will be laid down by the corporation and set out on a plan, to which the owners will be asked to adhere. (Wike 1913, p. 2)

Wike quite clearly saw the City Council as the successor to the landlords of the previous century acting in trust to the public interest in land which could override the purely selfish concerns of immediate developers. At Birmingham, the identification of the Corporation with the role of landowner is even clearer. A speech by the Lord Mayor announcing the intention to proceed with the Quinton, Harborne and Edgbaston planning scheme, in the event the very first to be approved, makes direct reference to the Calthorpe Estate and the 'beautiful suburb of Edgbaston which is the pride of the City and the envy of other towns'. While the scheme might not result in development at quite the same quality 'it could nevertheless be treated as a whole rather than individual owners being allowed to run wild with their own ideas'.[6] Perhaps significantly, the Calthorpe estate surveyor, E.H. Balden, sought the exclusion from the planning scheme of 85 acres of undeveloped land on the Edgbaston estate.[7] The local authority might be the successor to the great landlords, but it was not going to usurp their authority entirely.

Preparing the scheme for Quinton, Harborne and Edgbaston produced a protracted correspondence between Birmingham Corporation and the Local Government Board. The Corporation wondered, for example, whether it might be possible to have a clause which required houses to be kept in good order and

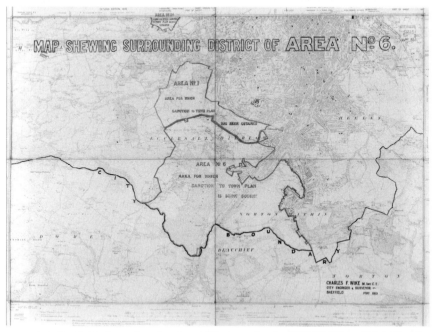

Figure 3.1. Sheffield. Areas for planning schemes under the 1909 Housing, Town Planning etc. Act in 1913. (*Source*: Public Record Office HLG5/1849)

to be 'used properly'; the Board was of the view that bylaws would be a better way of achieving this end. There was also some debate as to whether a scheme could include a clause itself allowing the corporation to make further bylaws, but the Board's view was that such a clause would exceed the powers of the Act. The general impression is that though the Board recognized that it had 'discretion of the widest possible character' to determine the provision of the scheme, it was quite another matter to confer discretion on local authorities even if elasticity would probably be needed.[8]

In the event, the Board did allow Birmingham a number of discretionary powers. They could, for example, depart from the standard dimensions laid down for building lines measured from the middle of the road, but only if the requirement was for less, not more, than the prescribed standard. There were also clauses which allowed the Corporation to identify how many non-residential buildings might be put up in a residential 'unit' (an area which the Corporation itself was at liberty to determine), and the expectation was that a developer would need to seek consent for such buildings. The same was true for residential development which was forbidden in certain areas except with the consent of the Corporation. There was a right of appeal to the Board against the refusal of consent, but there was also a right to appeal against the *giving* of consent.[9] So there was considerable protection for third party interests, although the intention was almost certainly to protect landowners rather than offer a general environmental protection. An appeal formed a useful check on the exercise of discretionary power.

Ruislip-Northwood and the Power to Control Design

The Ruislip-Northwood scheme is in some ways more interesting than the one for Quinton, Harborne and Edgbaston. It was by far the largest scheme to be prepared and approved under the 1909 Act, covering an area of more than 5900 acres (2390 hectares), or not far short of the area of all six of Sheffield's schemes. The area would have been bigger but for the fact that the Eastcote estate, already under development, posed insuperable problems for the service of notices on owners.[10] The scheme was further complicated by the inclusion of land in the rural district of Watford, something allowed for by the Act, but inevitably requiring inter-authority discussions. The general impetus for the scheme was clear enough. Ruislip and Northwood had been rural parishes until the end of the nineteenth century when the Great Central and Metropolitan Railway companies built the railway to Aylesbury which passed through Northwood and the Metropolitan Railway built a branch railway from Harrow to Uxbridge in 1904. This latter was almost immediately electrified and stations built at Ruislip, Eastcote and Ickenham. A third line, the Great Western Railway's link to High Wycombe, ran just south of Ruislip village. The area was rapidly becoming readily accessible to Central London.

There was a significant feature of the Ruislip-Northwood scheme which tied it neatly back to the history of estate development in the nineteenth century. Of the area of the scheme, no less than 1300 acres (526 hectares), which formed the lands of the Manor of Ruislip, were in the single ownership of King's College, Cambridge. The College was not slow to perceive that the new railway lines made the development of land likely and the earliest discussions on development appear to date from 1898 when the possibility of low-density housing on Copse Wood at the Northwood end of the estate was being considered. An initial building agreement was signed in early 1900. Another self-contained part of the estate at King's End Farm by Ruislip station was leased for building in 1907.[11]

In 1907, too, a prospectus was issued by a company formed of graduates of the College, the Ruislip Building Company, to 'assist the college in the development of its estate in Ruislip'.[12] This appears to have been a well meaning but ill-conceived attempt to move development forward; by 1911 the company had gone in to liquidation. No doubt realizing that the Ruislip Building Company did not offer much hope of success, King's had already in June 1910 entered into an agreement with another company, Garden Estates Ltd founded in 1909, whose managing director was Alderman Thompson, President of the National Housing and Town Planning Council. Thompson was, therefore, a protagonist of the low-density garden suburb,and this move represents a determination on the College's part to achieve a high quality of development. A central part of the agreement was that Garden Estates Ltd and King's College would jointly share the cost of preparing a general plan for development. The Company was then given the option to purchase the estate to implement the plan. A separate company, Ruislip Manor Ltd, was then set up to deal specifically with Ruislip. A competition for an estate layout was organized and won at the end of 1910 by the architects A. and J. Soutar whose layout received much praise at the time. The scheme was formed in the Beaux-Arts manner based on a major north-south axis crossing the Uxbridge line at a projected station for Ruislip Manor and creating a desired route across the District. The formal logic of the axis was disrupted where it met a reservoir and Copse Wood. In this new initiative, the College was undoubtedly prompted by Raymond Unwin who had been retained as an advisor to the College (Miller, 1992).[13]

While King's College was negotiating with the Garden City Estates Ltd, the newly formed Ruislip-Northwood Urban District Council, no doubt aware of

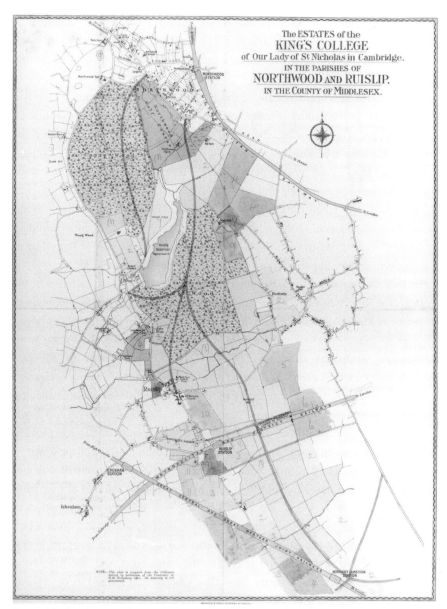

Figure 3.2. Ruislip Manor: the King's College estate. (*Source*: King's College, Cambridge, Modern Archive Centre, RUI 213)

the likelihood of development, announced their intention to prepare a planning scheme which would embrace the whole of the Ruislip Manor Estate. Such a move had the potential for conflict, and we have seen how the Calthorpe's surveyor asked for land on the Edgbaston estate to be removed from the Quinton, Harborne

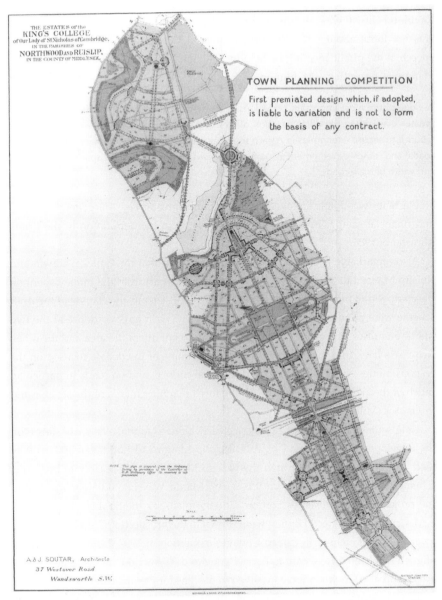

Figure 3.3. Ruislip Manor: the prize winning layout for the King's College land by A. and J. Soutar. (*Source*: King's College, Cambridge, Modern Archive Centre, RUI 213).

and Edgbaston scheme. At Ruislip-Northwood, however, there seems to have been a remarkable unanimity of purpose between the College as landowner, Garden Estates Ltd as developer and the Council as planning authority. Given that Alderman Thompson was a protagonist of the planning movement and that

Raymond Unwin was advising King's College this is not so very surprising. There was no doubt about what Ruislip-Northwood Council wanted to achieve. In a speech at the public meeting he held in 1910, the Chairman of the Council's Town Planning Committee, F.M. Elgood said:

. . . one of the most important provisions in the scheme would be that which would allow greater elasticity in the administration of the bylaws. [Hear, hear] This would enable the Council to secure economies in regard to character and width of subsidiary and residential roads, and, other development expenses, in exchange for huge open spaces and gardens and width of main roads.[14]

Elasticity was being invoked in the name of greater control, general amenity and financial saving, in exactly the same way as in the deputation to the Prime Minister of 1906.

Also remarkable is the immense amount of effort that the College, Unwin and Ruislip Manor Ltd all put in to the scheme. Quite apart from the money spent on the competition plan which was central to the final scheme, the clauses of the draft scheme were pondered endlessly by all three, and each gave evidence at the two public enquiries, one in 1911 to investigate the suitability of the area and the other, two years later, into the scheme itself. Though some of the debate focused on the responsibilities of the landowner and the local council, and on roads in particular, much of the exchange had to do with the town planning merits of the scheme and its clauses (Miller, 1992).

King's and Ruislip Manor Ltd were clearly anxious to make an early start with the development. By the end of 1911, Ruislip Manor Ltd had taken 100 acres of land and Thompson had formed the Ruislip Manor Cottage Society to prepare a scheme for low cost cottages on 9 acres on Manor Way immediately adjacent to the projected Ruislip Manor Station. Cottage plans by the Soutars, H.A. Welch, C.M. Crickmer and Cecil Hignett were shown in the prospectus. Crickmer had won awards at the Letchworth Cheap Cottages exhibition of 1907 (Miller, 1989), while Hignett had been an assistant to Barry Parker and Raymond Unwin at Letchworth. Welch and also Crickmer were involved in designs for Hampstead Garden Suburb, and J.C.S. Soutar was to become consultant to the Hampstead Garden Suburb Trust (Miller, 1992). The garden city credentials of the designers at Ruislip were impeccable. For building to proceed, Ruislip Manor Ltd needed agreement with the Council that the proposed building would not conflict with provisions of the Town Planning Scheme; without such an agreement the development would have been at risk from demolition once the scheme had been approved.[15] The scheme was built substantially as proposed.

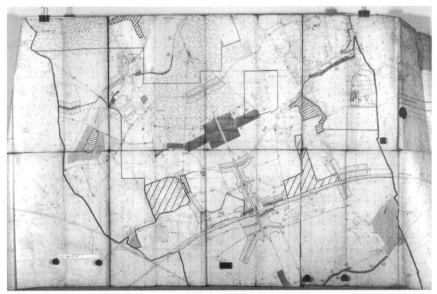

Figure 3.4. Part of the Ruislip–Northwood town planning scheme adjacent to Ruislip Manor station. (*Source*: Public Record Office, HLG5/1753)

Figure 3.5. Ruislip. Houses by Cecil Hignett in Windmill Way for the Ruislip Manor Cottage Society Ltd.

At the outset, King's College evidently wished to exercise a high level of control over development of their land. Towards the end of 1911, for example, in correspondence on the conveyance of King's Manor Farm to Ruislip Manor Ltd, the college proposed to specify the number of houses to be built per acre, to determine their character and value and to control the road layout. Alderman Thompson was quite prepared to accept these restrictions but believed the fifth requirement, to submit details of plans and innovations to the college for their approval, would result in endless discussions. The college stood firm on the requirement. As their surveyor put it in his comment on Thompson's letter: 'it is obviously necessary in the interest of all parties interested in the estate, that erections of new buildings should be controlled. Otherwise the beauty of a street or a district might be ruined by the buildings and alterations selfishly made by a few individuals'.[16] There is no evidence that the college exercised the power to any great extent, however. As the district council elaborated its planning scheme an increasing number of detailed clauses were introduced which meant that control would effectively be exercised by the public authority not by the landowner. As Miller (1992) notes, the clauses set standards for building line, for room sizes, and construction which were derived from Hampstead Garden Suburb, and most importantly laid down the basis for aesthetic control.

The imposition of building lines along streets was the subject of criticism from both Unwin and Thompson. Unwin was concerned that building lines would be too 'arbitrarily restricting [of] the architectural treatment of streets', while Thompson wanted them to be more flexible to allow for projecting end blocks and for shops to be set against the back edge of the pavement.[17] The clause on aesthetic control was far more contentious and involved an intensive exchange between the district and the Local Government Board. Aldridge (1915) cited with approval the clause as included in the final scheme and Punter (1986) has argued that it represents a major landmark in the control of design by local planning authorities. After several attempts to find a satisfactory form of words, the clause as finally approved reads as follows:

56. If, having regard to the nature and situation of the site, of any buildings or buildings proposed to be erected or altered or to the character of any buildings erected or in the course of erection in the neighbourhood of such a site, the Council are of the opinion that the character of the building or buildings proposed to be erected or altered would be injurious to the amenity of the neighbourhood, whether on the account of the design or the undue repetition of the materials to be used, the Council may require such reasonable alterations to be made in regard to the design or the materials as they think fit . . .

The clause also allowed for arbitration by the Royal Institute of British Architects (RIBA) in the event of a dispute.[18]

The clause is remarkable for the extent of the discretion it conferred on the Council, and for way that it explicitly used the word amenity, drawn from the Act itself, in relation to aesthetics. It is also important for the way in which it defined the field to which this discretionary power might be applied. In so doing it was to set the tenor of aesthetic control for much of the rest of the century. What was new was not the power itself but the degree of articulation and the fact that it would be the local authority that would exercise the power. For well before the scheme was approved, King's College had already intended to control the aesthetics of development on Ruislip Manor requiring the submission of plans for approval, just as the aristocratic estates had done in the previous century.

The Board very nearly refused to allow the inclusion of the clause at all. Raymond Unwin speaking on behalf of the RIBA at the second public inquiry in 1913 was in favour of aesthetic control, and had perhaps advised King's on the agreement with Ruislip Manor Ltd. Civil servants were clearly opposed, on the other hand. As Thomas Adams, the Board Inspector at both public inquiries, put it in his report:

I am doubtful if the Board can approve the Clause either in its original or revised form. The suggestion is to set up a censorship of taste in regard to the elevations of buildings.

The fundamental objection seems to have been a distaste for the growing power of local councils. A Local Government Board file note makes the point forcibly:

. . . the provision in Section 54 (5) [of the 1909 Housing, Town Planning etc Act] is so general that it seems to enable anything and everything to be included. If once included in the scheme and approved by the Board, the provisions are to have effect as if they are enacted by Parliament. I feel quite certain, however, that if the powers of D.C.s are unreasonably exercised some means will be found of quashing them. There are many points in the present scheme which would clearly be *ultra vires* if they were judged by the ordinary standard, i.e. if they could be brought before a Court of Law at liberty to deal with them as the Court thought fit.

The clause on aesthetic control was thought to go 'very close to the border in this respect'. In the end, the determining factor seems to have been the support of the Board's President, John Burns, which was in marked contrast to his officials' opposition. Ruislip-Northwood was allowed to retain the powers to control the design of buildings.[19]

The later history of the development of Ruislip seems to have been an anti-climax.Final approval for the scheme was not given until 7 September 1914, more than a year after the second public inquiry and by this stage the War had made development in the short term unlikely. By the end of the year Ruislip Manor Ltd was in financial difficulties and sought a reduction in ground rent. The Company survived the War but its option to purchase had been cancelled by the College in 1924, and in 1925 King's was considering the possibility of securing government subsidy for small houses. In practice the development was by small-scale speculative developers and, clause 56 notwithstanding, the architectural quality of the development did nothing to distinguish Ruislip from any other inter-war suburb. Vestiges of the Soutars' original layout, itself modified in the approved planning scheme, are still visible, but the architectural quality of the Ruislip Manor Cottage Society's schemes was not matched in later development. Ruislip became the very epitome of inter-war suburbia.

In 1931, King's College motivated, according to the *Middlesex Advertiser*, by the desire to 'do something big for Ruislip Northwood', offered the Council 236 acres (96 hectares) of Park Wood at a reduced cost as a public amenity. It was the tail end of a tradition exemplified by the Bedfords, the Grosvenors and the Calthorpes.[20] There is a footnote to the Ruislip-Northwood scheme, recorded by Punter (1986), which casts the use of discretionary power in the control of development in an altogether more sombre light. In 1933, the architects Connell and Ward who were in the forefront of the modern movement in England and had already designed the revolutionary scheme High and Over at Amersham, produced a plan for 300

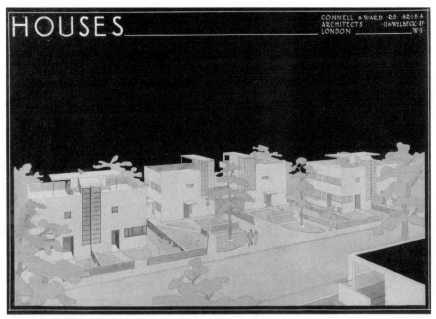

Figure 3.6. Ruislip. Proposal for houses by Connell and Ward in St. Martin's Approach and Park Avenue. (*Source*: King's College, Cambridge, Modern Archive Centre, RUI 448)

houses for the central part of the scheme area. The scheme followed relentlessly the aesthetic of the international modern movement. The Council using their discretionary power under Clause 56 of the scheme rejected the proposal and referred it to their Architectural Advisory Panel. The Panel's conclusion was that 'the duty of elected representatives [is] to have some regards to the feelings and wishes of the community which they represent, and, in our opinion, nine out of ten of the Ruislip population would view these houses in their proposed situation

Figure 3.7. Ruislip. House, Park Avenue, by Connell and Ward.

with active disfavour'.[21] The scheme then went to arbitration which upheld the Council's decision, but required Ruislip-Northwood to indicate to the developer the modifications which would make the scheme acceptable. The result was an Art Deco parody of Connell and Ward's project which was lambasted by the *Architects' Journal*. A modified scheme was finally given approval in mid-1934. In the end only three houses were ever built: a detached house and a semi-detached pair in Park Avenue.

Part of the *Architects' Journal's* attack on the Ruislip decision was couched in terms of the poor quality of the development that had taken place in the inter-war years. In response, the Urban District Council argued that King's College were responsible for approving low quality schemes, even though the Council held the power of aesthetic control in the planning scheme. No doubt this would be the last time a municipal council could blame a landowner for aesthetic delinquency.[22]

The Limits of the 1909 Act

The 1909 Act was both a heroic beginning and a heroic failure. It established a legal right for local councils to intervene in urban development by making plans. It was a failure in that its scope was limited and its procedures were cumbersome. Its impact in the 10 years to 1919 was limited. Nettlefold was in no doubt that this failure lay with the Local Government Board: fuelled by a desire to keep a watchful eye over local councils' behaviour, but nurtured in a tradition which constrained it from being too directive by leading from the front, it gave inadequate support to local authorities and yet agonized endlessly over the content of the schemes that came before it for approval.

For our purposes, however, several features of the way in which the Act was implemented are worth noting. The first is that the plans that were prepared for town planning schemes follow in a direct line of succession to the surveyors' plans for private landowners of the nineteenth century. There is little difference in the plans attached to George Wostenholm's agreements with Thomas Steade on the Sharrow estate in Sheffield and the Ruislip-Northwood planning scheme. Street lines and widths are laid down; for each street a building line is identified. The Ruislip-Northwood scheme did not prescribe building materials (although Clause 56 gave the Council power to reject plans on the basis of inappropriate materials), but unlike Wostenholm's plans it did identify building densities and not building values. Council surveyors not only saw their councils as successors to the great estates, they behaved like classic estate surveyors, too. Ruislip-Northwood is especially interesting in that it displays the almost imperceptible shift from private control by an institutional landlord to public control by the council which took place very largely without dispute.

The second point concerns the nature of control exercised. The 1909 Act set up the power to make plans for undeveloped land but made the assumption that the plan itself was the instrument of control. There was no separate system of planning permissions of the kind that was to be a key feature of the 1947 Town and Country Planning Act. The principle was that a development either conformed to a planning scheme or it did not. The developer who contravened the plan would face the threat of demolition as the ultimate sanction. But in fact matters were not so simple. Any developer, quite apart from complying with the scheme, would need bylaw approval, and so plans for buildings and development would be submitted as a matter of course to the local council. With a scheme in operation, a council would of course wish to be sure that a proposal did actually conform to the scheme at the point of giving bylaw consent. More importantly, both the Quinton, Harborne and Edgbaston and the Ruislip-Northwood schemes gave councils discretionary powers, and these implied that the councils would be regularly asked for consent and would be regularly making decisions on the individual merits of a case. This was self-evidently so in the case of Ruislip-Northwood's Clause 56. Birmingham also took discretionary powers in relation to land use and to determining the extent of a planning unit. A process of application to, and consent by, the public authorities, already established through the building bylaws, was being extended in those very few places with planning schemes in what looks remarkably like a blueprint for the post-1947 development control system.

The third point is that the schemes as finally approved were extraordinarily detailed. Nettlefold thought the Ruislip-Northwood scheme had gone too far (Nettlefold, 1914). F.M. Elgood, chairman of the Ruislip Town Planning Committee, could talk about the potential that planning schemes had for creating elasticity and this view was shared by the Local Government Board.[23] But if developers believed that greater elasticity would leave them with greater liberty to exercise their judgement, the reality was quite otherwise. Schemes clearly imposed far greater constraints on development than did bylaws, even if some leasehold covenants had been no less onerous. The elasticity gained was in the Council's power to decide, not in the developer's freedom to develop. The change was from a discretionary landlord to a discretionary local authority.

The fourth point concerns the object of control. In so many ways, the first planning schemes were surveyors' plans and bore little resemblance to the zoning plans of Germany which had nevertheless inspired them. But they did also contain the beginnings of a distinction between the control of building development and the control of land use. The Ruislip-Northwood plan set land aside for industrial and commercial uses and for public open space; the Quinton, Harborne and Edgbaston plan reflected a desire to balance residential and commercial development. To some extent this, too, had been foreshadowed in the control exercised by the landed estates, except that here a longer vision seems to be at work, and neither plan demonstrates any overt desire to maintain exclusiveness. Proxies for social control existed, even so. Variations in density allowed for different classes of development and for a different class of occupier. Aesthetic controls, too, had the potential for maintaining the exclusiveness of an area.

The final point has to do with the nature of the planning system produced by the 1909 Act. The first planning schemes may not have been zoning plans on the continental or American model, but they were legally binding. Schemes were laid before Parliament and then received the final approval of the Board at which point they carried legal weight 'as if they are enacted by parliament'.[24] This had two effects. One was that there could be no departures from an approved scheme except by modifying the scheme itself, a cumbersome procedure. In part, this was pre-empted by the kinds of discretionary clause we have already discussed, but it was to become an increasingly awkward problem. The other effect was more significant in the short term. If a developer put up a building after the decision to prepare a plan had been taken, there was a risk that it would be demolished if it contravened the plan as it was eventually approved. The effect was to bring all development to a halt during the period in which the plan was being prepared. Nettlefold was forthright about the problem:

. . . the immediate effect of the 1909 Act administered by the Local Government Board has been to stop building in areas where a scheme is under consideration, and to drive builders into other areas not yet protected. The total tendency has been to assist in creating a housing famine. The Board's regulations are all for delay and against progress. (Nettlefold, 1914, p. 136)

For Nettlefold, the problem was not so much the Act itself as the recalcitrance of the Local Government Board. The Land Enquiry Committee argued that more stringent bylaws had been a contributory factor to the housing shortage. The Committee proposed the rapid preparation of preliminary schemes to allow development to proceed more quickly with the possibility of builders entering agreements with local councils before the preliminary scheme was approved (Acland, 1914). The second proposal was no more than some developers had been doing already, as we saw in the case of Ruislip Manor Ltd in the Manor Way development. As Crow (1996) has described, the Land Enquiry Committee's proposals were taken a stage further by the Town Planning Institute in a memorial presented to Lord Rhondda, President of the Local Government Board. As with the Land Enquiry Committee proposal, the Institute argued for the rapid preparation of a preliminary scheme. After the approval of the preliminary scheme, no development 'should be proceeded with without the consent of the Local Authority' (Town Planning Institute, 1916). The germs of a new approach to control of urban development were in the offing.

The Beginnings of Interim Control

This widespread dissatisfaction with the way in which the 1909 Act had operated coupled with the scale of the housing problem that faced the country after the end of World War I made new legislation urgent. As with its predecessor, the 1919 Housing, Town Planning etc. Act was as much about housing as it was about planning and resulted in making local councils major providers of housing. The planning provisions of the Act were less radical. But it did require towns with populations greater than 20,000 inhabitants to prepare plans for their undeveloped land and it considerably streamlined procedures. Local authorities no longer needed approval from the Local Government Board or its successor, the Ministry of Health, for a resolution to proceed with the plan, nor did the completed scheme have to be laid before Parliament for 30 days before being approved.

A significant addition to planning powers was contained in Section 45 which enabled the Ministry to make orders which would allow building development to take place before a scheme was approved. This was a measure specifically designed to unblock the development process and speed the construction of much needed housing. The first General Interim Development Order was not made until 1922, but it provided for the possibility of 'permission to proceed' with development being granted by the local authority. This provision came into effect once the local authority had passed the resolution to start work on a scheme and ended once formal approval had been given to the scheme in its final form. It was not a mandatory power; builders could still start building without applying for permission under interim control, but receiving permission in effect indemnified the builder from any failure to comply with the scheme as completed. The power given the local authorities was overtly discretionary (the Ministry of Health took a more sanguine view of local authority discretion than did the Local Government Board) and local authorities were free to impose their own requirements when granting permission. The Ministry of Health was at pains to point out that local authorities should be judicious in their use of this control power:

The Minister considers it of the greatest importance that private development should not be arrested while a town planning scheme is in course of preparation and that areas should be able to proceed with genuine building plans without fear of the subsequent effects of the scheme . . . the local authority's requirements should be as few and as simple as possible. (Ministry of Health, 1922)

As Crow observes, this is an early expression of this policy presumption in favour of development (Crow, 1996). Interim control was an important step forward and Crow dates the 1922 order as the start of the modern development control system. It was an administrative expedient borne of a need to increase the rate of house building, but it came to have profound consequences for the character of the British planning system as a whole. Yet at the same time it can be seen as no more than a slight extension of the consent giving processes which were attached to bylaw regulation and, as we have seen, to the schemes themselves.

Interim powers were given a very considerable extension by the 1932 Town and Country Planning Act. This Act represented both a step backward and a step forward. The requirement to prepare plans was removed in 1932 and town planning regulations once again became permissive, not mandatory. The Minister was once more required to approve resolutions to proceed with the preparation of a planning scheme and the completed scheme had to be laid before Parliament for 21 days. A formal resolution of both Houses of Parliament was required if the scheme suspended any other legislation, although this did not include the public health or roads improvements Acts. On the other hand, the 1932 Act significantly extended the possibility for control by allowing plans to cover land that was already developed as well as unbuilt land. In fact, the Local Government Board and the Ministry of Health had taken a fairly generous view of the restrictions imposed by the previous Acts. At Poole, for example, the whole of the central area was included even though the land was partially developed.[25] However, during the 1920s there was a growing pressure from local authorities for the scope of town planning to be extended to existing built-up areas.[26] The government responded to this pressure and the 1932 Act allowed local authorities to plan for the whole of their area: plans could include land to be protected from development as well as existing built up areas. Interim development control was retained but an order was approved in 1933 which considerably extended the interim control powers.

Specifically, the Act went well beyond the 1909 vision of planning as being primarily about estate building. For the first time, the word development was defined to cover 'any building operations or rebuilding operations and any use of the land or the building thereon for a purpose which is different from the purpose for which the land or building was last being used' (Section 53). This reflects the growing interest in zoning which had developed at the end of World War I. Whereas lines of communication and density seemed to dominate the debate at the time of the 1909 Act, after 1919 there is significant reference to the zoning of land use. I.G. (later Sir Gwilym) Gibbon, an Assistant Secretary at the Ministry of Health, was already an advocate of zoning:

Considerable attention has already in the past been given to the questions of main communications in town planning schemes, and this line of development will be continued. In addition, however, it will be necessary to put particular emphasis on zoning, which has hitherto been neglected in this country. By zoning is meant to be assignment of districts for different industries, for residential purposes, for open spaces, and the like, according to their suitability, together with restrictions as to the height and density of buildings.[27]

He was to repeat the message at a conference a year later (Gibbon, 1922). It was this approach towards planning and the control of development that eventually became a central part of the government policy and found expression in the 1932 Act. Uses would be identified for all land, even if that meant no more than confirming an existing use, or even ensuring that no new development could take place. In this way the Act marks a decisive break with the old surveyors' estate layouts which date back to the eighteenth century. It suggests an approach to planning which is as much about the management of change as it is about new buildings.

The Local Government Board had conspicuously avoided producing the general provisions allowed for by the 1909 Act. As a result of an amendment to the Bill as it passed through Parliament, the 1919 Act required local authorities to prepare schemes in accordance with provisions made by the Ministry of Health, and Model Clauses were produced in 1922. This practice was continued with the 1932 legislation which, because of the emphasis on land use, led to Model Clauses that were considerably more detailed than their predecessors. In particular, Clause 27 of the 1935 Model Clauses introduced the distinction between uses that were allowed as of right and those which might be permitted only with the consent of the local authority. The 1933 Clauses considerably strengthened the scope for granting and refusing permissions within the context of an approved plan as well as in the period before the plan was approved. The distinction between 'as-of-right' and 'permitted' uses was retained in the Hong Kong planning system (see Bristow, 1984) and the distinction remains there to this day.

The interim control of development was also set to become a much more complicated affair. A ministerial circular (Circular 1305) was issued in 1933 which laid out the government's intentions for the implementation of the act as a whole. The circular notes that authorities 'have generally used their powers with discretion [i.e., judiciously]' but then sets about making sure that control is not exercised unnecessarily: 'it would probably be wise ordinarily to limit any control of this kind to preventing uses likely to be dangerous to health or detrimental to neighbourhood or were likely to involve the rate payers in unreasonable expense' (Ministry of Health, 1933). Control of design, which caused so much anguish to the Local Government Board in the Ruislip-Northwood scheme now became an accepted part of the planning process, and the phrase 'injurious to local amenities' used by the circular reflects the wording of Clause 56 (Ministry of Health, 1933). Indeed the Ruislip-Northwood clause had been the subject of continued debate during the 1920s. The issue had been not so much about the legitimacy of aesthetic control itself as the extent of control over design and the means by which decisions could be validated. By 1933 an official view on both seems to have crystallised.[28]

The practice of planning during the period between 1919 and 1939 suggests that problems still remained with the legislation. Though the procedures had been improved by the 1919 Act, progress with the adoption of plans remained slow. In spite of the requirement to prepare plans, of 262 urban authorities with populations greater than 20,000, 98 had not submitted plans by 1928 and 5 years later, when the 1932 Act came in to force, only 94 plans had been approved (Cherry, 1974). By contrast, after the 1932 Act there was a marked acceleration in the numbers of resolutions to prepare plans, even if the area covered by approved plans remained small by the outbreak of World War II. But the numbers of resolutions to prepare plans may well reflect the growing taste for the increase in power that interim development control offered.

The experience of Sheffield in the inter-war period is indicative of the general problem of putting the legislation into practice. After the initial frenzy of activity before 1914, the City Council appears to have found it very difficult to proceed beyond initial designation. In part this reflected the real difficulties of 'referencing', that is identifying the owners of land. The City Council returned to town planning with renewed energy in 1919 when they commissioned Patrick Abercrombie to prepare a civic survey of the whole city as the basis for future planning schemes (Marshall, 1993). This in turn led to a fresh start on plan preparation, and a preliminary scheme for the south-west areas, which combined four pre-war scheme areas, was eventually the subject of a public inquiry in 1923.[29] However 5 years later virtually no progress seems to have been made, and the city was arguing that the extensiveness of the areas covered by resolutions to prepare schemes meant that work was inevitably slow.

In 1935 a letter from the Ministry of Health proposed a programme of dates for the adoption of plans over a period of 2 years, but these dates were also not met.[30] Much of the problem seems to have been in setting up a satisfactory administration. Since the preparation of the Abercrombie plan, Abercrombie had been retained as a planning advisor but technical work on planning was carried out by the City Engineer and the Town Clerk. When, finally, C.G. Craven was appointed Planning Officer in 1936 official files suggest a clash of personalities and professional outlook that took its toll in the speed with which work progressed. Responsibilities of council members were also divided. Perhaps most damagingly, forward planning powers were vested in the Improvements Committee but plans submitted under interim control powers continued to be approved by a sub-committee of the Highways and Sewerage Committee. Craven complained that he was not consulted by the City Engineer on applications.[31] This problem was not finally resolved until 1944 when a Town Planning Committee was formed with responsibilities for both plans and the control of development.[32] Yet the 1930s did contain two notable achievements. First was the adoption in 1936 of a green belt to protect open countryside around the city. The second was the approval of a draft scheme for the city's central area in September 1939. This was a considerably more sophisticated scheme than anything which had preceded it and fully reflects the pre-occupations with land use rather than physical development.

Council minutes also reveal how Sheffield was using its power of interim control. The earliest explicit record of plans having been deposited with the Council for approval under the General Interim Development Order does not occur until 1930, when an appeal to the Ministry against refusal to permit the conversion of houses to shops was dismissed. From June 1931, minutes of the Plans (later Works and Town Planning) sub-committee record those decisions which were taken under planning rather than the bylaw powers. Given the extent of the city's planning schemes areas the numbers of 'deposited plans' seem small: in the 2 years from November 1934 986 applications were made, of which just over half were refused permission. Evidently, in Sheffield at least, the presumption in favour of development did not yet mean that the majority of proposals was approved.[33]

By the outbreak of World War II, the extent of control exercised by local planning authorities had increased enormously. Interim control, that administrative device to speed the building of estates, had by now become a major part of the armoury of the planning system. Approved planning schemes increasingly required formal consent for aspects of building and land use which were at the discretion of the local authority. Development was not formally defined to cover change of use as well as building. Extensive though these controls were, they still suffered from serious drawbacks. The first and most significant of these had to do with the system of compensation.

Compensation for the loss of development value as a result of the restrictions imposed by town planning schemes and the collection of betterment, the value that accrued to landowners as a result of being unable to proceed with development, was a major part of the debate on planning until the 1980s. The question is both intimately bound up with the evolution of planning control and something which has acquired a separate existence. Its ramifications have been fully explored elsewhere (see Cullingworth, 1980; Cox, 1984). The collection of betterment derives, as we have seen, from the growing sense of the injustice of large landowners benefiting from a 'an unearned increment' at the expense of their leaseholders, and the 1909 Act was designed among other things to allow the collection of betterment. Landowners could – and did – object that they also would suffer an injustice if they were deprived of the potential for development by the provisions of a town planning scheme. As a r esult, therefore, of an amendment to the Bill as it passed through Parliament, land-owners were able to claim compensation if they were denied the right to develop. This clause was to prove the Achilles' heel of the planning system until 1939.

A major difficulty concerned the reservation of open space. If a local authority wanted to restrict building on a given piece of land the likelihood of having to pay compensation was high. The alternative was to buy the land outright. Ministerial policy was clearly expressed in a minute of 1936 which argued that

. . . it is not worth paying a lot of money from the rates to keep land for a private use; if it is important that the land be kept open it is probably better to pay the extra and buy the land for public use. The authority can always let the land to a private club or farmer or whatever is appropriate, pending the public need of the land.[34]

Apart from the narrow interpretation of the value of reserved land, this highlights the local authority's dilemma. Sheffield had to resort to compulsory purchase to maintain its rural fringe (Marshall, 1993). And one can have sympathy for Greenwich Council who later built on land that they had compulsorily purchased for open space. Another alternative was for a local authority to enter an agreement with landowners over the protection of open space, as Ruislip-Northwood Council did with King's College.[35]

An even more worrying problem, also in Ruislip-Northwood, surfaced in 1919 in the *Ellis* (Re an Arbitration between Ellis and Ruislip-Northwood Urban District Council) case, a legal appeal that concerned the enforceability of a building line. In this case, the appellant argued that he was due compensation for being required to set back his building to the building line. Ruislip-Northwood relied upon Section

59 (1) of the Act which ruled out the possibility of compensation if a provision of the scheme could have been worded as a bylaw. The Council argued that a building line concerned space and buildings and was therefore potentially the subject of a bylaw, but the appeal judges did not agree and upheld the appeal (Hill and Nicholls, 1937).

The problems with the payment of compensation did not disappear with the 1932 Act. Nowhere indeed did the Act appear so limited as in the control of undesirable development along main roads. In theory, ribbon development could be controlled under the 1932 Act, but the risk of paying compensation was a real one and was a formidable deterrent for small district authorities. Moreover, there was a strong element of conflict between levels of local authority. Roads were the county councils' responsibility and the counties might be a good deal more concerned about ribbon development than were the districts, and yet be powerless to take action. The result was the passing of the 1935 Restriction of Ribbon Development Act which made all buildings within 220 feet of a classified road and all accesses to classified roads subject to consent by the highway authority. The counties were for the first time given a formal power in the control of development, something for which there had been growing pressure.[36]

The 1935 Act did not remedy the fundamental problems with the system of development control, it merely alleviated one of its worst effects. In a sense, the very success of establishing the principle that local authorities had a legitimate interest in the development of land meant that the shortcomings of the approach adopted between 1909 and 1939 could become increasingly apparent. The extension of interim control and of discretionary powers within approved planning schemes was paving the way towards a fundamental shift in the way planning control was perceived. It was a shift that would only come to fruition during and immediately after World War II.

Notes

1. PRO HLG29/96.
2. PRO HLG29/116. Department Committee on Building Byelaws/Minutes of Evidence, 1 July 1914.
3. PRO HLG4/1871. Letters dated 24 March 1911, 1 April 1911.
4. PRO HLG4/253. Letter dated 9 February 1911.
5. PRO HLG29/116. Departmental Committee on Building Byelaws, Minutes of Evidence, 1 July1914.
6. *Birmingham Post*, 21 July 1910.
7. PRO HLG4/251.
8. PRO HLG4/252. Minute dated 6 March 1912.
9. PRO HLG29/116. Departmental Committee on Building Byelaws, Minutes of Evidence, 1 July 1914.

10. PRO HLG4/1871. Inquiry held by Thomas Adams, 16 February 1911.
11. King's College, Cambridge, Modern Archive Centre. RU1 208.
12. King's College, Cambridge, Modern Archive Centre RU1 205.
13. King's College, Cambridge, Modern Archive Centre. RU1 211.
14. PRO HLG4/1871. *Middlesex and Bucks Advertiser*, 3 December 1910.
15. King's College, Cambridge, Modern Archive Centre, RU1 328, 16. Agreement dated 11 April 1911.
16. King's College, Cambridge, Modern Archive Centre. RU1 329(1), Thompson to Birkett, 15 November 1911.
17. King's College, Cambridge, Modern Archive Centre. RU1 329(1), Unwin 29 July 1912, Thompson 16 August 1912.
18. PRO HLG4/1875.
19. PRO HLG4/1873. Inspector's report 17/18 April 1913 and 1/2 May 1913; file note dated 13 January 1914.
20. *Middlesex Advertiser & Gazette*, 16 January 1931.
21. *National Builder*, **13**(12), July 1934, pp. 436–38.
22. *Architects' Journal*, **79** (2053, 2054), **80** (2071), 24 May, 31 May, 27 September 1934.
23. PRO HLG4/252. Minute dated 6 March 1914.
24. PRO HLG4/1873. Note dated 10 December 1913.
25. PRO HLG4/1749. *Daily Telegraph*, 13 August 1929.
26. PRO HLG71/1467.
27. PRO HLG52/912. Memorandum from Gibbon to the Minister, 10 February 1921.
28. PRO HLG52/559.
29. Sheffield City Council, Improvement Committee, 15 January 1923.
30. PRO HLG4/1988-1989. Letter from Sir William Hart, 14 December 1928; letter from W R Frazer 6 March 1935.
31. PRO HLG52/1986. Meetings 14 October 1937 and 27 October 1937; letter from C.G. Craven to G.L. Pepler 2 December 1938.
32. Sheffield City Council, General Purposes Committee, 28 July 1944.
33. Sheffield City Council, Works and Town Planning Committee, December 1934 – November 1936.
34. PRO HLG52/519. Minute dated 23 January 1936.
35. King's College, Cambridge, Modern Archive Centre. RU1 329(3).
36. PRO HLG52/588. Letter from Middlesex County Solicitor. PRO HLG52/591. Minute dated 10 November 1938.

Chapter Four

Towards Universal Control

The extent to which all the elements of the modern development control system were in place by the mid-1930s is not often realized. The 1932 Act made control over land-use change as well as building development possible, and the definition of development prefigured the classic distinction in the 1947 Town and Country Planning Act and its successors. Though the phrase 'other material considerations' had not yet appeared, there was unlimited power to impose conditions 'such . . . as they think proper to impose' (Section 10). In the General Interim Development Order there was a clause which identified certain types of development that were always permitted, while the Act itself fixed a two-month period within which an application had to be dealt with by the local authority. There was, finally, a right of appeal to the Ministry of Health against a refusal of permission under interim control and that right extended to any decision taken under discretionary powers within an approved scheme. Certainly there were differences. There was an absence of any means of enforcement other than the sanctions imposed by failure to comply with an approved planning scheme. Though a local authority could get agreement in writing to extend the two-month period for processing an application, failure to decide in the absence of an agreement resulted in a deemed permission after eight weeks, not a deemed refusal.

The 1932 Act in Practice

What little evidence is available in the professional press confirms the impression of a system that was developing its own momentum. While Crow (1996) is right to note the marked absence of a professional commentary on development control as opposed to planning schemes, one or two references in the *Journal of the Town Planning Institute* give the flavour of practice in the 1930s. The County Planning Officer of Worcestershire, H. Robinson, laid emphasis upon the need for systematic administration to be in place before a resolution to proceed with a plan was taken, and in doing so he prefigured the concern for the management aspects of development control that, as we shall see, were to come to dominate the debate from the 1970s onwards. Robinson recommended a standard list of conditions, although these were expressed as dimensional norms (Robinson, 1936). The fullest account comes in a paper given to the Housing and Town Planning Conference in 1937 by the Chief Engineer of Leeds (Cameron, 1937). The paper is concerned primarily with procedure and deals with various categories of development that were perceived as problematic, including petrol filling stations, public houses, cinemas and industrial buildings. Yet implicit in the paper are values which were to inform planning control after World War II. The reference to amenity and character which had been the subject of agonized debate in the making of the Ruislip-Northwood planning scheme are internalized in Cameron's paper: they are assumed to be the appropriate criteria for development control decision-making. Cameron's paper also makes clear how much was to be vested in the judgement of the decision-maker. But although he frequently invokes the planning committee of elected representatives, his article does not explore the balance of power between the committee and the planning officer.

Another paper, under the title 'Is town planning a failure?' (Moss, 1935) is rather more explicit about the values that should underwrite the system of control. Moss argued once again for elasticity in the drafting of the planning scheme, in recognition of the fact that control under an operative planning scheme was 'more effective' (p. 158) than interim control. Perhaps most telling is his criticism of the way in which planning had gone wrong: '. . . instead of having a planning personnel composed of able and sympathetic administrators, we have a collection of building inspectors enforcing a set of bylaws which goes under the guise of a planning scheme'. The old bogey of the public health Acts had clearly not been laid to rest. But for the future, development control would be exercised by far-sighted and intelligent professionals who would be in charge of applying the 'elastic' provisions of planning schemes. The safeguard would be the right of appeal.

These quotations almost, but not quite, articulate the change that was being induced in the planning system. Official thinking at central government level demonstrates, too, a growing awareness of the consequences of the evolution of the planning system in the period immediately before the outbreak of war. Insofar as there is much evidence two schools of thought are apparent. In 1933, for example, a file minute on the need to amend the Model Clauses reflects on whether development that had taken place after a resolution to prepare a plan had been taken and was not in accordance with the approved plan might nevertheless be considered on its merits. In other words, non-conforming development should not automatically be demolished: a process of application and appeal should be available to test the merits of the completed development. The argument was given force at Blackpool where the council had issued a large number of contravention notices on buildings which were apparently 'not rigidly excluded by the zoning provisions'. There was merit in the idea of allowing an application after the event.[1] The same insistence on the ability of the planning system to reflect on specific circumstance rather than apply rules by rote is present in the minutes of the Office Committee on the Model Building Bylaws:

Miss [later Dame Evelyn] Sharp explained that the term planning clauses were concerned with *amenity* and controlled (*a*) the proportion of site covered; (*b*) the density; (*c*) overall height and angular measurement; and (*d*) breaks in buildings. The limits specified were discretionary and dependent on the locality and the circumstances of each case.[2]

Sharp was trying to draw a very clear line between bylaw control and the flexible case-by-case approach that was becoming the hallmark not only of interim control but also of control within approved schemes. This not only had implications, of the kind noted by Moss, for the way in which decisions would be reached, it also suggested something fundamental about the nature of planning control.

E.R. Abbott, who as town clerk to Ruislip-Northwood Urban District Council had taken a pioneering role in the planning scheme for the district and who was by the late 1930s a respected figure within the profession, perhaps understandably, took an opposing view. Anything, he argued, 'which gave the public or the Ministry of Health the idea that certain local authorities were trying to deal with all their plans under interim development procedure would do an enormous amount of harm to planning in general' (*Journal of Town Planning Institute* 1937, p. 303). And, indeed, interim control raised serious questions about the nature and value of the planning scheme itself.

Towards the Nationalization of Development Rights

The full logic of the move towards ever greater discretion and ever greater control in the absence of an approved scheme was only fully explored during the war years. The pressure came from two directions. The first was in the form of those great reports published during the war by Barlow, Scott and Uthwatt whose role in shaping the British planning system after 1947 is very well known. Of these, the Uthwatt Report (1942) was by far the most significant in framing the debate about development control because of its attempt to solve the problem of compensation and betterment once and for all. But the Barlow Report published in 1940 was important for advocating the purchase of development rights by the State. For Barlow, compensation was no longer to be seen simply as the means of redressingpotential injustice to landowners, it would represent a fundamental shift in the State's role in relation to land. We have already seen how the development of bylaw control and then of town planning implied that local authorities had an interest in land in their control. Barlow's proposals were far more overt: he specifically identified a formal property interest whose nationalization he advocated. Such a suggestion was only possible in a culture which had for centuries recognized that there could be concurrent interests in land and that future development could also be a current interest (Barlow, 1940). Barlow's proposals and Uthwatt's development of the idea sat squarely within the conceptualization of property that derived from the Middle Ages. There is something of a paradox that the move to nationalize future rights to development should become at the very moment when property rights in general had been simplified as never before.

Cullingworth (1975) has presented in detail the slow maturing of central government thinking in town planning that was to reach fruition in 1947. The path was not an easy one, but involved essentially four elements: the problem of compensation and betterment; the move to the control of all development; the question of the role of central government; and the appropriate level for the making of plans in the control of development. The starting point for the whole war effort on planning was driven by the self-evident need for reconstruction once peace was declared. Arthur Greenwood was appointed as Minister in charge of reconstruction in December 1940. However it was Lord Reith, Minister of Works and Building, who raised the question of town planning with the War Cabinet and was invited to report. His report argued on the basis of three assumptions:

(a) The government will be favourably disposed towards the principle of planning, as part of national policy, and some central planning authority will be required. (b) In planning the physical reconstruction of town and country, the planning activity will be able to proceed in the light of a positive policy in regard to such matters as agriculture, industrial development and transport. (c) The central government would itself arrange for the planning by the central planning authority or other government agency of service and other matters requiring treatment on the broadest national scale. Matters calling for treatment on a regional basis would be planned by a regional authority.

To that final assumption was later added the words:

It will be important to maintain unimpaired the character and independence of existing local authorities, but it will be found necessary to readjust their present functions so as to enable certain of their powers to be exercised on a wider basis. (cited by Cullingworth, 1975, pp. 15, 58)

These assumptions then formed the framework of the committee appointed to advise Reith which in turn sought expert advice on aspects of the planning problem. From this arose the commissioning of the Uthwatt Report on compensation and betterment. Less well known, because they were never published, were the reports from the committee chaired by T.D. Harrison who was charged with reviewing existing planning legislation and, as Cullingworth observes, was to be a major influence on the way legislation was to develop.

The debate on compensation and betterment that was engaged between 1940 and 1947 was immensely complicated and has been fully presented by Cullingworth (1975, 1980). It was bedevilled by an interlocking of political and technical objections to the principles and practice of taxing the increase in land values and the paying of compensation. Radical options favoured collecting betterment value to the full while minimizing the payment of compensation. Conservatives were not in favour of collecting 100 per cent betterment value and wanted to ensure that compensation was calculated in a way that did no injustice to property owners. And, as we have already noted, the question of compensation and betterment was no longer conducted simply in terms of a fair return to government and a just deal for landowners who were adversely affected by planning schemes, it had become a question of nationalizing development rights. The only measure of agreement seemed to be that there was a need for some form of universal control and that the compensation provisions of the 1932 Act militated against effective planning.

The nationalization of development rights in Uthwatt's proposal would have related only to unbuilt land on the edge of towns, not to all land. Compensation in these terms would be the means of buying out development rights and solving the problems of floating and transferred value that his report expounds. But simply dealing with undeveloped land quickly came to be seen as too limited and official thinking came to favour the idea of nationalizing development rights in all land. This in turn led to discussion on whether and how the right to compensation might eventually be limited. The question was partly a matter of economics as the unlimited rights to compensation would be immensely costly; partly, a desire to extinguish development rights which were not accorded by the State. A radical line of thought wondered why compensation need be payable at all. Frank Schaffer, an official at the Ministry of Town and Country Planning during the war, noted that as the transfer of development rights did not convey a legal or equitable interest to the State, there might formally be no case for the payment of compensation at all (Schaffer, 1974). Certainly at the time, Schaffer declared himself to be 'deeply disturbed' by proposals to fix compensation at a level of 60 per cent put forward by the Whiskard Committee set up to look at the development rights question in 1943.[3] In the end, the problem was only resolved in the 1947 Act with a 100 per cent tax on betterment and compensation only payable where the value of land was depreciated by the activity of planning: compensation was no longer automatically payable on the refusal of planning permission.

The Harrison Committee recommended the extension of control to all areas. The Committee's interim report in May 1941 also argued for the possibility of immediate enforcement of interim control, for planning permission to be limited and for deemed permissions to be replaced by deemed refusals when the local authority had failed to determine an application within the prescribed two months. In this, the Harrison Committee was on the face of it doing no more than proposing marginal changes to the existing system.

But within the Ministry the understanding of where such moves were taking the system appeared by then to have developed. An internal memorandum of October 1941, apparently a response to the Harrison Committee's report, is particularly interesting. It notes as an accepted fact that traditionally owners were free to do what they liked with their property and if that right was to be limited the restriction should be specific. The first planning schemes fell into that category of restraint on individual freedom, and control was exercised solely within the constraints imposed by the scheme itself. For the author of the memorandum, extending interim control might in fact lead to a rather different concept of the planning scheme itself:

The alternative proposal would be that a local authority should draw up a plan on the lines of the present map which forms part of a scheme but which unlike the present scheme map would have no legal effect. Owners would continue to be under the obligation to make applications in respect of all development but the fact that the development proposed was in accordance with the plan would not be conclusive in their favour nor would the plan be conclusive against them if the proposed development did not conform to it. The plan would not do more than give a general indication of the intentions of the local authority at a particular time and could be changed at any time without formalities.

The author proceeds to investigate the disadvantages of this new form of 'elastic control' and 'control by consents' and concludes that they are few. Buyers and sellers of land would find themselves in the same position as they were currently under interim control. Local authorities would need enhanced powers, some of which, such as dealing with contravening buildings or uses or the compulsory purchase of land, might be difficult to establish in the absence of plans carrying legal weight.[4] The idea of an indicative system of plans and universal control was already well developed in official thinking.

Although the ideas may have been well developed in 1941 they did not result in immediate legislative action. Shorter-term pressures led instead to the implementation of the proposal to extend interim control to all parts of the country which was given statutory force in the 1943 Town and Country Planning (Interim Development) Act. The failure to take more radical action reflects both the cautiousness of Ministers and the fact that the wide discussions on compensation and betterment, the development rights scheme and the central planning authority were threatening to delay legislation when there were immediate problems to be resolved.

The short-term issue was that bombing had created a risk of speculation in land and the prospect of redevelopment that would prejudice a coherent planning of war damaged areas when peace was declared. Abercrombie, for example, wrote to George Pepler, Chief Planning Advisor at the Ministry, of his concern about the redevelopment of shops in Oxford Street, Plymouth and Peckham, where road plans were insufficiently advanced.[5] Abercrombie's point was taken up by Stafford Cripps in a letter to Lord Portal who was Minister of Works and Planning:

I was very disturbed to be told by a fairly reliable person the other day that in some districts – including London – plans are being passed for rebuilding which will gravely interfere with any new and imaginative planning. If this is true, surely there should be a 'stop order' put upon such things until the machinery for new planning is worked out and in control. Otherwise a host of 'vested rights' will grow up which will interfere severely with decent post war development.[6]

In 1941 following the bombing raids which badly damaged the city, George Pepler visited Sheffield and the City Council's Town Planning Committee pressed him to strengthen the powers of interim development control, particularly by extending control to the re-erection of buildings on existing sites. They also asked for control over decisions by government departments taken in the national interest without regard to local planning policy. A case in which 13½ acres of green belt were selected for a factory without notification had particularly angered the Council. The Committee also asked Pepler for wider powers of compulsory purchase, and for a removal of the prohibition on compulsory purchase for real sale to third parties. The following year, another report by the Planning Officer proposed that interim control should be made directly enforceable, and reiterated the concern about the lack of control over rebuilding on existing sites. It ran the risk of perpetuating an unacceptable use and the removal of such buildings could only be achieved once the planning scheme had been approved and on the payment of compensation. Since Sheffield had no approved planning scheme for its builtup area and only the central area plan prepared in draft, the Council was far from being able to take action. On compensation and betterment, the Sheffield Committee took the view that the Council should become owners of land on which development was proposed.[7]

The 1943 Town and Country Planning (Interim Development) Act did not respond fully to these concerns: it did no more than to extend interim control to the country as a whole and tackled neither the question of enforceability nor that of the establishment of rights. In presenting the Bill to the War Cabinet, W.S. Morrison, Minister of Town and Country Planning, acknowledged that the proposal did not go far enough but argued that action was necessary immediately to prevent prejudice to future planning.[8] The Act did at least introduce powers to ensure that development that was refused permission in the interim period did not go ahead and brought the re-erection of existing buildings under control. The enforcement power could only be applied in areas subject to a resolution to prepare a plan and the power was permissive. Local authorities were only to take enforcement action if it was necessary or expedient in the light of the provisions of the proposed plan, and the Act specifically required the local authority to prefer alterations to demolition if possible. It also allowed local authorities to refuse to entertain an application on the grounds of prematurity, in order that rights to development were not created. The final change made by the Act was to alter the deemed permission for development that resulted from a local authority's failure to deal with an application within two months, to a deemed refusal with a right of appeal to the Minister. The major criticisms of the Act did not lie in the provisions for the control of development so much as in its failure to implement proposals for the nationalization of development rights and to link planning to local government reform.

The weakness of the 1943 legislation led inevitably to demands to strengthen powers to deal with the outstanding problems. The Uthwatt Report had been published in 1942 and had argued for universal control of development as well as the nationalization of development rights in land that was undeveloped. While the issue of development rights and compensation and betterment were to exercise minds throughout the war and did not find a resolution until the 1947 Town and Country Planning Act, the idea that all development should be subject to control had begun to take root in official thinking. Thus a memorandum by Malcolm Trustram Eve (Chairman of the War Planning Commission) took as a starting point the idea that universal control was a prerequisite of satisfactory planning at national as well as at local level. The acceptance would then frame the way in which the machinery was set up.[9] The following year the Whiskard Committee was set up and its first paper in June 1943 reiterated both the necessity of universal control of changes to land use and the need for the State to acquire development land. Universal control would need to be linked to increased powers for local authorities to buy land to pave the way for positive planning.[10]

Official minds began to be exercised as to what the change of use in land might amount to. Did it mean only using land for an entirely different purpose? Or did it include the use of a site in a different way, as for example, by increasing the height of a building? E.S. Hill thought there should be some changes so minor that the Minister ought to be able to issue a general consent by order.[11] But although there now appeared much agreement on the need for universal control and for a viable scheme for paying compensation and collecting betterment in order to nationalize development rights, the practicalities proved defeating. The 1944 Town and Country Planning Act did not become the all-embracing legislation originally hoped for and did not in fact extend the provisions of interim development control already enacted.

Much of the Act concerned areas of extensive war damage and some of the most important provisions concerned the widening of local authorities' compulsory purchase powers to 'areas of bad layout and obsolete development' as well as to land needed for certain classes of development (Sections 9, 10). For the interim control function, Section 33 did allow local authorities to refuse applications for development which would otherwise be allowed by an approved scheme and to permit development which contravened an approved scheme, if a resolution to modify the scheme had been made. Such permissions needed ministerial approval. Though this added flexibility to planning schemes, there was no general change to the system of plans in the 1944 Act. Silkin, who was to become Minister of Town and Country Planning in the Attlee Government after the war, attacked the Bill on the grounds that 'it contemplates that towns shall be redeveloped piecemeal' and abandoned any idea there might be national planning.[12] The law did not yet reflect the full consequences of introducing planning by consent which had been recognized, as we have seen, by 1941. It had plainly failed to solve satisfactorily the question of compensation and betterment or the relationship of development control to development plans.

On the other hand, the wartime legislation did make two marginal but important contributions to the extension of planning control. One was in the introduction of tree preservation orders. The other was in the protection afforded to historic buildings and the introduction of the list as a means of identifying buildings of significance. Both have often been thought of as innovations in the 1947 Act; both were in fact introduced as amendments to the Interim Development Act of 1943, with the provision for historic buildings carried forward to 1944. These contributions may not have made any fundamental difference to the development control system as it then existed, but they did significantly extend the objects of control in a way that was to become increasingly important after 1947.

The Power to Control: Central or Local?

The other issues that were the subject of considerable debate were the establishment of some kind of national planning authority and the appropriate tier of local government to deal with planning. Of the two, the creation of the central planning authority was by far the most difficult. The origins of the idea appear to lie in a letter from Raymond Unwin to the Minister of Health in 1935 in which he argued strenuously that a central authority was vital to securing the proper coordination of activity at the local level and the carrying out of projects on a large scale. In 1935, the view from within the Ministry of Health was that national planning led by a central board would cut across all existing patterns of administration and property and could only be achieved by 'bitter compulsion'.[13] Nevertheless, the Barlow Report commissioned a mere three years later (and with Unwin as one of the committee's members) proposed a central planning authority as an essential prerequisite for the redistribution of the country's activities. By the early 1940s, Unwin's proposal which had been unthinkable only a few years before was becoming a respectable part of government thinking. Uthwatt, for example, actually foresaw in his interim report that a central authority would be responsible for all control of development, with the possibility of delegation to local authorities or joint committees (Uthwatt, 1941). The Harrison Committee rejected that approach in favour of the extension of interim control powers, but did at least envisage a central planning authority having oversight of that control. Lord Reith, Minister of Works and Buildings, on the other hand, argued for the setting up of a central body 'forthwith' and evidently favoured Uthwatt's recommendation.[14]

The actual implementation of this proposal had to wait for the 1947 Act and even then the Central Land Board as it became took a rather different form from that envisaged by Uthwatt. In the meantime there was a rather unsatisfactory shuffling of ministerial responsibilities and personnel. Before the war, the responsibility for planning rested with the Ministry of Health, even if the planning of the highway network remained with an increasingly powerful Ministry of Transport. With the onset of war the planning task was transferred to the Ministry of Buildings and Works, which became Works and Planning under Lord Reith. Lord Reith did not remain in post long enough to consolidate his Ministry as the champion of a radical approach to planning. His successor, Lord Portal, according to Sir William Jowitt was 'equally as anxious to rid himself of "planning"'. In turn, Sir William Jowitt, appointed to the position of Paymaster General as successor to Arthur Greenwood in 1942, agonized about what planning was and should be, but was responsible for setting up a Ministry of Town and Country Planning under W.S. Morrison in 1943.15 The creation of the Ministry was clearly seen as an alternative to setting up the central planning authority envisaged by Uthwatt.

Not very much progress towards national planning by a central government agency was made during the wartime years, then. Yet there was an increasing involvement of central government in local planning decisions. The 1943 Act enabled the Minister to determine applications if it was necessary in the national interest, and required ministerial approval for agreements between developers and local authorities. The 1944 Act introduced further control by the Minister, over local authorities' powers to revoke or modify interim permissions and over the new power to permit departures from approved schemes.

The question of the appropriate size of local authority to be given planning powers was an issue that also began to surface in the 1930s. Recognizing that districts might be too small to reflect on questions of strategic importance, the government had encouraged the formation of joint committees and regional planning studies had been undertaken under their guidance. But the power of control remained with the district authorities, and this became a source of friction by the 1930s. Devonshire County Council complained that district councils frequently ignored the advice of the County Planning Officer, and the County Solicitor of Middlesex made much the same point. This lack of consultation was particularly serious in that counties had been given a formal role as consultees in the preparation of planning schemes by the 1929 Local Government Act.[16] In 1941, the Harrison Committee was recommending that interim control should pass to the joint committees, although already the idea was being advocated that counties might replace districts as planning authorities.

The official response in the first instance was that such a move would only be possible if the planning system were being created from scratch and if introduced now would anger the districts. In the same year political initiatives were beginning to move the thinking forward, however. Lord Reith, announcing the commissioning of the Uthwatt and Scott Reports, took as a working assumption that existing local authorities would continue to survive, with their independence unimpaired, but that the functions might be distributed differently. By 1942, Malcolm Trustram Eve was recommending that planning powers should be given to the counties and county boroughs as a means of ensuring that the local authority units were big enough to coordinate development needs.[17] Yet this approach did not surface in the 1943 Act. W.S. Morrison took as cautious a line on local authorities as he did with the rest of the Act. Districts were to remain as local planning authorities but they were given strength and powers to create joint committees. Morrison's report to the War Cabinet resulted in a stinging riposte from the Home Secretary, Herbert Morrison. Berating the failure to implement the Scott and Uthwatt Reports, he argued strongly that counties were the proper level for planning and that the joint authority was 'a clumsy instrument of public administration – there is too much "joint" and not enough "authority" about it'.[18] And just as the 1944 Act had disappointed Silkin in its failure to address the issue of national policy in its implementation so, too, it failed to make any change to planning authorities.

Within the complicated history of the evolution of town planning in the war years, two tendencies emerged. One was looking for radical change that would result in the nationalization of development rights (and ultimately also of development land). It placed a heavy emphasis upon the need for national planning and control vested in a national commission to mitigate the effects of parochialism in the districts. Within this tendency was a desire to replace the districts by the counties as planning authorities and the institution of regional authorities to oversee regional policy. This tendency was as centralizing as it was radical. The other tendency favoured incremental change of existing structures in order to deal with immediate problems created by the war and the inadequacy of pre-war legislation. This tendency favoured the extension of the interim control powers and the maintenance of districts as planning authorities. It led to the successive pieces of legislation in 1943 and 1944. It was born of official caution and the need to balance opposing political views in the wartime Coalition Government. Yet to characterize one as radical and the other as conservative is only a partial representation of truth. For the incremental extension of development control was also to have a radical effect on the planning system which was beginning to be understood by the early 1940s. 'Planning by consent' was to divide the right to current enjoyment irrevocably from the right to future use of land, quite apart from the vexed questions of how to collect development value and what compensation might be due. The issues that remain to be worked through – as much present in the incremental as in the radical approach to planning reform – were what relationships could be established between the plan and the consent and between national policy and local circumstance.

Implementing Planning by Consent

Of course planning by consent did not necessarily require a reform of the 1932 planning schemes. These schemes did indeed carry the force of law, but we have already seen that they could carry within them discretionary clauses that made further consent from the local authority necessary. Universal control as enacted in 1943 did not require a new sort of plan to be effective. But official thinking began to see these planning schemes as insufficiently flexible in the face of change: the fight for elasticity that had begun at the beginning of the century was being continued. There were two major problems with the existing legislation. If a proposal conformed to an adopted planning scheme in every detail there was no need for a further consent and no grounds on which it could be opposed. At the same time a local authority could not give consent for a proposal that did not conform to the scheme unless the scheme itself was modified. The modification procedure was slow and cumbersome. These two problems were enough to suggest that a change in the system of plans was also necessary. The modifications brought by the 1944 Act were only a very partial solution.

Universal control, whether simply of interim development, as in the 1943 Act, or of all development, which was becoming the increasingly accepted option for the future, did not actually need the existence of a scheme or a plan at all. Pepler evidently saw this as a problem and stressed the necessity of having planning schemes in order to ensure that there was some kind of security for developers and for the public at large. Pepler's view seems to have been that the problem with existing planning schemes was not that 'they were too rigid but because they were too elastic' (cited by Cullingworth, 1975, p. 97). Delay had been caused by 'protracted negotiations' with landowners. This appears to follow the kind of professional thinking from the 1920s when the virtues of American zoning were being promoted. Yet the prevailing view was that plans should be more, not less, flexible. In 1945 the Whiskard Committee thus came forward with a proposal for outline plans which would prescribe a general framework for policy: it would act as a guide for private developers, and for central government in relation to the compulsory purchase of land for public needs. Within these outline plans detailed development plans would be created to amplify policy for areas of extensive redevelopment and new development. Such a system would, it was argued, serve to defeat the negativity and cumbersome procedures of the 1932 Act planning schemes.

The Whiskard Committee did not envisage a complete transfer of plan-making powers to the counties but did nevertheless argue for the strengthening of existing powers to grouped authorities and for districts to transfer their authorities to counties. The committee also envisaged an enhanced role for central government. The Minister would be able to direct on matters of national and regional importance as well as prepare codes for the satisfactory drawing up of detailed plans. Ministerial approval would be necessary for both sorts of plan. There had been discussions earlier on whether plans should also be laid before Parliament. Here there was initially some disagreement. A minority view which eventually became to be accepted was that parliamentary approval was inappropriate for indicative plans, and that parliamentary control of ministerial powers would be adequate to ensure accountability. An inquiry before a plan was approved would not be mandatory, but the Minister should be given discretion to hold an inquiry if necessary (Cullingworth, 1975).

The Resolution of Problems: The 1947 Town and Country Planning Act

Out of this essentially confusing pattern of debate and disagreement was eventually born the 1947 Town and Country Planning Act. It did what neither of the wartime Acts had done, in laying the basis for the planning system as a whole. The incoming Labour government under Clement Attlee made a fresh start in trying to resolve the issues that had been tossed back and forth endlessly during the war. Silkin as Minister of Town and Country Planning invited Sir Geoffrey Whiskard to investigate once again the basis for a scheme for compensation and betterment and, by extension, for the planning system as a whole. From within, the process that led eventually to the 1947 Act looks extraordinarily protracted and the discussion circular. But with the benefit of hindsight it is possible to see how much thinking had crystallized by 1945 and how much had been achieved through a process that at the time had seemed agonizingly slow. There was broad agreement that universal control of development was necessary. Plans should be indicative, and statutory only in the sense that they would be a point of reference sanctioned by statute for development decisions. There needed to be oversight by central government both of the content of plans and of decisions by local authorities that would depart from plans. Above all, there needed to be a satisfactory system for the collection of betterment and the payment of compensation that would ensure that development rights would only be exercised with the consent of government.

Some aspects at least of these broad areas of agreement had already been enacted. The chief innovations of the 1947 Act were in the system of plans and in the provisions for compensation and betterment. The development plans of the Act were indeed indicative, although they did not quite include the distinction between the outline and detailed plans envisaged by the Whiskard Committee. Departures from the plan had to be referred to the Minister but did not require the modification of the plan as a whole.

In the end, the development plan system came to be seen as flawed. As Cullingworth observes, there is a paradox in the fact that the Whiskard proposals look remarkably like the distinction between Structure and Local Plans introduced in 1968, and yet the Planning Advisory Group Report (1965) was to criticize the 1947 development plans for precisely the inflexibility that they were supposed to have resolved. The Act nevertheless established the principle of a mandatory system of plans which would be based upon research and survey and which would be concerned with land use as much as with built form. They represented the culmination of the move away from the surveyor's plans of the beginning of the century.

The provisions for compensation and betterment have been fully explored elsewhere (see Cox, 1984) and in practice also proved to be flawed. What they did do was to underwrite the intention to nationalize development rights, even if compensation and betterment were not fundamentally necessary for the concept; the need for consent to carry out any development was enough to ensure such a nationalization. For the Labour government, the nationalization of development rights was only a prelude to the nationalization of development land, and hence a much more formal acquisition of an interest in the future use of land. In this light, the need for a planning consent for all development was seen as a temporary rather than a permanent measure which would be replaced by direct implementation. Uthwatt had already proposed that development land should be leased to developers and local authorities and this concept was retained by the Labour administration. In place of the great estates of the nineteenth century would be central and local government once again controlling development through binding covenants. The Labour administration did not achieve this end and the Conservatives repealed the provisions for the recovery of betterment. The two subsequent attempts by Labour to control betterment value also ended in failure. But the nationalization of development rights has never since been questioned.

The provisions for the control of development in the 1947 Act were perhaps the least radical part, because they already existed in embryo in previous Acts. Consent would now be required for all development, whether or not there was an approved plan. The provision for appeals to the Minister against decisions of local authorities was perpetuated. The enforcement provisions of 1943 were reintroduced and strengthened. The additional powers for historic buildings and trees were re-enacted and to them were added new powers to control advertisements. The most striking aspect of the Act was the way in which it formalized the distinction between land use and physical development and the discretionary powers of decision-makers. The definition of development in Section 12 has remained virtually unaltered to the present day. It extended the term 'operations' to embrace not only buildings but also engineering and mining. It also introduced the concept of a 'material' change of use without establishing criteria for what was and what was not material. The definition was wider and more clearly expressed than in the 1932 Act and ensured, among other things, that a local planning authority could deal with the problem created by rebuilding on an existing site.

Section 14 of the Act contained the main discretionary powers of the universal development control system. As we have seen, discretionary power of one kind or another had in fact been available to local authorities from the outset. The infamous Clause 56 of the Ruislip-Northwood scheme was one early example as was the power to impose conditions in interim control. Section 14 generalized the discretion. In determining applications for planning consent, the local authority was required 'to have regard to the development plan and to any other material considerations'. The use of the phrase 'other material considerations' effectively served two purposes. It ensured that development plans could only ever be indicative, because considerations might dictate a decision not authorized by the plan. It also enshrined a case-law approach to dealing with planning applications: each application would have to be, in the time-hallowed phrase, considered on its merits. Particular circumstances of place and time might influence the decision and after 1947 the site visit would become a staple of the development control officer's work. The power to grant permission conditionally was retained, but not substantially modified from the 1932 Act. Yet it reinforced the discretionary power of local authorities, and discretionary power was in turn to reinforce the unwritten but shared system of professional values that we have seen emerging already in the 1930s.

Secondary legislation under the Act also had a significant place in the control of development. The old General Interim Development Order was replaced by the General Development Order, the first example of which predated the coming into force of the Act itself. In the same way as the pre-war orders, the General Development Order set out the administrative procedure for planning applications, and covered some details, such as the time limit for processing applications, which had previously been in the primary legislation. Finally, the Order set out a schedule of development for which permission was granted by the Order itself. This was little more than an extension of Article 4 of the 1933 Order, but one innovation was that the Act itself allowed the Minister to make orders for the granting of planning permission which embraced not only the General Development Order but also the possibility of Special Development Orders for permission in particular circumstances. Another innovation was the power under Article 4 of local authorities to recover control over any aspect of permitted development, provided they had had the Minister's approval.

The original General Development Order was considerably less generous in granting permitted development rights than its successors were to be. As the first report on the operation of the 1947 Act put it:

The first General Development Order under the 1947 Act had to be framed before the Act came into force and the 'block' permissions it gave were deliberately on the cautious side; their chief aim was to assist the routine operations of local authorities and statutory undertakers, and the tolerance allowed to the private developer was small. The householder, for example, might do little more without permission than put up small sheds and shelters in his garden (but not his garage) and build a wall not more than seven feet high (so long as it did not abut a road); the farmer might erect without permission only buildings which were not more than 300 square feet in area, 13 foot high and 150 feet from the principal farm block. Eighteen months experience has shown that a number of relaxations might be made particularly to give greater freedom to householders and farmers. (Ministry of Local Government and Planning, 1951b)

The question of unsightly garages and sheds had worried the authors of the early planning schemes and both the Quinton, Harborne and Edgbaston and the Ruislip-Northwood schemes had attempted to control what householders did in their own back yards. With the shift in emphasis towards the control of land use rather than simply of estate layout a rather more relaxed attitude to such extensions appears to have been possible in the post-war period.

As a result, the General Development Order was revised in 1950 to give the now familiar rights to extensions expressed as a percentage of the cubic volume, or of the floor area for industrial buildings, and the general principles on which permitted development rights were based have not been substantially varied since. The second statutory instrument was the Use Classes Order whose aim was to categorize generic uses such that change within a given class would not be considered 'material' and would not, therefore, constitute development. As with the General Development Order 2 years of experiment led to change, with an original 22 classes being reduced to 18 in 1950. The Use Classes Order was the direct answer to the administrators' concern to be able to identify a change of use, and as with the General Development Order the principle has remained unchanged even if the classes were substantially reconfigured in 1987.

So a universal system of development control that nationalized development rights and was related to, but not absolutely bound by, a system of plans was now in place. A delicate balance between local authorities left free to decide applications in the best interests of their locality and a proper desire to achieve national policy objectives through ministerial reserve powers had been achieved. The passage of the 1947 Act remains a formidable achievement.

What is striking about this discussion of the events that led up to the imposition of universal control is the extent to which the focus was upon process and not upon content. It was as though everyone knew what control was to be used for and what it could achieve. Nevertheless, there is enough within the official memoranda and the policy documents to give an idea of the conception of development control that informed official thinking. In part the emphasis on an ordered environment seems to have remained current throughout the first 50 years of the twentieth century. John Burns, the President of the Local Government Board at the time of the passing of the 1909 Housing, Town Planning etc. Act had declared to Parliament in a memorable speech that the Act would:

. . . secure the home healthy, the house beautiful, the town pleasant, the city dignified and the suburb salubrious. It seeks and hopes to secure more houses, better houses, prettier streets, so that the character of a great people in towns and cities and villages can be still further improved and strengthened by the conditions under which they live. (Address to Parliament 1908, cited by Minett, 1974, p. 679)

Here was a vision that could only be delivered, it came to be realized, through the control of individual projects as well as through the preparation of planning schemes. It was a vision that had not died by the 1940s, but one that had certainly evolved in the 40 years following the passing of the 1909 Act. An unsigned file note of 1943 whose main aim was to review the issues of compensation and betterment started with a declaration of the objects of planning:

In town planning the aim is to remove squalor and congestion, to promote the welfare of the worker in his everyday life by bringing work and residence nearer together, to secure adequate open space for rest and recreation, to replace ugliness by architectural beauty and civic dignity; to prevent a jumble of incompatible activities in the same area, to secure a road system which avoids traffic delays and promotes safety, to prevent the overgrowth of towns and the social and economic disadvantages which follow from it . . . It will be apparent that to secure the results outlined above two essential conditions must be fulfilled: 1. all development must be controlled in town and country . . . 2. that local authorities should have wide powers to purchase land wherever necessary to secure development or re-development in accordance with the plan.[19]

There is perhaps no clearer indication of official thinking on the purpose of development control than this. Physical form remained an object of control, therefore, but the control of land uses was now an essential part of the vision as a means of creating economic and social well-being. And the ordered, utopian view of the future was to be achieved by State intervention both to control development and also to promote it through the purchase of development land. It represents the fulfilment of one strand of thinking about development control, but it does not recognize at all the potential of development control for dispute resolution and the vision is as potentially authoritarian as it is utopian.

One measure of the achievement of the 1947 Act is the extent to which the legislative framework for development control has remained unchanged since 1947. That suggests that the framework was fundamentally robust and has been able to adapt to the enormous changes that have taken place in Britain since 1947. On the other hand, this lack of change could reflect a kind of administrative inertia in rather the same way that the 1774 London Building Act remained unaltered for 70 years, because a sufficiently complex piece of legislation had created vested interests that ensured its survival. This is an issue to which we shall return in looking at the way in which the development control system was applied over the next 50 years.

There are other points to be made about the Act. In vesting the rights to the future use of land in the State, the Act was creating a tension between the role of the local authority as an impartial arbiter of the public interest in determining planning applications and the local authority as an entity having an interest on a par with that of the current occupier of the land. In one sense, this is no different from the trustholder who acts selflessly on behalf of a beneficiary; except that in the case of local authorities, there might be a direct pecuniary advantage to the authority of the decision it takes. This has, in particular, bedevilled the issue of planning agreements.

The second point is that nationalizing development rights led to a system of checks and balances that were primarily there to redress potential injustice to landowners. So the right of appeal was only given to the private sector owners and developers who wish to contest a local authority's decision and not to third parties, and the appeal system was set up in a way that ensured is was adversarial. At another level, the extension of permitted development rights was explicitly designed to ease the burden of the householder. In some ways, then, the Act served to further entrench the private property interest, just as, McAuslan (1980) argues, the courts were also to do in trying to define the limits of planning. In nationalizing an interest in property, the checks and balances in the system were geared to defending the remainder of the private property interest. We need now to turn to the way in which the Act was used in the next two decades.

Notes

1. PRO HLG52/587. E.S.Hill and R.J. Simpson, 13 October 1933; Divisional Memorandum, 16 August 1934.
2. PRO HLG58/202. Minute dated 23 October 1936.
3. PRO HLG81/40. File note dated 3 July 1943.
4. PRO HLG29/268. Memorandum dated 18 October 1941, initialled E.H.S. Since no other memorandum carries these initials and since other material on this and related files include work by E.S. Hill, it is reasonable to assume that this memorandum was also by Hill.
5. PRO HLG29/268. Letter dated 21 April 1942.
6. PRO HLG 29/268. Letter dated 9 June 1942.
7. Sheffield City Council, 18th and 23rd Report of the Special Committee on Town Planning and Civic Centres, 21 April 1941 and 20 July 1942.
8. PRO CAB117/133. Memorandum of the Minister of Town and Country Planning for the War Cabinet/Legislation Committee, 12 March 1943.
9. PRO CAB127/164. Memorandum dated 3 April 1942.
10. PRO HLG81/40. Memorandum dated June 1943.
11. PRO HLG81/43. E.S. Hill to Sir Geoffrey Whiskard, 30 November 1943.
12. Hansard, House of Commons, 12 July 1944.
13. PRO HLG52/1206. Letters between Sir Raymond Unwin and Sir Arthur Robinson, 25 July 1935 and 23 August1935.
14. PRO HLG29/268. Interim report of the Harrison Committee, 21 May 1941; CAB87/1. Memorandum from Lord Reith.
15. PRO CAB127/164, CAB127/169. Memoranda by Sir Malcolm Trustram Eve, Sir William Jowitt.
16. PRO HLG52/588. Letter from County Solicitor, Middlesex. HLG52/591. Memorandum dated 10 November 1938.
17. PRO CAB127/164. Memorandum dated 3 April 1942.
18. PRO CAB117/133. WP(43)117, 23 March 1943.
19. PRO HLG81/40. Unsigned file note dated June 1943. Handwritten marginal note: 'further revise by Sir R. Hopkins and Sir Malcolm T[rustram]-Eve'.

Chapter Five

Control by Consents: the 1947 Act and After

The 1947 Act was decisive in giving legal form to 'control by consents' that had begun to emerge as the way forward from the late 1930s. In that light, the absence of debate about development control in the 20 years after the passing of the Act is all the more remarkable. While plan preparation and the surveys that would be undertaken as a necessary part of the process were the subject of government policy and professional comment, development control received a meagre share of either. Not until the late 1960s did development control begin to attract as much policy attention as plan making, and critical comment only followed in the 1970s. Certainly plan making remained the more glamorous end of the new planning system. The application of social science methodology to the survey work began to point planning in a very different direction from the physically deterministic planning schemes of the previous legislation. The Ministry on the other hand was intent on bringing some coherence to the plans that would be prepared for the country as a whole, by advising on standards for physical layout and use of land.

Development control by contrast seems to have become stigmatized as a bureaucratic chore and, in McLoughlin's (1973) words, its practitioners the 'Cinderellas' of the profession. The logic of planning by consent had not been fully assimilated into the practice of planning and appears to have been regarded as a secondary activity. The effect was to obscure some of the issues that were to become increasingly problematic from the 1970s onwards: the nature of the relationship between the development plan and development control decisions; the nature of the decision-making process; the degree of certainty that the system could offer to its users.

Why development control should have sunk into relative obscurity requires explanation. A first reason has to do with the continuity of control. For though the 1947 Act established an important principle in requiring that all development everywhere should be subject to the need for planning permission, the effect in practice was no more than to enlarge the frontiers of an existing activity. Seventy-three per cent of England was covered by resolutions to prepare plans by 1942; a very substantial majority of local authorities were already engaged in development control work. Sheffield is a good case in point: in 1947 it had no approved plans for any of its area, but the whole of the built-up area was covered by a resolution to prepare plans. As we have seen, the City was pressing the Ministry for increased control over development, particularly in view of wartime damage. And already by 1944 a town planning committee had been established as a standing committee of Council, with its own sub-committee for the approval of plans under the planning acts.

A second reason is that in the control of development as it was being understood in the 1940s, the process of determining planning applications was only one part of a larger scheme. Thomas Sharp in his readable popularization of the case for town planning argued strenuously for the new planning to be positive and not negative (1940), and that view was being echoed by ministerial officials. Planning permission was intended to be part of a system that encompassed the nationalization of development rights, the collection of betterment and the purchase of development land by local authorities so that they could carry out their own schemes. Whether it was actually believed that development control would wither away entirely in the face of the nationalization of all development land is not clear, but if development land was to be nationalized as the Labour government originally intended, then the control process might take on a very different complexion. At the same time, of course, in the economic crisis of the late 1940s private sector development was still at a very low ebb: less than a quarter of all permanent housing put up between 1945 and 1950 was built by private builders (Ministry of Local Government and Planning, 1951b).

A third reason is that quite apart from the subsidiary nature of the control process, the provisions for compensation and betterment proved extraordinarily troublesome. In theory, by limiting compensation to those who could claim that their land had been 'dead-ripe' for development (the colloquialism sits curiously in the midst of the official writing of the period) and by taxing betterment value at 100 per cent, the difficulties of previous schemes were overcome. The betterment provision was designed to ensure that land would change hands at existing use value. In the event, the effect was to discourage landowners from selling. It also encouraged buyers to pay a premium in order to secure land for development. This was far from the intended result, but is explained by the system of licences which were required for all building construction as part of the austerity measures in the aftermath of war. Such licences were time limited and as a result placed a pressure on developers to acquire land if the right to build was not to be lost. Nor did the collection of betterment enjoy universal political support. The Conservatives had never really favoured the tax on betterment, and when they were returned to power in 1951 moved to abandon the tax and wind up the Central Land Board. This was eventually done in the 1953 and 1954 Town and Country Planning Acts which also limited the compensation payable to the loss in value as at 1947; subsequent increases in land value could no longer be compensated. But there was also no about-turn on the principle of universal control. As Westergaard (1964) has explained, the effect of these acts was to denationalize development *value* but not development *rights*. The idea that the state had an interest in land remained intact.

The final reason has to do with the renewed emphasis on plan making. Part of that work was undoubtedly innovative. The Middlesbrough Plan of 1944–45 by Max Lock and Partners involved an analysis of socio-economic factors that was without precedent in British planning, as was the fact that the sociologist Ruth Glass was employed in the plan's preparation. The Ministry's report of 1951 lists a number of surveys which the Ministry itself had commissioned and which it commended to local authorities. But if survey techniques suggested a whole new approach to plan making (and one far removed from the process of development control), ministerial advice on the plan itself tended in a different direction. Certainly the Ministry put much effort into advising local authorities on what plans needed to be and no fewer than four major circulars were issued between 1947 and 1949 (Ministry of Town and Country Planning, 1947, 1948a, 1948b, 1949b). Perhaps this is hardly surprising. If interim control powers had already become universal by 1947, the experience of plan making was much more limited with only 5 per cent of the country subject to an approved plan by 1942. Universal plan making by local authorities rightly required an input from central government.

What is striking is the highly prescriptive nature of the advice given. Normative standards and measurable criteria were seen as an important part of a plan, and precise instructions were given as to how these should be represented. Standard colours and notation were identified. With this emphasis on physical criteria, the development plans began to look more like an extension of pre-war planning schemes than an innovative approach to policy-making. The concept of an indicative plan seems to have been somewhat lost, perhaps in a desire to create a firm base for local authorities' own development and for the process of development control. If the standards were clear enough in the development plan, then the process of development control would take care of itself. The reasons why such a prescriptive approach should have continued after 1947 probably lie with yet another of the wartime committees. For while the broad outlines of 'control by consents' were being established and the issue of compensation and betterment explored, the Pound Committee was reviewing the Model Clauses under the 1932 legislation in very much the terms of the advice that was to be given by the Ministry after 1947 (see Home, 1992). The Pound Committee was yet another of the ways in which the continuity between planning before the war and universal control after 1947 was assured.

The Early Years of Universal Control

These reasons begin to explain why development control had a low profile in its first two decades. It was either not recognized as a separate sphere of activity or, if it was, it was accorded a more lowly status than the positive powers of implementation that the 1947 Act brought in. In this respect the Schuster Committee *Report on the Qualifications of Planners* (Committee on the Qualifications of Planners, 1950) is revealing. The report was highly influential in identifying the nature of the planning task, the values that it perceived as fundamental to that task, and the type of education that as a consequence a new breed of planning professional would require. In particular, it presented the decisive break with the architectural, engineering and surveying origins of planning in the first half of the twentieth century. Yet its references to development control are extremely limited. It identifies the three stages of the planning process as survey, formulating the plan and implementation. Although it recognized that implementation was to a large extent a matter of control over private development, much more space is devoted to the 'positive' aspects of implementation. And much of the work of development control staff is regarded as 'requiring a certain amount of knowledge and common sense, but no high degree of specialist skill' (Committee on the Qualifications of Planners, 1950, para 7b).

Yet at the same time these first 20 years of universal control were formative even if the focus was elsewhere. Though ministerial policy on development control mainly concerned procedures, some policy advice was forthcoming on specialist topics, including gravel workings, agricultural land and a brief circular on the need for a 3-year housing land supply. Two rather more general circulars begin to set a policy tone for development control. Circular 67, for example, tried to define the term development, by noting that demolition was not covered and that for a doctor to establish consulting rooms in his own house did not constitute a change of use. Though both of these were no more than a matter of policy opinion, they nevertheless influenced practice thereafter (Ministry of Town and Country Planning, 1949*b*). The other circular offered advice on the drafting of permissions and in particular on the proper use of conditions. Local authorities were advised to keep conditions to a minimum and to ensure that they were enforceable:

. . . the attempt to guard against every contingency and regulate every trifle is not only a sign of fussy administration but frequently defeats its own ends, (Ministry of Local Government and Planning 1951*a*, para. 10)

Moreover conditions were not to be used to acquire material advantage such as the payment of cash or the cession of land for road widening. By 1953, the advice articulated in rather more detail the presumption in favour of development. A refusal of planning permission was only justified if there was demonstrable harm to an interest of acknowledged importance (Ministry of Housing and Local Government, 1953). And then in 1955 came the circular on green belts which spelt out the nature of the constraint in those areas which were designed to prevent the inexorable outward growth of towns and cities (Ministry of Housing and Local Government, 1955). By so doing, it was to lay the basis for a major element in development control policy for the next 40 years. The idea that the development control process would have a life of its own is given some impetus by the relatively few professional commentaries on control. George Pepler looking back in retirement on the first 10 years of universal control could reflect at a Town Planning Institute conference with some satisfaction, complacency even, on the 'growing necessity' for control (*Journal of the Town Planning Institute*, 1959). Lewis Keeble, whose textbook *The Principles and Practice of Town and Country Planning* (1952) was to appear in three editions and was the staple of planning courses in the 1950s, devoted three chapters to control, albeit out of a total of twenty-three. His treatment of the subject is worthy of comment. Control was there, certainly, to implement the plan, but:

Besides this, development control involves regulation of the detailed aspects of development, about which no guidance is given by the development plan, so as to achieve convenient and sightly results.

He continues:

Powers of development control are so wide, and as regard some subjects, so vague, that the framing of a clear policy based upon definite principles is essential if control is not to degenerate into either, on the one hand, an irritating policy tyranny, or, on the other, into an ineffective and formless confusion unlit by either principle or precedent. (p. 411)

Keeble does not quite make clear why precedent should be important even if the parentage of this approach in common law is evident. The rest of the section on development control is devoted to enunciating the principles, which are all connected with the values of 'sightliness' and 'convenience'. Sketches help the reader to understand the way in which buildings may appear intrusive in the landscape, how trees may contribute to a setting and when infilling is acceptable. All the principles thus exemplified (they exist only by reference to a specific example) are to do with physical development. But unlike the Ministry's standards for development plans, these are not normative or measurable and depend upon arcane judgement informed by values which are not articulated.

Keeble's approach is echoed by others. E.A. Powdrill, Assistant County Planning Officer for Surrey, like Keeble, was of the view that the development control officer would have certain principles constantly in mind. Speaking at a branch meeting of the Town Planning Institute, he said:

These principles should be such that, when set against the rather loose background of the development plan, they could stand by themselves and thus achieve what would have otherwise resulted in the lack of effective consideration which would have inevitably led to piecemeal development. (*Journal of the Town Planning Institute* 1960, p. 124)

Both Keeble and Powdrill were identifying the development plan as an inadequate base for decision-making and advocating the need for principles based on concepts of physical development to underpin the work of control. The separate existence of development control was being established, with its own justifications and its own touchstones of performance.

This did not serve to enhance its status with the profession and to some extent both Keeble and Powdrill contributed to the lowly image that development control acquired. Keeble in particular seems to have taken an increasingly jaundiced view of development control as a time-wasting activity, and both castigated the ineffectiveness of planning officials, inspectors and even Ministers in trying to determine appropriate policy base for a decision. Keeble might insist that development control was a task 'of great complexity requiring special qualities, not least a delicate feeling for diplomacy, and long experience' (1957, p. 175). But its image was to remain determinedly down-market.

Development Control and Legal Interpretation

The system was also being moulded from without. In particular, the courts came to play a significant role in defining the scope of development control. McAuslan (1980) argues that those who drafted the 1947 Act might have assumed that the terms 'other material considerations' and conditions 'such as the local authorities thinks fit' left enough freedom for local authorities to act without judicial interference. Given the courts' interest in defending private property interests, such a view was hardly realistic. The *Ellis* case of 1920 (see p. 84) was already an indication of how the courts reacted to planning law. Though planning case law in the post-war period is relatively limited, there is a small number of planning cases which have been significant in constraining local authorities' discretionary freedom. The legal doctrine of *ultra vires* (literally 'beyond the powers', which in a legal context implies the powers granted by Parliament) has been crucial in testing the limits of the otherwise unbridled power of the administration to take action. In planning, the courts' determination to uphold property rights has been articulated particularly in relation to those points where the law is most open-ended: in the definition of what might be taken as a material consideration, and in the nature of the power to impose conditions.

In the limits to the power to impose conditions, a succession of judgements refined what it was, and what it was not, proper for local authorities to do. The *Pyx Granite Co Ltd v. Minister of Housing and Local Government* case of 1958 was the first to establish the principle that the condition had to be related to the permitted development:

The planning authority are not at liberty to use their powers for an ulterior object, however desirable that object may seem to them to be in the public interest. (Lord Denning, cited by Grant, 1982, p. 338)

Later cases extended that definition. So in the *Mixnam's Properties v. Chertsey Urban District Council* case in 1965 (to do primarily with caravan licensing rather than town planning) the court ruled that conditions had also to be related to 'planning considerations' and to be reasonable if local authorities were to act within their powers.

Beyond this establishment of general principles, particular cases give insight into the impact of the courts on the limits on the power to control development. The case of *Hall and Co. v. Shoreham-by-sea Urban District Council* in 1964 was a good example of the court setting very tight limits on the ability to grant conditional permission. In the Hall case, the local planning authority had given consent for industrial development on condition that the applicant provided a service road which traffic from adjoining properties could be allowed to use as the industrial area was developed in its entirety. In planning policy terms, the argument in favour of the condition was unimpeachable. The local authority wanted to stop the proliferation of accesses to the main road running alongside the site. The judge took the view that the local authority was requiring the company to give up some part of its interest in the land (i.e. by allowing others to use the service road as of right). The authority had, he argued, the power under the Highways Acts which could have allowed them to achieve the same end, with proper compensation to the owner. The condition as it stood was in his view unreasonable.

A decade or so later, the Royco Homes 1974 judgement (*R. v. Hillingdon London Borough Council* ex parte *Royco Homes Ltd*) tended in the same direction. Here the London Borough of Hillingdon imposed a condition which required the developer to build flats, which were part of a larger housing scheme, to the minimum standards and costs laid down by the Ministry of Housing and Local Government. The flats were then to be offered to housing waiting lists tenants. The court ruled that this condition was unreasonable in that Hillingdon was requiring the developer to shoulder what was described as a 'significant' part of the local authority's responsibilities, although as McAuslan (1980) remarks, the use of the word 'significant' to describe a mere thirty-six flats said more about the court's attitude to conditions than it does about the actual scale of the task.

The *Fawcett Properties Ltd v. Buckingham County Council* case of 1960, as much cited in legal textbooks as the previous three, appears to suggest a very different attitude. Buckingham County Council imposed a condition which required two cottages in the green belt to be occupied only by agricultural workers. This on the face of it was in direct opposition to the concept that planning was about the use of land and not about the nature of the occupants. But here the court upheld the local authority's conditions on the grounds that it would serve to maintain the green belt. As McAuslan puts it:

Green belt preservation is the archetypical planning policy – it's about amenity, it's easy to understand, its philosophy is accepted by judges and so passes the test of a proper planning policy. The condition itself is acceptable because *looked at from the point of view of the landowner* it did not unduly restrict his freedom of action. This is a crucial matter for the courts (the point of view of the landowner) and it helps to explain the ready acceptance of green belt policy. (p. 164)

The point that McAuslan is making here is that the courts have acted to protect private property interests in the face of the growing power of public authorities. But more than that: the criterion of acceptability of control is whether or not a private landowner might not have acted in the same way. The Hall and Royco cases fail by that measure because the local authorities required the developer to act positively on their behalf in a way that no landowner would have done. The Fawcett conditions sit squarely within the tradition of negative covenants on leasehold agreements, and is of a piece with those restrictions which ensured houses were kept exclusively in residential use.

The Fawcett judgment gave judicial authorization to a policy that was already deeply entrenched in the popular imagination. Attitudes to positive conditions seem to have modified somewhat, however. In 1984 the court ruled that Grampian Regional Council in Scotland were within their powers to impose a condition that prevented a supermarket development proceeding before a road closure had been completed (*Grampian Regional Council v. City of Aberdeen District Council*). In the Grampian case the judge was satisfied that the council intended to carry out the closure and that it was in an approved programme of work. It was not, therefore, quite comparable to either the Hall or the Royco Homes case because it did not involve the developer giving away some part of their property rights (*Journal of Planning and Environment Law*, 1984). The government advice in the early 1990s to local authorities to achieve affordable housing in their areas by securing agreements with private developers seems to suggest the achievement of the Royco objective by other means (Department of the Environment, 1992). There has of course been no attempt to set internal space standards in such agreements, but the major difference is that this is control by agreement and not by the imposition of a condition on a planning permission.

There is a larger point to make about the role of courts as well. What is clear from the case law is that the courts have been very largely instrumental in defining the scope of local planning authorities' powers and in defining the meaning of terms such as 'material considerations'. The courts nevertheless sometimes have had recourse to government policy in shaping their decisions. In a case at Coleshill in the West Midlands (*Coleshill and District Investment Co. v. Minister of Housing and Local Government*, 1969) in which the judge ruled that the demolition of embankments did not constitute development, he noted that the applicants had relied on the advice of the 1951 circular referred to earlier. In turn, that case law has been repatriated into the planning system through advice from central government to local authorities. In 1968, for example, the government issued a circular which defined a six-point test for conditions. They had to be necessary, related to planning, related to the permitted development, precise, enforceable and reasonable (Ministry of Housing and Local Government, 1968). Of these, the second and fifth had already appeared in a circular in 1951 and three others derived from the Mixnam Properties judgement. The test of necessity is evidently another form of the policy presumption in favour of development: conditions are only to be used if planning consent would have been refused without them. The planning process may have become legalized in the period since 1947, but the courts have also accorded a status to government advice which seems to take them beyond the role of mere opinion.

Public Inquiries in the Control Process

The other significant event in the otherwise quiet years of development control was the report by the Franks Committee on administrative tribunals (Committee on Administrative Tribunals and Enquiries, 1957). Although it was not only concerned with planning inquiries, the report nevertheless made much reference to them. In that, the Franks Report recognized the extent to which inquiries had become an important part of the structure of decision-making within the planning system. We have already seen how inquiries were used by the early system when a planning scheme was commenced and when the draft scheme had been finalized. The possibility of appeals to the Minister, and the possibility of inquiries in connection with appeals was part of the set up for the interim control of development.

Two rather different traditions were combined in the system of appeals before 1947, however. For approved planning schemes, the preferred form of appeal against the local authority's use of its discretionary powers was to the magistrates' courts, where the role of the magistrates was clearly adjudicatory. But appeals on aspects of the scheme before it was approved and on interim development control decisions were to the Minister, who was empowered to hold an inquiry. The rationale behind this distinction was that the Minister acted as ultimate decision-maker on planning schemes and it was therefore appropriate for him to hear appeals: the Minister's role was perceived as administrative and not judicial. The inquiry was an instrument of government that had originated in the early nineteenth century and was essentially a means of informing central government about the proper basis for its decisions; they were not intended to be adjudicatory (Wraith and Lamb, 1971). The role of the inspector sent out by central government to investigate was a relic particularly of public health legislation. In practice the distinction between the role of the courts and the role of the Minister in dealing with appeals was never very clear-cut. The Quinton, Harborne and Edgbaston scheme allowed for both appeal to the magistrates court in the case of street widths, but to the Local Government Board on the size of land units and the number of houses that might be built.[1]

In spite of some reluctance on the part of the Ministry in the inter-war years, the appellate role of central government grew and that of the magistrates' courts declined. With the introduction of universal control from 1947, the calls on a system of administrative appeals were inevitably set to become much larger. Between 1943 and 1951 the Ministry of Town and Country Planning Inspectorate dealt with 10,000 inquiries although these covered much more than just appeals against refusal for a planning permission (Ministry of Local Government and Planning, 1951b). The system was in many ways a satisfactory one in that it gave appellants a reasonably simple means of redress against an unfavourable decision. Its limitations lay in the confusion of an administrative, decision-making function with an adjudicatory function. The principle was that an inquiry was a means of informing the Minister on the decision to be taken, but the Minister was also in effect being called on to judge the merits of the case being made by the local planning authority and the appellant respectively. The procedure of inquiries rather supposed the former, not the latter, role. Though the inquiry itself was public and the inspector was free to hear anyone who wished to make a case, there was no sharing of information before the inquiry and the inspector's report was confidential.

The Franks Committee was appointed to look at administrative tribunals in general not so much because of these specific weaknesses of the inquiry system in planning, as because of the increasing concern about the nature of administrative behaviour and the exercise of administrative discretion. The Committee was set up in the wake of the notorious Crichel Down case of 1954, although its terms of reference were to look only at those tribunals set up by statute. In the Crichel Down case, the Ministry of Defence had bought land in Dorset for a bombing range during the Second World War and then, when peace was declared, the land was transferred to the Ministry of Agriculture. The son-in-law of the original owner believed his offer to repurchase the land had been overlooked when the Ministry of Agriculture were considering selling it. Much concern was expressed at the time at the apparently unlimited discretionary power wielded by civil servants who were criticized in an informal inquiry set up to investigate (Wraith and Lamb, 1971).

The Franks Report took as its starting point the promotion of good administration; and the characteristics of good administration would be openness, fairness and impartiality. Its recommendations were that procedure before inquiry should be open and in particular that local authorities should give advance notice of their case; that central government should set out a policy context for the decision to be taken; and that inspectors' reports should be published. Franks also recommended that some decision-making at inquiries should be delegated by the Ministry to the inspector. Although the Franks Report was accepted by Parliament, it took time for the proposals to be implemented by the Ministry of Housing and Local Government. Dame Evelyn Sharp was opposed to the publication of inspectors' reports and delegation of decisions to inspectors did not begin until 1969 (Barker and Couper, 1984). Nevertheless, the remaining recommendations were acted upon, and procedural rules for inquiries were laid down by statutory instrument. Statements of the policy context of decisions did not become standard, however. Yet policy in government circulars, already an important element in the communications between central and local government, was further developed by the publication of a series of Development Control Policy Notes from 1969 onwards

(Ministry of Housing and Local Government/Department of the Environment, 1969–1977). This form of policy directive was to become increasingly significant in the 1970s and 1980s.

The Franks Committee recommendations did not greatly add to the rights of third parties to contest planning decisions. They still could not easily challenge a local authority's decision to give planning permission. But opening up the inquiry procedure allowed for a far greater possibility of meaningful participation by the public at large in an appeal against a refusal of the local planning authority. McAuslan (1980) saw the changes brought about by the Franks recommendations thus:

Between them they [the publication of the reports of inspectors and other officials inside the Department of the Environment, and the creation of statutory rules of procedure] have decisively shifted the balance in public local inquiries in the land use planning field from the inquiry processes being merely one part, albeit the most public part, of the administrative process of making a decision in the public interest on a planning issue, to being the forum in which a greater degree of public participation can take place, in which a decision is increasingly being reached and through which the courts can exert a much greater control on the planning process, usually but not always in the interest of, and in accordance with the ideology of private property. (p. 47)

Creating procedural rules for inquiries not only allowed for a greater degree of public involvement, it also ensured that administrative behaviour was potentially brought under a greater degree of judicial control. Planning was increasingly no longer simple division between a private property interest and a public interest. It was no longer enough to say that local authorities could act on behalf of the public at large and a much more complicated set of relationships was beginning to emerge. McAuslan (1980) saw the change in terms of three opposing ideologies: those of public interest, private property interest, and public participation. In his view, the courts, wedded to the protection of private property against the arbitrariness of the state, nevertheless also have sometimes come to defend participation by the public at large. For McAuslan, too, the three ideologies were continuously in tension, and the tension was the cause of confusion in the planning system. Grant (1982) has argued that the tension was simply a sign of the normal processes of evolution in public law, but does not deny its existence. It was a tension that was to become increasingly acute in the 1970s and 1980s.

The Cinderella of the Profession

Evidence of what was happening at the grassroots during the first two decades of universal control is far harder to establish. The first full-scale studies of development control were not undertaken until the 1970s. Yet the belief that development control was a professional task in its own right, and not one that simply required administrative skills began to develop in the 1950s. Harrison (1972) argued that the terms in which the legislation has been couched has ensured the creation of a professional mystique. The interpretation of words such as 'amenity' or the characteristics of high quality landscape became by statute a matter of professional judgement.

The development control task might call on special skills and required a foundation in a set of principles, but its status within the profession was as low as it was outside. The popular perception of development control was that it was a mind-numbing bureaucratic process, a perception that was partly fuelled, as we have seen, by commentators like Keeble who, for all his talk of special skills, nevertheless also referred to the way in which development control 'inexorably filled the time available for its performance' (Keeble, 1983, p. 105). This not very encouraging prospect seems to have been translated into staff who had fewer professional qualifications than their colleagues in development plan and policy research work. According to McLoughlin (1973) development control staff were also less well paid, tended to be either younger (trainees and students) or middle-aged. There may also have been another element in the traditional dislike of development control work. More than in any other sphere of planning, development control brought planners into direct contact with elected representatives and members of the public. In this way, 'pure' planning judgement had to be continually adjusted or compromised in a way that was undermining of professional values. It was easier to remain untainted in development plan work.

The studies by McLoughlin, and by Underwood (1981) a decade later, demonstrate how development control officers sought ways of delimiting the task of recommending decisions. Faced with the open-ended discretion offered by the need to have regard to other material considerations, McLoughlin and Underwood noted how officers tried to find rules to guide their behaviour. Part of those rules would involve reference to the development plan and ministerial advice, but Underwood found development control officers' attitudes to development plans as ambivalent as Powdrill's had been more than 20 years before. Principles had then to be acquired by a process of osmosis from colleagues; there was recourse to precedent as a guide, and most decision-making appeared rooted in a reliance on visual criteria. Social and economic effects were 'almost completely ignored' (McLoughlin and Webster, c.1970, p. 17). And for Harrison (1972), this portrayed a continuation of pre-war values in the post-war system. Precedent became an important guide for future decisions. The site visit came to occupy a central place in the process of reaching a decision. Rules for decision-making, most conspicuously in the use of standard conditions, helped remove the inherent uncertainty for the decision-maker.

In behaving in this way, development control officers were not unique, as other studies in the use of discretion make clear (Adler and Asquith, 1981). Faced with apparently unfettered discretion, administrators have regularly tried to establish rules, which would ease the difficulty of managing unconstrained freedom. For the existence of wide discretion is evidently stressful for decision-makers and rules are a way of reducing not only uncertainty but also the stress of taking decisions which an uncertain environment imposes. Arguably, the open-ended nature of the development control task as it emerged in the 1950s and 1960s actually encouraged a certain conservatism in practitioners. The known solution was less difficult than one that was untried. Maybe, too, decisions by reference to physical criteria and neighbourhood interests were easier than by reference to the more abstract nature of policy. Development control was undoubtedly establishing a system of decision-making in parallel to the making of policies and plans. But it was not a very comfortable process and not yet one that had attracted much professional attention.

Towards Breakdown

McLoughlin, and even more Underwood, were writing at a time when development control was beginning to undergo major changes; indeed they were writing precisely because from the 1970s onwards, development control came under increasing scrutiny. The call for reform which became ever more strident as the 1970s progressed, owes it origins, paradoxically, to the dissatisfaction with the 1947 system of development plans. In 1963 the Planning Advisory Group was set up by the Ministry of Housing and Local Government to investigate the apparent limitations of the Town and County Maps which were the mainstays of the system. The Group's report published in 1965 advanced the not uncontested view that the detailed Town Maps were not in fact sufficiently fine-grained to respond to the complexity of urban areas and that County Maps were too much constrained by their ordnance survey base to be sufficiently strategic. Whether their criticisms were correct or not, there are grounds for wondering whether the 1947 Development Plans were quite the kind of indicative plans that the wartime administrators had envisaged. The report's recommendation was for the system of Structure and Local Plans which was introduced with the 1968 Town and Country Planning Act and has remained the basis of the plans system to the present. Structure Plans would be truly strategic and indicative and would not carry precise boundaries. Local Plans would be prepared at a level of detail that would enable a proper consideration of the intricacies of urban development.

The Planning Advisory Group were not specifically asked to look at development control. However, they did report briefly on the control system and took a view that was largely positive: the problems of British planning lay with the system of plans not with the means by which those plans were implemented. Nevertheless they argued that the system was too complicated and too slow and that there were problems of management that needed to be addressed. This recommendation led in turn to the commissioning of a study, which was published in 1967. The management study was conducted by a team led by N.R. Mitchell of PA Management Consultants Limited. The other three members of the team were also appointed for their management expertise. Their task was to consider the organization of local authorities in the exercise of the development control function in relation to the prescribed time limit and 'general requirements of public policy that they shall operate fairly, openly and impartially' (Ministry of Housing and Local Government, 1967, brief to consultants). They were also particularly charged to look at consultation arrangements. The resulting report was a careful assessment of the management dimension of development control and contained a large number of detailed recommendations, many of which were acted upon. The report was, for example, the source of the proposal to time-limit planning permissions to 5 years, enacted in 1968. It also urged that all planning committees be given delegated powers, and that some decision-making should be delegated to chief officers. Minor amendments were suggested to permitted development rights. The quality of decision-making was not addressed at all, although in fairness this was not part of the team's remit (Ministry of Housing and Local Government, 1967).

The Planning Advisory Group report and the Management Study together appear innocuous enough; perhaps they even served to legitimate the concept of development control as a separate part of the planning system. But in fact the refusal to see development control as anything more than an administrative exercise was to colour the debate that ensued during the 1970s. It placed the emphasis upon performance not upon objectives. It gave credence to the idea that delay was a major problem. It created the unacknowledged context for the two major inquiries into development control of the 1970s.

One other factor emerged in the late 1960s that was to have significance for the debate on development control. It was widely assumed that local government reform would lead to a pattern in most of the country of unitary authorities, which would be responsible for strategic and local planning and for development control. The original Redcliffe-Maud proposals of 1968, the year in which a new Town and Country Planning Act was passed enacting the revised development plan system, were in the end rejected after two subsequent reports. The local government structure finally approved in 1972 and which came into force in 1974 retained the pattern of counties but created a new structure of districts which were very much larger than their predecessors. Planning powers were divided between the two tiers. Districts acquired a statutory, rather than a delegated, power to determine planning applications and became responsible for preparing Local Plans. Counties were to be responsible for Structure Plans. In order to uphold strategic policy, counties were given the power to direct decisions on what were regarded as county matters. This was not a recipe for harmonious relationships, and the result in some parts of the country was conflict which undoubtedly added to the time taken to process planning applications. Development control became mired in an increasingly acrimonious debate about local government.

The Crisis in Development Control: The Dobry Report

The Dobry Report was commissioned in 1973 against a background of local government reform in process and a view of development control that had emphasized procedure rather than quality of decision-making. The immediate reason for commissioning was the failure of the planning system nationally to deal with the immense upsurge of applications that accompanied the inflation of property values in the early 1970s. Within a period of two years the numbers of applications received in England and Wales had increased by more than 50 per cent. In the end the real estate bubble burst and by the time the final Dobry Report was published, the volume of applications had returned to the level of the late 1960s.

George Dobry, a planning QC, was given the widest possible terms of reference to his study. These were:

- to consider whether the development control system under the Town and Country Planning Acts adequately meets current needs and to advise on the lines along which it might be improved;
- to review the arrangements for appeals to the Secretary of State.

The resulting reports (there were interim and final reports and a separate report on the control of demolition) were not the work of a committee although Dobry was assisted by a large advisory group. The result was in many ways a remarkable achievement. It was by far the most comprehensive description of the development control system ever attempted. It contained numerous recommendations for improving the system, the most important of which had they been implemented, would have had a considerable impact on the way in which the system worked (Dobry, 1974a, 1974b, 1975).

The first of the two major recommendations was that applications should be divided into two categories. Class A applications were to comprise simple cases, applications conforming to an approved development plan and applications for reserved matters on outline permission. These applications were to be processed in 42 days rather than the 8 weeks allowed by the General Development Order, and a failure of the local authority to decide in 42 days would result in a deemed permission. All other applications would be classed B and a 3-month time limit was proposed and 'strict compliance with the time-limits would be demanded'. Local authorities could transfer Class A applications to Class B within 28 days of receipt.

The second major recommendation was that all demolition should be brought under control. Dobry's view was that demolition might result in the loss of buildings which still had a useful life, lead to vacant sites, and could be used by developers as a lever on local planning authorities to permit redevelopment which might not otherwise be acceptable. Indeed so important did Dobry consider this recommendation that he issued a separate report to deal with demolition in advance of the final report. He believed passionately in the proposals he was making.

Given that these two major recommendations were not in fact acted upon, the logic that lay behind the recommendations is perhaps more significant than their substance. Like the Management Study report 8 years before, although rather more radically, Dobry emphasized the administrative weaknesses of the system. Unlike the Management Study the problem of delay is quite explicitly seen as the major challenge. The introduction to the report makes his approach clear:

1.9   The system is potentially very good, but its procedures 'do not adequately meet current needs'.

1.10   The planning system has achieved a great deal. The countryside, for instance, has been well defended, considering the enormous pressures upon it; the impact of suburban sprawl could easily have been catastrophic.

1.11   Regrettably the system is slow, even at times desperately slow, because the procedures are, as at present used, too cumbersome. (Dobry, 1975, p. 5)

Dobry's attitude to the policy base for development control decisions also reveals the extent to which the administrative view of development control was deeply rooted in his thinking. Plans were 'no more than a necessary instrument of planning control' and should 'be applied fairly rigidly' (p. 92), even though he welcomed the greater flexibility of the new system of Structure and Local Plans. The approach is essentially mechanistic: the major function of plans seems to be to facilitate the speedy processing of planning applications. The one thing Dobry did not recommend was an extension of permitted development rights. He argued that such a relaxation would lead to:

. . . some unsatisfactory development which would damage the amenity of the neighbourhood. It could only be accepted if we were to regard it as the price for freeing the planning control system from too much clogging detail. (p. 102)

Dividing applications into two categories would have been, in his view, a more certain way of reducing delays without the same potential for harm. Procedural streamlining would ensure that the amenity objective could still be met while at the same time delays were reduced.

There appears to have been very little general criticism of Dobry's approach at the time. Harrison's (1975) was a rare voice urging that a more thoroughgoing investigation of development control as an instrument of social policy was necessary. He argued against the reliance on 'ill-defined amenity objectives' and advocated an approach based upon estate management in which development control would only be one aspect of a local authority's development policy. This was in part a return to the vision of the late 1940s. Yet although there was little criticism of the approach that Dobry had adopted, the government showed itself reticent on Dobry's major proposals. It did not wish to extend the scope of control by including demolition in the need for planning consent at a time when the system was under pressure. It found the proposal for dividing applications into two types with the possibility of deemed consent to be not self-evidently a simple or effective system to operate. Class A and Class B applications would not necessarily equate with uncontroversial and controversial development; there would be conflict and potential for delay in the way in which the applications were categorized (Department of the Environment, 1975). The one change the government did try to make was the very thing that Dobry had rejected. An amendment to the General Development Order containing a relaxation of permitted development rights was laid before Parliament and, exceptionally, gave rise to a largely hostile debate in the House of Lords. Faced with opposition on all sides, the government was forced to withdraw the amendment (*Journal of Planning and Environment Law*, 1978).

There must be some sympathy with the government's rejection of Dobry's major proposals. But the reluctance to make changes is partly explained by other changes within the planning system. Control over demolition had in fact been extended by the passing of the Town and Country Amenities Act of 1974 which required consent for the demolition of any building within a Conservation Area.[2] Of course not all buildings were covered, but it did very substantially extend the control exercised by local authorities. A second factor was the government's intention to legislate for the control of development land. A White Paper was published as Dobry was conducting his review, and this led in 1976 to the Community Land Act which was to be the final attempt to tax betterment value and to bring development land under public control. By giving local authorities the power to acquire development land on favourable terms, central government believed that demolition would be less likely to take place prematurely: developers would no longer use the leverage of demolition to secure development if a local authority was able to acquire the land.

The Expenditure Committee Report: The Crisis Continued

If the government of the day was not prepared to implement the proposals it did not refute the central argument on delay. The failure to act in turn led to a renewed pressure for action. Fifteen months after the publication of Dobry's final report, the Environment Sub-Committee of the House of Commons Expenditure Committee launched its own inquiry into the development control system. The immediate impetus to do so was likely to have been the second of the two ministerial circulars which followed the publication of the Dobry report. The feeling that both of these circulars had been inadequate was widespread. The 8th report of the Expenditure Committee was published a year later in May 1977 (House of Commons, 1977). It took as its brief to identify 'reasons for delay and the resource costs that such delays create' (p. xix). More explicitly than either the 1967 Management Study or the Dobry Report, the Environment Sub-Committee work was focused on the procedural inadequacies of the system and there was no shortage of people who were prepared to give evidence on the inefficiency and time wasting of local authorities. Unlike the Dobry Report, the written and oral evidence was all recorded and in this way gave an unparalleled insight into official thinking and the thinking of the development industry in the late 1970s.

The Sub-Committee was advised by H.W.E. Davies who undertook an extensive survey of local authorities in England and Wales. The survey was to provide the first firm data on the handling of planning applications and the costs involved. It showed that 61 per cent of applications were determined within the 8-week period laid down in the General Development Order and 95 per cent were determined within six months. Decisions on county matters were found to take much longer, with only 20 per cent determined in 8 weeks. For the rest, Davies's report notes the diversity of administrative arrangements and the difficulty of devising a quantitative measure of performance. But in the end, the Environment Sub-Committee work appears to have been informed more by the unshakeable belief that the system was failing than it was by the results of the survey of local authorities. The presence on the Sub-Committee of Michael Latham, a former Director of the Housebuilders Federation and at the time still Managing Director of the housebuilders, Lovell Homes, goes some way to explaining the approach.

Though the Environment Sub-Committee may have been receptive to criticism there was no shortage of critical comment. The overwhelming impression of the report was of the immense anger expressed by the professionals of the building industry at the way local authorities used their powers. Criticism was of substantially two types. Part was directed at the question of delay within the process. Part was to do with the nature of the control exercised and was primarily to do with aesthetic control.

Looked at objectively, the quality of evidence on delay was unsatisfactory. Much of it was assertion rather than demonstrable fact, and the case studies, though sometimes well documented, indicated particular, rather than necessarily general, problems. The British Property Federation, for example, with a membership of 30,000, brought forward evidence which was based on replies from 50 of its members. When challenged that the evidence was anecdotal rather than concrete the Federation's Director-General agreed: the evidence was about creating an impression rather than establishing an irrefutable case. The Housebuilders Federation took much the same stance. They recorded their 'grave disappointment' at the 'virtually complete rejection' of the Dobry Report by central government, and the wide gap, as they saw it, between the Department of the Environment's 'wishes and intentions' and the practice of local authorities. C.D. Mitchell, the president of the Federation, in his opening comments said:

. . . the general opinion throughout membership is that the planning procedure is falling down. It does nothing but create an enormous amount of delay, it increases our costs to a very considerable degree, and that, in turn, must affect the ultimate price of the article that we provide for people generally in the country; and it does slow down the whole process. (House of Commons, 1977, Vol. 2, p. 154, evidence of the Federation of British Housebuilders)

Housebuilders provided a valuable social function and by implication the planning system was acting anti-socially in the delays it caused. Other members of the Housebuilders Federation's group could not understand why it took so long to obtain planning consent:

All we are really talking about is vetting [the scheme]. What we need to know in the first place are the requirements relative to particular areas. We produce the scheme. All we are asking them to do is to vet it. I just cannot understand why it should take all this time just to vet something. (House of Commons, 1977, Vol. 2, p. 173, evidence by D.A. Moody)

Moody had a particular reason for feeling aggrieved with the development control system. His company had waited 16 months for approval of the Queen's Park development at Billericay and had become caught in the crossfire of a quarrel between the district and county councils about whether the Essex Design Guide should apply in the district. That the application took longer to process than it need have done is beyond doubt. Whether the problem with Queen's Park was part of a larger problem with the way in which development control powers were being used is open to question. But for many of the witnesses who gave evidence to the Environment Sub-Committee cases of this kind were ample proof of the system's unhealthiness.

Evidence to the Sub-Committee was supported by published material from outside. Slough Estates produced a report which purported to show that for a factory of 50,000 ft^2 (5,000 m^2) achieving planning consent took 26 weeks in Britain compared with 4½ weeks in the United States and 16 weeks (the next longest period) in France (Slough Estates, 1979). The methodology for this study was questionable but it made the point for industrial development that Queen's Park did for housing. Another study looked at the performance of one local authority, the London Borough of Islington (Price, 1975). Price, a property developer, was arguing once again that the planning system was slow and cumbersome, and that the impact of delay was to hold up badly needed urban regeneration in the borough. The report gives detailed case histories of 10 prime examples of the difficulties of developing in Islington. A further 62 examples are dealt with more summarily. Delay was not the only factor. Eighteen cases were said to have involved an anomalous use of the borough's policy on office location. Overall, Price concluded that Islington was using development control in a way that was not sanctioned by the planning Acts:

. . . to frustrate people or projects of which the Council disapproves, for reasons which have nothing to do with town and country planning. (p. 4)

Price clearly believed himself to be the innocent victim of that disapproval.

The argument on aesthetic control was in part linked to the question of delay. Unnecessary quibbling over design detail might lead to lengthy processing times for planning applications. But there was also a philosophical basis for objecting to detailed design control in that it interfered with matters of personal taste and usurped the professional judgement of those whose sphere of competence it properly was. The Royal Institute of British Architects was particularly vehement in this respect. Its then President, Eric Lyons, inveighed against 'immoral' requirements of local planning authorities. He argued that lay committee members would be unable to read architects' drawings and that in any case they were being advised by staff who were not qualified to make comment. The Royal Institute of British Architects evidence as a whole was couched in terms of high-minded principles confronting ignorant prejudice.

Another strand to the argument concerned the still relatively recent Essex *Design Guide for Residential Areas* already referred to in the context of the Queen's Park case (Essex County Council, 1973). Debate had raged about the Guide, since its publication in 1973. The Royal Institute of British Architects in its evidence to the Environment Sub-Committee declared itself to be strongly opposed to design guidance. The Housebuilders Federation was more ambivalent in its attitude. Moody thought that design guides were 'fundamentally alright' (House of Commons, 1977, Vol. 2, p. 158) but that their content was too regulatory and their application was too rigid. Flexibility was what was needed. One member of the Sub-Committee, Eric Moonman, clearly detected an inconsistency, in that elsewhere the Federation had also called for a greater degree of certainty in the policy base for development control. But the housebuilders seemed oblivious to any ambiguity in the call for certainty and flexibility. As so often for developers, the desire to minimize risk by asking for clear guidance was offset by an equally strong desire to negotiate the most favourable end result.

Given the enormous weight of resentment against the way in which the development control system operated, the response from those who might have been expected to support the system was curiously flaccid. The Royal Town Planning Institute's submission accepted that delay was a serious problem that needed confronting, although it noted that delay was difficult to define and preferred the euphemistic phrase 'unnecessary time'. The submission called for a relaxation of permitted development rights to allow concentration on major planning applications. In the oral evidence, Andrew Thorburn argued that development control had become 'bogged down in bureaucratic processes' (House of Commons, 1977, Vol. 2, p. 47). It was scarcely a very positive picture of the system. Individual local authorities gave evidence about the efficiency of their procedures, which was no doubt intended to distance the virtuous few from the inefficient many. The North Southwark Community Development Group argued that, so far from being too slow, for community groups development control decisions were taken too rapidly and were surrounded by an unacceptable level of secrecy. The overall picture was not very encouraging.

The only really spirited defence of the system came in the evidence presented by the Town and Country Planning Association and to some extent by the Civic Trust and the Council for the Protection of Rural England where the essential argument being made was that delay was the 'reasonable price to pay for a better environment' (House of Commons, 1977, Vol. 2, p. 86). But even their submissions were to a large extent focused on contingent remedies rather than ultimate justifications. For the rest, supporters of the development control system were content to point to elements of delay that were not the responsibility of the local authorities or lay beyond the development control system. The failure to complete development plans was widely perceived as a problem, and by developers, too. The appeals system led to delays within central government. And poorly conceived schemes and inadequately presented applications for planning consent could also produce delay.

Compared with the histrionics of the evidence, the report that eventually emerged was something of an anti-climax. It made 14 recommendations which appeared very largely to give credence to the idea that local authorities were guilty of time wasting. The difficulty the Sub-Committee faced was that the evidence it had received against local authorities was largely circumstantial and did not lend itself to specific remedies. The first recommendation was the appointment of planning assessors:

. . . to give help and advise the local planning authorities and to monitor their performance by continual and informal contact. (House of Commons, 1977, Vol. 1, para 62)

The second recommendation was that:

. . . inefficiency should be penalised by being made an additional reason for the award of costs on appeal. (para 64)

and third, that costs should be awarded when the Secretary of State revoked a decision

. . . which blatantly contradicts national policy expressed in a circular. (para 65)

Other recommendations called for a clarification of the roles of counties and districts and for a review of the system of plans.

The planning profession greeted a proposal for assessors with predictable horror. Central government showed itself to be little more responsive to the proposal than it had been to the Dobry Report. It was prepared to undertake discussions with local authorities on assessors but not to review as a whole the system of plans. Nor would it undertake to award costs punitively. The Environment Sub-Committee was clearly unimpressed by this response and reconvened to take further evidence during 1978 publishing a further report in June (House of Commons, 1978) which reiterated the call for planning assessors and a review of the development plan system. Yet still nothing happened. The country's economic difficulties and the build-up to a general election meant that the government's priorities were elsewhere. Within planning itself the Community Land Act and the problems of inner urban areas were of more significance. The failure to amend the permitted development rights in the General Development Order perhaps further dampened the government's enthusiasm for dealing with development control. Change required a new government.

Community Interest and Public Involvement

There was a conspicuous omission in the Environment Sub-Committee report: the involvement by the public in the decision-making process was largely ignored. Dobry, it is true, had considered the mechanics of public consultation, but this did not really begin to address the problems that were beginning to emerge. Yet development control – indeed planning as a whole – was coming under considerable attack from both individual members of the public and community groups, just as it was from the professionals of the building industry. Feeding the groundswell of discontent was a feeling that insufficient weight was being given to legitimate public concern and that planning authorities were taking arbitrary decisions in an unaccountable fashion. In some places, there was a particular fear that deals were being stitched up between local authorities and developers in a way that excluded public comment.

One measure of public discontent was the rate of complaints to the Commission for Local Administration (the Local Government Ombudsman) created by the 1974 Local Government Act. During the 1970s a third of all complaints received were to do with planning and almost all of these had to do with development control (*Planning*, 1978). The Ombudsman was of course only able to entertain complaints that had to do with administrative process, not with the content of decisions, so that many complaints could not be investigated. But the fact that the complaints were made at all suggests a public fear that decisions were neither transparent nor fair.

Complaints to the Ombudsman were by their very nature concerned with individual loss and private advantage. However, the 1970s also witnessed attacks on the development control system from community groups whose concerns were collective rather than individual. Several cases during the decade brought the confrontation into a wider public arena. There was, for example, the notorious series of inquiries into proposals to develop Coin Street on the South Bank near Waterloo in the London Borough of Lambeth. Community activists, backed by the borough council, wanted low-density housing for local residents. Developers, on the other hand, saw the potential of the site for office development and produced grandiose plans, one of them by the architect Richard Rogers. By the beginning of the 1980s the planning applications for office development were rejected by the Conservative Secretary of State for the Environment, Michael Heseltine, on *aesthetic* grounds, that the schemes did not match up to the significance of the site for London as a whole.

Such a decision was not much more comfort to the community activists than a grant of planning permission would have been. In his decision, Heseltine identified the site as suitable for a mixed-use development. However, the recently approved Local Plan for the area specifically allocated the site for housing. Heseltine appeared to be overriding not only a locally expressed preference but also the formal instrument of policy that should have informed a development control decision (*Planning*, 1980; Ambrose, 1986).

In more general way, Ambrose and Colenutt (1975) showed how the property industry works to the disadvantage of local communities. They did so by virtue of their involvement in the North Southwark Community Development Group which we have already noted as having given evidence to the Environment Sub-Committee. For them, the particularly worrying aspect of the system's failure was the way in which local planning authorities were often all too eager to secure high-value development in the face of local opposition. Ambrose and Colenutt identified the development of Hays Wharf on the South Bank to the east of Coin Street as the classic case of a deal which effectively excluded the public. Here, the original landowner and a potential developer were given encouragement to proceed with office development on the basis of an informal strategy produced in 1970. Southwark Borough Council had put together this strategy without public consultation, as a means of encouraging the development of land that it feared would remain derelict. The local community's interests, potentially a 'material consideration' had been brushed aside.

How far the attack on the system by members of the public and community groups represents naked self-interest or something which transcends the purely personal and individual is a matter of debate. Nevertheless, the picture that Ambrose and Colenutt paint is of a property industry that is able to carry considerably more clout in a process in which a range of considerations must be taken into account and may manipulate the development control system to its own ends. But the accusations go further than simply suggesting that local planning authorities were being overwhelmed by the superior weight of developers and landowners. Planning authorities were sometimes colluding with developers in a way that smacked of corporatism, a point made by Reade (1982) in relation to the use of negotiated agreements.

The Ground Prepared

Concern for community involvement and community interests remained firmly in the background, however. The striking feature of the debate on development control that lasted throughout the 1970s was the extent to which it centred on the question of delay. Equally striking was the fact that at no stage did anyone try to define what delay meant. The one yardstick used loosely throughout both the Dobry and the Environment Sub-Committee studies was the statutory 8-week period. That of course had remained the same since 1933 when it had been increased from one month in the first General Interim Development Order. There was no reflection at all on whether or how the task had changed in 45 years. The Royal Town Planning Institute's definition of delay as 'unnecessary time' was in the end no more than elegant variation in that it begged the question of what might be necessary. The only proper note of caution in dealing with delay as some kind of absolute comes in H.W.E. Davies's admirably circumspect memorandum in which he draws attention to the very considerable difficulty in making meaningful comparisons between the performance of different local authorities on the basis of either time or cost (House of Commons, 1977, Vol. 3, pp. 707–732).

Why should delay have become the overwhelming preoccupation in the 1970s and indeed subsequently? Seen from without, the system does not appear to be particularly slow. The French Conseil d'Etat in a memorandum on planning in Britain that formed part of a critique of its own system, declared itself amazed that delays should be seen as a problem at all (Conseil d'Etat, 1992). Part of the answer lies, as we noted earlier, in the belief in the Planning Advisory Group Report, that problems in development control were largely a question of administration not fundamental weaknesses. There was a failure to address the question of what purpose the development control system served. And when crisis came, the planning profession was ill equipped to choose the terms on which the argument would be fought out. The major crisis was of course the speculative boom in the property market in the early 1970s and the following slump which left the development industry in a state of considerable disarray. The second crisis, which was maturing more slowly in the same period, was the growing discontent of community activists who increasingly came to view the planning system as being weighted firmly in favour of the development industry not of the public at large. With the exception of the North Southwark Community Group's evidence, this aspect of development control hardly surfaces in the Environment Sub-Committee's report. The final and probably the least significant crisis was the reform of local government and the division of planning responsibilities between counties and districts. In the short term at least this led to the kind of conflict threatened at the Queen's Park, Billericay case which served no one very well.

There is yet a more fundamental reason why the question of delay should assume such critical proportions in development control which has to do with the very nature of 'planning by consent'. In planning systems which create zoning plans as legally enforceable documents, the plan itself conveys, at least in principle, a right to develop for a certain purpose in a certain form. This was even true of the British system until 1947, but is more especially characteristic of American zoning ordinances and continental European planning systems. By introducing universal development control and nationalizing development rights, plans gave no guarantee of the acceptability of a project and no control was of course possible in the absence of any plan. The effect has been to place a considerable premium on planning consent as the only guarantee of a right to develop. By the same token, the premium on the consent places an exaggerated emphasis on the time taken for consent to be given. This, coupled with the presumption in favour of development, is probably more surely explanatory of the preoccupation with delay than are any of the more immediate causes.

As we have seen, neither the Dobry Report nor the Environment Sub-Committee's recommendations had much impact on the Labour government. But the discussion of the 1970s undoubtedly built up a head of unsatisfied criticism of the development control system. The Conservative government elected under Margaret Thatcher in October 1979 proved far more receptive to the complaints. The debates of the 1970s paved the way for reforms in the 1980s. It is to the 18 years of Conservative administration that we must now turn.

Notes

1. PRO HLG29/116. Departmental Committee on Building Byelaws. Evidence by J.A.E. Dickinson, 1 July 1914.
2. Partial demolition control in Conservation Areas had been introduced two years previously.

Chapter Six

Development Control in a Market Economy

Over the course of nearly two decades, there has been much speculation about the actual impact of Conservative philosophy. How far did the unwavering belief in the efficiency of the market affect a planning system rooted in a concept of social welfare? The most thorough analysis is Thornley's (1993) patient examination of Conservative beliefs, of the way those beliefs were translated into a national planning policy and of the impact of that policy in practice. There is no intention within the space of a short chapter to replicate the achievement of Thornley's work. However, there is scope for considering the way in which Conservative philosophy affected development control in particular. And here, as with the planning system more generally, we face a problem. As Allmendinger and Thomas (1998) argue, commentators have tended to divide into those who conclude that the planning system has survived 18 years of Conservative government more or less intact and those who argue that, on the contrary, the system has undergone a profound change.

The first argument is easy enough to rehearse. The 1947 system, the argument goes, has survived very much as it was first conceived, in spite of some legislative nibbling at the edges. But the fundamentals remain: the universal control of development; a system of plans which is indicative not binding; a reliance on 'other material considerations' to inform development control decisions; above all, the nationalization of development rights. This persistence of the system can be read as a tribute to the thinking of the 1940s and the robustness of the mechanisms created in 1947. Other commentators have taken a less sanguine view. The second argument depends on a reading, not of legislation and procedures, but of policy and process. Thornley summarizes the unease succinctly:

Certain elements of the planning system are surviving . . . However, it is not simply the outward form of planning that is important. It is absolutely crucial who has control. The trends identified in this book show a clear process of centralisation and a narrowing of legitimate criteria and values. A major change in the control and purpose of planning has taken place even though certain policy instruments remain. (Thornley, 1993, p. 219)

The point is clear: because the British development control system deliberately leaves space between parameters which are in effect filled by policy interpretation much can change without any need for new legislation. Moreover, the possibilities for interpretation offered by planning law also permit a shift in the balance of decision-making power as well as in the content of decisions. Thornley's point is that the 1980s saw an increasing shift towards central government control of planning, as part of the general centralization of power that political commentators have noted. This chapter must, then, necessarily deal with two sets of ideas. One has to do with the nature of change within the statutory system. The other is about shifts in policy content of decision making and the transfer of the power to control.

Reducing the Stranglehold: Modifying the System

The 18 years of the Conservative administration do not form a cohesive whole from the point of view of the planning system and contain three clearly defined periods. The first is the period to about 1986 which is marked by the apparently clear policy direction and some legislative change necessary to implementing parts of that policy. The second period, from 1986 to 1991, is characterized by policy confusion and conflict in development control. The third period whose start was defined by the passing of the 1991 Planning and Compensation Act appears to suggest a new certainty and a considerable shift in policy stance.

This chronology reflects a second point. The underlying Conservative belief in the efficacy of the market as the best regulator of human affairs with central government intervening as necessary to ensure that the market could operate to best effect did not change in 18 years in spite of a change of leadership. Moreover, this political philosophy was in itself coherent. What the Conservatives had not done was to think through how this philosophy would be translated into practice within the planning system or what its impact would be on a system conceived within a very different political context. This may be explained by first, the fragmented character of policy change to the development control system in the first period and secondly, the ambiguity of attitudes to planning of successive Secretaries of State. It also explains why the second period in the chronology outlined above should have been one of conflict that the government found very difficult to weather.

We need also to recognize that although the Conservative government is credited with changes both in policy and to procedures, and indeed with the confusion and incoherence of the later 1980s, much of what it did to the development control system was no more than to give substance to the thinking that had matured during the 1970s. The debate then, as we saw in the last chapter, focused heavily on delay and on the unnecessary interference of local authorities in development decisions. Many of those who put the case to the Environment Sub-Committee will have shared the Conservative philosophy of the efficiency of the market. But, again as we saw in the last chapter, these criticisms go beyond the question of New Right ideology to something more deeply rooted in the system itself. In tackling the symptoms of a problem in a particular way, we can argue that the Conservatives were relying upon pre-conceived solutions as much as upon an application of their own political philosophies.

Although there may not have been a consistent view about how market philosophy might be applied to the planning system, attitudes to the system, and to development control in particular, were fuelled by two strands in Conservative thinking. One of these was that the private sector was too heavily regulated and that the duty of government was to reduce this burden of regulation in order that free enterprise could flourish. The other was a rooted suspicion of local authorities who were accused of politically motivated meddling to control economic activity to the detriment of the country as a whole. It was, of course, a criticism that was primarily aimed at the Labour-controlled urban authorities. Both attitudes were summed up in the words of William Hague, then a 16-year old school boy, at the 1977 Conservative Party Conference, that the duty of a Conservative government would be to 'roll back the frontiers of the state'. This emotionally charged but essentially ambiguous phrase nevertheless carried a telling resonance, and Ministers after 1979 were entirely clear as to what it should mean in practice. Ways would be found to loosen the perceived stranglehold of local authorities on the development of land necessary for economic recovery. Economic regeneration would only occur if private enterprise were given its head.

The policy stance of the Conservative government was spelled out in three White Papers. Although all of them were declarations of intent, all followed at least some of the changes to the planning system explored below. Their objective was clearly announced by their titles: *Lifting the Burden* (Cabinet Office, 1985), *Building Businesses . . . Not Barriers* (Department of Employment, 1986) and *Releasing Enterprise* (Department of Trade and Industry, 1988). Free enterprise was weighed down by a series of regulations among which figured planning control. Yet the proposals for deregulating planning were in the main relatively modest, and a relatively minor part of the whole. Changes to the General Development Order and to the Use Classes Order were first advocated in these White Papers, as was the review of the development plans system and the introduction of Simplified Planning Zones. Other changes were aimed at administrative efficiency rather than at fundamental reform.

There were essentially three ways in which the Conservative government sought to deregulate development control: by legislating to modify the planning system; by attempting to remove control from local authorities altogether; and by the nature of policy advice given by central government. The first of these can be dealt with relatively quickly. Apart from the Planning and Compensation Act which will be dealt with later, legislation which directly modified existing development control powers was limited in the 1980s. The first significant change came with an amendment to the General Development Order in 1981 which in fact followed closely the detail of the Labour amendment of 1977. Its principal feature was to increase the size of extensions (in general from 10 per cent to 15 per cent of the volume of the existing house) that householders could build without the need for planning permission. The intended impact was to reduce the number of applications being dealt with by local authorities, and so speed the planning process. While it certainly reduced the number of applications its affect on processing time was harder to establish. This was at least in part because the retention of lower limits for terraced housing and in Conservation Areas, National Parks and Areas of Outstanding Natural Beauty actually made the General Development Order more difficult to apply, by creating distinctions where none had existed before.

The second legislative change to the development control system came with the revised Use Classes Order in 1987. The government had suspected that control over changes of use was hampering the activities of developers who would otherwise be able to contribute to the economic development of the country. Michael Heseltine, the first Conservative Secretary of State for the Environment, had set up the Property Advisory Group within the Department of the Environment as a means of broadening the advice that he received, and the group was called on to report. Some of the work they did was a necessary modernization of categories of use that had a clear parentage in eighteenth- and nineteenth-century prohibition on tripe boilers and tallow chandlers. The establishment of a new food and drink class, to cover restaurants, snack bars, cafes and pubs was another useful change that recognized the changing nature of eating and drinking. This much lay well within the original intentions of the order.

One major recommendation for change was incorporated into the new order, however. The group agreed that new economic activity, represented by the ideal of the small business, often went through rapid change which could be harmed by bureaucratic control. So a small-scale research and development activity might generate the need for production capacity which in turn might be carried out equally suitably in connection with either office or industrial uses. To that end, a new use class was introduced which covered everything from office use to research and development establishments and high technology industrial production. The new use class, identified ever since by its number B1, operated on exactly the same principle as any other, in that change within the class would not be a material change and so would not require local authority consent. The circular accompanying the order explained that micro-engineering and the pharmaceutical industry were particularly within the government's sights, because their need for rapid change was great and because their impact on their surroundings could be slight (Department of the Environment, 1987). But of course Class B1 was a significant extension of the general principle embodied in the order. The original intention had been to define generic similarities between uses and clear lines of demarcation from other uses. B1, on the other hand, deliberately broadened the scope of the class to make it a genuinely deregulatory measure, not an aid to definition. It was very much the type of Conservative market-led reform.

The actual impact of Class B1 is harder to assess. Local authorities feared with some justification that it would lead to the proliferation of offices in areas in which they hoped to encourage industrial activity. It would prove impossible to refuse a B1 use in an industrial area and there would be no control over a subsequent change from an industrial to an office use. The effect was to give far greater freedom to the developer to determine the appropriate mix of uses for a given site and by the same token, therefore, to switch control from the local authority to the private sector (Home, 1992). In London, the impact was to drive out traditional industries such as tailors in Savile Row and jewellers in Hatton Garden (Bell, 1992). However, Bell did find that with new developments some London boroughs were using legal agreements in order to ensure a minimum proportion of industrial use in a B1 development, even if the success was varied.

A final, apparently minor, change to the legislation introduced by the 1980 Local Government, Planning and Land Act was the provision to charge developers for planning applications. It was of a piece with the market philosophy in that it required users of the development control system to pay for the service they received. Criteria for charging were established; the principle on which a scale of charges was to be drawn up was that it should be simple to understand and to apply, reasonably related to the scale of development for which permission was being sought, and not so great that it would act as a deterrent to development. It was also intended to cover the costs incurred by local authorities. The scale that was introduced in 1981 only partially met the criteria set. Its application was not necessarily straightforward and later amendments made it increasingly complex (Harrison, 1984). It was only partly related to the scale of development, but in any case scale of development did not necessarily reflect the cost of processing applications. And the sums that it would generate did not appear to cover the total cost of running the development control system. But the most telling criticism was that offered by the Town and Country Planning Association. Charging applicants did not reflect the fact that development control was a service in the interest of the community as a whole, not just a contract between applicant and local authority (Town and Country Planning Association, 1980). We can argue that it was instrumental in creating a perception of development control as a 'customer service'.

Overall, the effect of these changes was to limit local authorities' powers to control development and in so doing contributed to a general objective of reducing their overall powers. However, legislating to change the planning system was rather less important than the attempt to remove development from local authority control altogether. Some of these attempts did also require new legislation: such was the case with Enterprise Zones and Simplified Planning Zones discussed below. Some were consequential upon changes to the system of local administration, such as the imposition of Urban Development Corporations to replace local authorities. But one significant attempt to circumvent local control relied on a mechanism that was possible under the existing legislation.

One of the features of the 1947 Act and its successors was the wide powers they gave to Ministers to act in place of local authorities. The calling in of applications is the most obvious of these, and is characteristic of the ambiguous relationship between central and local government: a more or less unlimited power to deal with any application which successive Ministers of whatever political party have used only very sparingly. The Act also gives powers to the Minister to make orders to 'provide for the granting of planning permission'. This power (now contained in Sections 58 and 59 of the 1990 Town and Country Planning Act) was used to create the General Development Order. But the Act specifically permitted the use of special orders for particular sites. Until 1979, Special Development Orders were used infrequently. When they were used, it was for development that was believed to have clear national importance. Development in National Parks and Areas of Outstanding Natural Beauty and, more controversially, the Sellafield nuclear processing plant had all been the subject of special orders. Like all ministerial orders, they had to be laid before Parliament and could be annulled by resolution (Cullingworth and Nadin, 1997).

Almost immediately after the Conservatives had been returned to power, the Housebuilders Federation met Michael Heseltine to argue the case for using Special Development Orders to speed the processing of applications for residential development. At the same time, Coopers and Lybrand recommended their use for industrial development. The impact was not immediate, but in June 1981 the Department of the Environment produced a consultation paper which proposed the much wider use of orders which would cover extensions and changes of use in existing industrial estates and outline permissions for land allocated for both industry and housing in local plans. The paper also proposed a curious exemption for low-density housing 'where market forces can be expected to bring high standards in every respect' and full planning permission 'for urban sites of special significance where the developer is prepared to proceed by way of open competition' (*Planning*, 1981a).

Heseltine was quoted as saying that the use of orders:

. . . enabled a degree of involvement much earlier that might lead to a greater degree of certainty for the developer if he works from the outset within a planning brief that has my support. It may also lead to savings in time. Further, the procedure would encourage a wider public debate about the range of choices and solutions for a particular site that is not normally available when only one scheme is the subject of a planning application. (*Planning*, 1983; Thornley, 1993)

The message was clear: Special Development Orders would remove the obstacles to development by ensuring greater speed in decision-making and a greater likelihood of a favourable decision. There were also other messages. The Secretary of State would be playing a far larger role in identifying the terms on which planning permission was granted. Public accountability would be achieved through public comment on schemes, not through the decision made by councillors answerable to a local electorate.

The first attempt to use a Special Development Order came later in 1981. The Effra and Green Giant site in the London Borough of Lambeth had already had a complicated planning history and consisted of two sites which had been the subject of earlier, rejected, proposals. 'Green Giant' referred to a project for a tower block to be clad in green glass. A new proposal had been prepared for the combined sites by the developer Arunbridge Ltd., which was under negotiation with the Lambeth planners. Heseltine called the application in, however, and Arunbridge agreed to an open competition for the site on the promise that permission would be granted by Order. An Order was duly laid before Parliament and approval granted in 1982.

The case was highly controversial. As Thornley notes, John Finney, then Junior Vice-President of the Royal Town Planning Institute, condemned the use of an Order for a site which had no implications for national policy, yet was significant for the locality, because it prevented local debate. *Planning* also rather gleefully reported that by calling in the application, at a point where only 'one or two technical matters' were unresolved with Lambeth, Heseltine had almost certainly delayed development (*Planning*, 1981b). In fact the scheme never went ahead: by 1983 Arunbridge was in liquidation.

A second attempt to use Special Development Orders was made by Heseltine's successor, Patrick Jenkin, in the equally controversial Hays Wharf development on the South Bank in Southwark. A public inquiry had been held in 1981 and Heseltine refused part of the application on the grounds of excessive office floorspace, and in effect laid down criteria for a renewed application. In the meanwhile, the London Borough of Southwark with the support of the Greater London Council was preparing a local plan for North Southwark which rejected office development in favour of housing and industry. However, the developers negotiated with the London Docklands Development Corporation which was by now the development control authority, for a scheme which had more office floorspace than in the one rejected by Heseltine. The scheme was then submitted for approval by Order which neatly avoided the need for local consultation and effectively deprived Southwark and Greater London Council of the power to object. As *Planning* wryly noted, planning permission was granted in less than 8 weeks (Thornley, 1993, *Planning*, 1983). Thereafter the enthusiasm for architectural competitions and the use of Special Development Orders waned. The fuss that followed the competition for the extension to the National Gallery was probably more significant than the Effra site in leading to a reconsideration of the virtues of competitions.[1] And Hays Wharf may have suggested that using Special Development Orders posed too big an electoral risk to be repeated.

In any case, other attempts were being made to reduce local authority power and to adapt the development control system to the needs of a market-led economy. The introduction of Enterprise Zones and later Simplified Planning Zones was of rather more significance than the use of orders and ostensibly these were more successful in their application. Enterprise Zones were introduced by the 1980 Local Government, Planning and Land Act. They were deliberately designed to enable the private sector to operate freely in the creation of jobs and to assist in the economic regeneration of the country. They were to be the embodiment of the new spirit of deregulation by offering developers freedoms, of which by far the most significant was the freedom from payment of property taxes for the first 10 years. They were also to be removed from the normal process of development control, in that the initial document creating the zone would itself give planning permission for given categories of development. It was the Special Development Order procedure – albeit one generated in consultation with the local authority – allied to tax breaks.

Thirty-two Enterprise Zones were created in all, and there has been debate since as to how far they had in fact achieved their objective. Freedom from local rates and enhanced capital allowances were the major elements in the attractiveness of these zones rather than freedom from planning control, even though firms considered the reduction in control as beneficial. Their success in creating the opportunity for new enterprise is more doubtful. Nationally, almost half of all firms were either in the zone before it was created or relocated from the local area (PA Cambridge Economic Consultants, 1995).

Simplified Planning Zones were an attempt to generalize the freedom from planning control in Enterprise Zones without the accompanying fiscal advantages. Introduced in the 1986 Housing and Planning Act, they were to be created by local authorities who would set out the permitted uses and the general conditions for new development, in an initial document. Thereafter, any development conforming to the general requirements needed no further consent. The Act also contained powers for the Secretary of State to create Simplified Planning Zones if local authorities showed themselves reluctant to do so and if there was pressure from developers. Progress with Simplified Planning Zones was even slower than with Enterprise Zones and in the 10 years following the 1986 Act, only thirteen zones were created.

The final means by which local authorities were divested of the power to control development was through the Urban Development Corporations which also came into being with the 1980 Local Government Planning and Land Act. They were significant in that in general they represented the belief that local authorities were unequal to the task that confronted them in declining urban areas and that they were reluctant to associate with the private sector in solving problems. Among the powers transferred to Urban Development Corporations was the control of development within the area for which they were responsible. Such a transfer clearly undermined the principle that development control decisions could be made by a democratically accountable body, for the lines of accountability of the Urban Development Corporations were undoubtedly attenuated. It also led to the prospect of conflict between the Urban Development Corporation and the local authority in which it lay. That conflict was most acute in the London Docklands and the example of Hays Wharf is an illustration of the scant regard that the London Docklands Development Corporation had for local authorities. Elsewhere, and particularly later in the decade, a rather more concerted effort was made to consult and the conflicts were less severe. Also, local authorities could act as agent for their local Urban Development Corporation in the control function. Such was the case in Sheffield. An agency arrangement of this kind gave the potential for an informal oversight of Urban Development Corporation decisions and thus for the informal resolution of problems.

Reducing the Stranglehold: Policy Shifts in the 1980s

The long-term impact of Enterprise Zones, Simplified Planning Zones and Urban Development Corporations in the development control system as a whole is not easy to discern. At the time they were introduced they were regarded with some fear as part of a concerted campaign to dismantle the planning system and to reduce, if not entirely remove, local authority control. Later it was recognized that the effect of these various instruments was strictly limited: in principle they did not call into question the general application of the planning Acts. Such a conclusion gives credence to the theory that the planning system has been robust enough to withstand the onslaught of economic liberalism – or at least that the system had a requisite degree of inertia to withstand change. What such a conclusion conceals is that these legislative changes, relatively innocuous in themselves, were part of a broader policy shift whose impact was indeed profound. This is essentially the conclusion of Brindley, Rydin and Stoker (1996) in their study of policy shifts in the 1980s. Focusing on legislative change alone is insufficient.

For the development control system, then, the most significant means of modifying control powers was through the advice and policy directives issued in government circulars. The first period of Conservative government, to 1987, saw the publication of a series of circulars whose impact was considerable because it was generalized. To understand why the circulars of the 1980s should have had such an impact, we need to reflect on the nature of government circulars in general. Circulars have several functions within British administration. They may simply be used to elicit information. Or they may announce changes in legislation. But their third role is the most significant. They have frequently been used to spell out how the government thinks that statutory powers should be used or to offer technical advice. In principle, this last use of circulars appears innocent enough:

they offer policy advice and so reflect the opinion of government, but they are not in theory equivalent to legislation, even the secondary legislation of the orders which the Acts empower Ministers to make. Yet judges do refer to circulars, as we saw in the Coleshill case where the judge relied on earlier advice in a circular to confirm that demolition was not included in the definition of development. As McAuslan (1975) puts it,

Even though circulars on planning have not been classified as delegated legislation it appears that some could be classified as custom and thus eventually 'ripen' into law . . . (p. 92)

So the boundary between law and policy is essentially blurred in this kind of government circular. There is a second reason why circulars carry particular weight in development control. The courts have ruled that circulars may indeed be a 'material consideration' to which local authorities must therefore 'have regard' in determining planning applications. But it is not only local authorities: planning inspectors will also have regard to circulars in considering appeals. This leads to the potential for local authority decisions based, rightly or wrongly, on local considerations being overturned at appeal by reference to national policies in circulars.

The use of circulars in the 1980s and their impact on development control was not the result of a major change in government practice after 1979. Circulars have been used throughout the post-war period, and indeed even before. We have already seen how Circular 1305 played a major role in defining how the 1932 Town and Country Planning Act should be used. Moreover, as Grant (1982) notes, the Act which created a Minister of Town and Country Planning in 1943 specifically required the Minister to 'secure consistency and continuity in land-use policy' and circulars were the obvious vehicle by which to achieve consistency and continuity in development control. The publication of a series of Development Control Policy Notes from 1969 onwards was a logical further step towards formalizing central government policy (Ministry of Housing and Local Government/Department of the Environment, 1969–1977). The circulars of the 1980s were in a direct line of succession to an established practice.

What was new about the circulars of the 1980s was their tone and their content. In one sense, the question of tone is of little significance in the long term, except in so far as it reveals the attitude of the government in power. Nevertheless, the way in which the circulars were written was dismissive of the activities of planners and led to an undermining of morale. If the planning system had a function, it was to be subservient to the needs of wealth-creating enterprise: it was not there to call the shots. Development control was about enabling development, not restricting it. Planning committees and the professional planners who served them were obstructionist in their reliance on values at odds with neo-liberalism. Town planning was not of course alone in being demonized in this way. The 1980s saw a concerted attack on the hegemony of the professions, notably teaching, but also medicine, architecture and even the law. The reference to arcane expertise and to an unwritten value system was perceived as essentially destructive.

The policy intent of the government circulars of the 1980s was more significant, however. The first of the series, Circular 22/80 (Department of the Environment, 1980) showed how far the Conservative government was prepared to pick up the criticism that the development industry had levelled at the development control system in the evidence to the Environment Sub-Committee of the House of Commons. Four major themes run through the circular: the need for speed and efficiency; the promotion of small businesses; the availability of land for housing (subject to another circular earlier in 1980); and aesthetic control. In all of these, the circular makes clear the government's intention to tackle the problem of delay and to underline the presumption in favour of development:

The planning system balances the protection of the natural and built environment with the pressures of economic and social change. The need for the planning system is unquestioned and its workings have brought great and lasting benefits . . . But the system has a price, and when it works slowly or badly, the price can be very high and out of all proportion to the benefits . . . This circular is concerned with planning applications. It has two aims – the first to secure a general speeding up of the system. The second is to ensure that development is only prevented or restricted when this serves a clear planning purpose and the economic effects have been taken into account. (Department of the Environment 1980, paras 1, 2)

The overriding preoccupation with delay had at last found a place in the centre of government thinking. What this extract also reveals is how that preoccupation had impoverished the debate on development control. Benefits are construed only in terms of protection, and the price of protection may be out of proportion to the benefits. An implied value system is not properly articulated. In the section on aesthetic control the circular quotes extracts from a speech by Michael Heseltine which he gave to the Town and Country Planning Summer School in 1979:

Far too many of those involved in the system – whether the planning officer or the amateur on the planning committee – have tried to impose their standards quite unnecessarily on what individuals do . . . Democracy as a system of government I will defend against all comers, but as an arbiter of taste or as a judge of aesthetic or artistic standards it falls far short of a far less controlled system of individual, corporate or institutional patronage or initiative . . . (para. 18)

In one sense, this is no more than the concern of the Local Government Board over the Ruislip-Northwood aesthetic control clause surfacing 70 years later. But much had changed in those 70 years. The trouble with Heseltine's speech was that it failed to understand the real nature of planning by consent, both in terms of the process and in terms of its outcomes. What this vision offers is really the replacement of one set of imposed standards with another, those of 'individual, corporate or institutional patronage' – or of course of those of the Secretary of State in Special Development Orders. The question of community involvement is entirely absent in this analysis.

Circular 22/80 represents the general influence of this debate about delay and design control that had dominated the 1970s. In a much more direct way Conservative policy was also being guided by the forces that had led to the debate before 1979. Heseltine appointed as a special adviser Tom Baron, Chairman of Christian Salvesen Properties and Secretary of the Volume Housebuilders Group. Baron had not himself given evidence to the Environment Sub-Committee but he undoubtedly shared the views of those housebuilders who had. In 1980 in a speech to the Town and Country Planning Summer School, he argued that housebuilders were 'planning's biggest and most regular customer' and that housebuilders required of the planning system that it delivered an adequate supply of land and 'an efficient and speedy service' in dealing with planning applications. He offered a ringing endorsement of the unequivocal advice, as he saw it, in Circular 22/80 (Baron, 1980). Since he presumably had had a major influence on the circular's contents, his endorsement of it is hardly unexpected.

The circulars of the mid-1980s saw a further development of the government's attitude. The first of these took up once again the theme of housing land availability. Rather more stringent requirements were developed for identifying available land, by now in consultation with housebuilders. This is no more than an extension of policy which pre-dates 1979. The significant aspect of Circular 15/84 is the weight that it gives to these studies of land availability in relation to the development plan in determining planning applications. The circular stressed that local authorities needed to consider the development plan *and* other material considerations. The italicized *and* is in the original and land availability studies were a material consideration. A first draft of the circular went further: the fact that a local plan was in the process of alteration would not in itself be grounds for refusing a planning application for new housing. Local authorities must use the discretion given to them by the law to permit necessary housing development to proceed (Department of the Environment, 1984a).

The circular on industrial development which followed in the same year made the point rather more forcefully. It suggested once again that local authorities needed to consider both the development plan and other material considerations (the conjunction was printed in bold this time). The circular then went on:

> In the modern economy, it is not always possible to anticipate in the development plan all the needs and opportunities which may arise. Thus where a developer applies for a permission for a development which is contrary to the policies and proposals of an approved development plan this does not, in itself, justify a refusal of permission . . . While the decision will obviously be more difficult than in cases which conform to development plan policies, the onus nevertheless remains on the planning authority to examine the issues raised by each specific application and where necessary to demonstrate that a particular proposal is unacceptable on specific planning grounds. (Department of the Environment, 1984b, para 9)

The circular on development and employment of a year later was even more trenchant. A whole passage on the presumption in favour of development was printed in italics and the paragraph on the importance of other material considerations went further than ever in suggesting that plans could not anticipate every need and might be based on outdated assumptions (Department of the Environment, 1985). The overall impact of these three circulars was to call into question the role and relevance of development plans, in particular for development control. The policy to promote economic development by allowing the free market to operate with the minimum constraint may have been internally consistent, but the attitude towards planning that it generated was incoherent.

The attitude to planning may have been incoherent, but it made an impact on the system all the same. Thornley, for example, found in a study of thirty-three appeal decisions that there was:

> . . . a narrowing range of criteria used to refuse permission . . . in well over half of the reported cases . . . Circular 22/80 was successfully used to win an appeal. (Thornley, 1993, p. 150)

And Davies, Edwards and Rowley (1986) pointed to the increasing number of appeals being allowed by reference to circulars rather than to locally approved development plans. For them, this represented a significant weakening of the British planning system. Local policy, prepared in the knowledge of local circumstances by a democratically elected council, was being replaced by generalized policy not subject to the same democratic scrutiny.

Tillingham Hall and Foxley Wood: the Test of Conservative Policy

The results of that incoherence were exemplified in two cases which were to be instrumental in changing the government's attitude to the planning system. They also demonstrate how the insistence of the circulars on local authorities' discretion, far from creating greater certainty by increasing the likelihood of permission being granted, could in fact lead to confusion and delay. Both cases represented an attempt by housebuilders to test the limits of the policy insistence on making land available for housing. In 1983, nine members of the Volume Housebuilders Group, recognizing they had a common interest in promoting housing development, came together to form Consortium Developments Ltd with the specific objective of promoting what they called 'new country towns'. These, the consortium intended, would ease the pressure upon new housing in the South-East and would be 'balanced, comprehensive communities built to a high design standard and sympathetic to the environment'. The new country towns would have about 5,000 houses catering for 12–15,000 people on sites of up to 1,000 acres (420 hectares). Employment would be provided as would services (Consortium Developments, 1984). Conran Roche were retained as advisers, and by 1986 ten potential sites had been identified (Potter, 1986).

The starting point was the belief that a Conservative government would look favourably on proposals which would otherwise meet local authority reluctance to give permission for development in open country. The calculation went further than that, however. Consortium Developments by proposing 'new country towns', were both tapping into an honourable tradition of new settlements and evoking an idealized rural past. The Town and Country Planning Association, with its roots in the Garden City movement, was enthusiastic about the concept. The intention was that the quality coupled to the idea of self-contained new settlements would be a sufficiently strong material consideration to outweigh other policy objections, and at the same time guarantee a measure of public support.

The first site for which Consortium Developments prepared a proposal was at Tillingham Hall in Essex. From a developer's point of view the site was ideal. It was flat and undeveloped. The agricultural quality of the land was not high and the scenic value was limited. On the other hand it lay alongside the London-Southend Railway and the existing station at Horndon. It was also within easy reach of two major roads, the A127 and the M25. Its one important constraint was that

Figure 6.1. Tillingham Hall, Essex. Consortium Developments' first 'country town' proposal which was rejected because of its incompatibility with green belt policy. A central feature of the scheme was a lake which was intended to assist with the drainage of the site.

it lay in the Metropolitan Green Belt halfway between Upminster and Basildon. Work was already underway on the proposal in 1984 and by March 1985 was in a form to be submitted for planning permission. The proposal was very close to the specifications set out in Consortium Developments' manifesto. There were to be 5,100 houses, commercial and industrial floorspace and schools. High quality landscaping of a water feature used to assist drainage of the site was an integral part of the proposal.

Given its location in the green belt, the response of the local authority, Thurrock District Council, to the proposal was predictably negative and their attitude was consistent throughout the period. They refused the application in September 1985 on nine grounds, the first two of which were based on the violation of green belt policy. Thurrock had another reason to oppose Tillingham Hall, however. They were actively seeking to secure the development of disused chalk workings, Thurrock Chalklands, and an application for developing 4,000 houses there was lodged in August 1985. Unlike Tillingham Hall, it had obvious planning advantages. The site was derelict, not working farmland, and had been identified in the Essex County Structure Plan. It was also close to Grays town centre. Whether Thurrock feared that the viability of the Chalklands development would be threatened if Tillingham Hall went ahead is not clear, but they could demonstrate that, with other sites in the district, at least as much housing could be created in the district as would be provided by Tillingham Hall.

The inevitable public inquiry was held in 1986. The inspector concluded that Consortium Developments had not in fact justified their case that there was a crisis in the supply of housing land and that even if they had, that in itself would not have justified the choice of a site in the green belt. Nor was any settlement necessary to support the regional policy for growth in south Essex. The Secretary of State, who was by this time Nicholas Ridley, referred back in his decision letter to Circular 15/84 and the need to ensure that 'the planning system catered effectively for the demand for private sector housing and that there is an adequate supply of land available for house building'. But he nevertheless supported the inspector's conclusions that no case had been made for taking green belt land.[2]

So green belt policy proved stronger than the exercise of discretionary power in favour of development. More significant was the reaction of a wider public to the proposal. Tillingham Hall served to bring together a coalition of local residents, Members of Parliament from both the Conservative and Labour parties and local authorities of different political complexions. The opposition, it is true, was in part orchestrated. Thurrock canvassed support from neighbouring local authorities, most of which not only offered moral support but also either made written or oral representations at the inquiry. The local Members of Parliament, Oonagh McDonald (Labour, Thurrock), Harvey Proctor (Conservative, Billericay) and Robert McCrindle (Conservative, Brentwood) tabled a motion in the House of Commons to get Patrick Jenkin, Ridley's predecessor as Secretary of State, to give assurances that the green belt was inviolate, something he signally failed to do. The ground swell of public outrage was clearly embarrassing and was only stemmed by the final refusal in February 1987.

By that time, however, battle was about to be joined elsewhere. Consortium Developments had identified sites in north-east Hampshire as having potential for new settlements in an area that was subject to considerable pressure for growth. Consortium Developments had evidently held preliminary discussions with officers of the Hampshire County Council, and it seems likely that officers were supportive of a proposal for development at Bramshill Plantation. Although located close to Reading, Wokingham and Aldershot, Bramshill Plantation was curiously remote from other centres and the major transport networks. On the other hand, it had the advantage of having been used in part as a gravel pit which by the time of the application was almost worked out and, by virtue of being a largely conifer plantation, set apart from surrounding farmland. Unlike Tillingham Hall it was not in the green belt, but had not been designated for development in the Local Plan. Part of the site had considerable ecological interest and had been declared a Site of Special Scientific Interest.

Bramshill Plantation seems to have been identified for possible development even before Consortium Developments expressed an interest in it. In 1981, Hampshire county planners had prepared a report identifying sites for development of which Bramshill Plantation was one but the report had never been approved by the appropriate committee. The *Planner* (1989b) also reported that the planning authority, Hart District Council, had itself identified Bramshill Plantation for a new settlement in preference to expanding existing settlements in the same year. In the next 5 years attitudes evidently hardened. Consortium Developments' proposal was in preparation during 1986, and by the time that two applications were lodged in 1987 Hart felt able to refuse both applications (to prevent an appeal against non-determination) in spite of its earlier support for development on the site. The applications were refused in August 1987 and a public inquiry took place in June and July the following year.

Consortium Developments' proposal for the settlement they were to dub Foxley Wood was little different from that for Tillingham Hall. There were to be 4,800 houses, 5.6 hectares of land for employment uses, and schools and community buildings. There was to be the usual emphasis on high quality landscaping. If Consortium Developments thought they would have an easier task in getting planning permission for a new settlement on Bramshill Plantation than they had had at Tillingham Hall, they were wrong. Hampshire County Council officers may have encouraged them initially but the opposition from elected members and from the public at large was if anything more vociferous than at Tillingham Hall. Foxley Wood was to become one of the *causes célèbres* of the late 1980s.

Figure 6.1. Bramshill Plantation, Hampshire. 'Foxley Wood' central area.

Part of the opposition came, as at Tillingham Hall, from a united front of local authorities and from local politicians, in this instance all Conservative. The adjoining Basingstoke and Deane, Wokingham and Surrey Heath districts lent their support and both Julian Critchley, MP for Wokingham, and a local councillor gave evidence against the scheme in person at the public inquiry. But the most important part of the local opposition came from the highly organized action group, SPISE, set up to fight the case. SPISE – Sane Planning in the South East – from its formation in 1986 tried to avoid any accusation of nimbyism. It argued against Foxley Wood not only in terms of the unsuitability of the site and the immediate loss of amenity that the new settlement would bring but also in the light of regional forecasts for population growth. In this, they were acting in the awareness that Foxley Wood was not likely to be a one-off fight. The area between the M4 and M3 motorways was one of intense development pressure, with schemes built and proposals for other major housing development in the offing. SPISE was also helped by having public relations expertise within its ranks which allowed it to present its case forcefully. It proved a remarkably effective campaign.

Foxley Wood was a good deal more complicated than the Tillingham Hall case. Unlike Tillingham Hall, there was not the presumption against development in the green belt that ensured that Consortium Developments would always have the more difficult task in Essex. Indeed, rather the reverse: in the light of policy in Circular 15/84 the presumption was from the outset in favour of the development of Bramshill Plantation. The fact that it was unallocated in the Local Plan was not a bar to its future use for housing. Hart District Council's hurried modification of its Local Plan to extend an 'area of natural conservation' to cover the whole of the north of the District including the Bramshill Plantation was dismissed by the inspector in his decision later as 'a surrogate green belt policy', a polite way of saying it was a last ditch ruse. Much of the argument then centred on the regional forecast of housing need prepared by SERPLAN (the Standing Conference on South-East Regional Planning), Hampshire's Structure Plan allocations and the part that Hart District should be required to accept. At all levels the inspector was to find evidence of a housing shortfall, and noted that the Structure Plan alterations, the second of which was in draft, were designed 'to rein back the growth momentum' established in the previous 20 years. Consortium Developments argued that they were catering for growth in what would now be called a sustainable way. Foxley Wood would be self-sufficient. However, the fact that they were willing to make improvements to the railway station at Winchfield suggests that they, like the objectors, foresaw that residents of Foxley Wood would be largely commuters.

The inspector's report was dated 9 January 1989 and his conclusion was not as inevitable as in the Tillingham Hall case. The case that he made against the development of Foxley Wood hinged on two issues. One was the loss of 'a significant ecological interest and the urbanization of an attractive rural area of value for its

Figure 6.3. Bramshill Plantation, Hampshire. Nicholas Ridley, as Secretary of Sate for the Enviornment, earned the wrath of local activists when he declared he was 'minded to approve' the development of Foxley Wood. On 22 July 1989, his effigy was burnt in a field adjoining the site as a protest against this decision. (*Source: Reading Evening Post*)

recreational opportunities'. The other was the fact that in the words of Planning Policy Guidance Note 3, para.5 [Foxley Wood] 'would not be well integrated with the existing pattern of settlement'. The specifics of the site were paramount. If the inspector recommended refusal of the proposal, six months later Nicholas Ridley, by now Secretary of State for the Environment, announced that he was 'minded to allow' the development to proceed. As the *Planner* reported at the time, Ridley did not dispute the inspector's findings of fact, but did argue that those facts had to be weighed against the provision in the Structure Plan alterations for a large housing increase in north-east Hampshire. At the same time, his planning Minister, Michael Howard, made a strong statement in support of new settlements (*Planner*, 1989a). Conservative policy looked as though it remained intact.

Two weeks later, an effigy of Nicholas Ridley was burned in a field next to Bramshill Plantation. The event was witness both to the strength of local feeling and to SPISE's ability to organize an event that would attract media attention. Ridley was moved to the Department of Trade and Industry shortly afterwards, and following unguarded comments about Germany in the *Spectator*, left the government altogether in the autumn of 1989. Ridley was succeeded as Secretary of State for the Environment by Chris Patten who reversed his predecessor's decision, as he was widely expected to do. The fact that his 'minded to refuse' letter was issued six days before the Conservative Party Conference was no doubt directly calculated to head off any revolt among the ranks. A final decision letter was issued in December, but not before Consortium Developments had undertaken to protect the whole of the Site of Special Scientific Interest.

Neither the Tillingham Hall site nor Bramshill Plantation have been under threat since the development proposals of the 1980s were rejected. In Thurrock, Chafford Hundred went ahead on the Chalklands and became the site not only of housing but also of the extensive Lakeside Shopping Centre. In its district-wide Local Plan approved in 1997, the green belt boundary remains unchanged and Tillingham Hall is identified as an area of landscape improvement. So, too, in Hart's District Plan, Bramshill Plantation is now part of a countryside protection area, and housing needs are being met on infill sites and by an extension to the town of Fleet. SPISE did not regard its work as complete with Patten's decision, however. It continues to fight for 'sane planning' and celebrated the tenth anniversary of the burning of Ridley's effigy albeit in a rather less flamboyant fashion than in 1989.

Two aspects of the inquiries into the development proposed for Tillingham Hall and Foxley Wood require further comment. At the Foxley Wood inquiry, considerable outrage was caused by the unannounced intervention of the Department of Trade and Industry. In a written statement, the Department argued that the release of Bramshill Plantation for housing was essential for the continued prosperity of the South-East. In particular, the statement noted the high concentration of high technology and industry and the lack of skilled staff. The outrage that this caused was both because it was unannounced and because, as a written statement, it gave no opportunity for opponents of the proposal to cross-examine the Department. In the end, it appears to have carried little weight with the inspector whose decision did not rest on the shortfall of housing land but on the nature and location of Bramshill Plantation. At the time, it looked like a flagrant attempt by the government to influence the final decision of a supposedly independent procedure. Certainly it was an intervention that was consistent with other attempts by government to assume control of decision-making in order to advance a political philosophy. It was a classic example of the directive, authoritarian state at work.

The other aspect of the process was present in both inquiries. Opponents of the schemes argued that the appeals were in effect trying to establish a new settlement policy for their areas, something that was an inappropriate use of development control appeals. Policy on new settlements was properly the preserve of the structure and local plan process which was more democratically accountable than an inquiry. Neither inspector was prepared to accept the argument; both believed that an appeal inquiry was no less democratic than the preparation of plans. As the inspector in the Foxley Wood case put it:

In my view the general issue is not whether a new settlement would conform with the distribution of housing in the approved Development Plan . . . but whether such development would be harmful to the reason behind that distribution: this principle applies, in my view, to any alleged 'non conforming' use . . . I do not accept that permission [for a 'non conforming' use] would necessarily undermine local democracy or imply a review of established policy. (para 589)[3]

In one sense, this argument does little more than point to the fact that there is always the possibility of tension between strategic policy and local implementation whenever a development decision has a more than immediate impact. The decision may, as in these cases, call into question a hitherto agreed strategy. Or local constraints may be found to militate against a strategic presumption in favour of development, which at Foxley Wood might have been the central government's interpretation of what eventually happened. This tension is inherent in British development control because of its discretionary nature. The appeal system has by and large dealt effectively with the need to reconcile strategy with particularities of site and if the process is not necessarily democratic it has commanded respect because it is transparent. Indeed, with the focus particularly upon site characteristics, the appeal and inquiry process could be expected to be essentially conservative. But the concern for the appropriateness of the development control process to determine the location of new settlements also revealed the wider concern about the role of development plans. The significance of the Tillingham Hall and Foxley Wood cases was the way in which they highlighted the government's confusions about the nature of policy in the development control process. By insisting on local authority discretion and downplaying the value of Structure and Local Plans in identifying sites for development, the government had neither created certainty nor reduced delay.

Rethinking Policy: Towards the Plan-Led System

The disarray within Conservative ranks that these cases created led to considerable heart-searching and to a re-evaluation of policy in the later 1980s. This re-evaluation took two forms. One was the amplification of technical advice offered by central government. The circulars of the mid-1980s were characterized by the very general nature of the advice they offered coupled with what looked like thinly veiled threats. Realizing that the circulars had not really achieved their objective, from 1988 onwards the Department of the Environment collated technical advice in the form of Planning Policy Guidance Notes. These PPGs, as they came to be known, had an equivalent force to the circulars they superseded in that they were a material consideration and existed at the same boundary of policy and law as did circulars. But the PPGs, though sometimes criticized on specific points, have achieved a general acceptance among the planning and development professions because they offer a level of detail absent in the circulars that preceded them. Over the course of the next 10 years, these guidance notes came to represent a formidable body of policy which has helped to clarify what central government thinks that local authorities should be doing. By the beginning of the 1990s, the policy framework offered by central government was radically different from that of 10 years before, but the introduction of PPGs had done nothing to shift the centralizing tendencies of the beginning of the decade.

The other form of re-evaluation was in the thinking about development plans. Here, the ambivalence of government attitudes was rather greater. In spite of the way in which the circulars of the mid-1980s emphasized other material considerations, the Conservatives at no stage advocated the abolition of all development plans. There was a continuing recognition of the role of plans in environmental protection, an acknowledgement both of public support for countryside protection and of landed interests in the Conservative Party. There was equally a belief in the Local Plan as a facilitator of private sector development. Structure Plans, on the other hand, had never had much support from the government. The first attempt to review the system of development plans came with the publication of a consultation paper in 1986 (Department of the Environment, 1986). This proposed the replacement of Structure Plans by regional guidance from central government and county policy statements. At the same time, it also proposed the requirement for a complete coverage of the country by Local Plans. These Local Plans were to be stripped of extraneous content and the time for public consultation was to be reduced in the interests of speed and efficiency of production. This, then, at last, was a response to the repeated assertion in the evidence to the Environment Sub-Committee in 1977 that the absence of up-to-date plans was a significant factor in delaying development control. But as Thornley (1993) notes, reference to community involvement was once again conspicuously absent.

The proposals of the 1986 consultation paper followed the logic of the view of government as an enabler of free market activity but sat oddly with the advice that stressed the limitations of plans when it came to determining planning applications. In that sense, the 1986 paper and the White Paper of 1989 (Department of the Environment, 1989), which incorporated the 1986 proposals largely unchanged, might be said to represent a modest change of heart from the circulars of 1984 and 1985. They nevertheless still entailed a considerable dismantling of the system of plans that had been put in place in 1968. However, by 1990 there were signs that the government was having second thoughts on reform. On the face of it surprisingly, the Housebuilders Federation came out in support of Structure Plans (Humber, 1990), and within the government Chris Patten was said to have 'made no secret of his reservations about being the midwife to proposals which dramatically diluted strategic planning' (*Planning*, 1990). When new legislation was presented to Parliament, the abandonment of Structure Plans was no longer an option.

The major change of heart came with the passing of the Planning and Compensation Act in 1991, legislation designed to modify the consolidated provisions of the 1990 Town and Country Planning Act. It was a change of heart which came almost by accident, however. At the report stage, the Opposition tabled an amendment which required the development plan to be a 'first consideration' in determining applications for planning permission. Rather than rejecting it out of hand, the government promised to incorporate the spirit, if not the wording, of the amendment in the final bill (*Planning*, 1991). In fact the clause as it was finally drafted went a good deal further by suggesting, as the *Encyclopaedia of Planning Law* (1991) puts it, a 'substantive requirement' that development should be in accordance with the development plan. In this way what was to become Section 54a of the 1990 Town and Country Planning Act was born:

Where in making any determination in the planning acts, regard has to be had to the development plan, the determination should be made in accordance with the plan unless material considerations indicate otherwise. (Planning and Compensation Act 1991, S.26)

This coupled with the requirement to prepare local plans, which was also part of the 1991 Planning and Compensation Act, seemed to give development plans a new and important role in the development control process.

Certainly the new clause was welcomed by the defenders of the planning system as an important shift in favour of planning. For the first time in a dozen years, the planning profession appeared to have been given a renewed remit. But a belief in planning may not have been the only reason that the clause was attractive to the Conservatives. One of the problems of insisting on local authorities' freedom to approve planning applications was that it required them to use the administrative discretion that was also a hallmark, in the Conservative view, of the unacceptable face of local government. Insisting on plan preparation and on the primacy of the plan in development control was a way of ensuring that local authorities were less likely to act on whim or take 'politically motivated' decisions.

What the amendment actually achieved is quite another matter. In many ways, Section 54a is the classic example of something which appears to offer a very great deal and in practice makes very little difference. For its wording did not mean that other material considerations would no longer have an important role in development control decisions. The apparent primacy of the development plan could always be overturned by reference to particular circumstances. But it did represent a shift in policy. Where before the policy presumption was in favour of development, Ministers now began talking of a policy presumption in favour of development in accordance with the development plan, and that wording has now been formalized in the revised PPG1 (Department of the Environment, 1997). The courts appear to have upheld this policy interpretation, although judges have varied in the emphasis they have laid on the development plan (Purdue, 1994). The impact on day-to-day decision-making has been slight, however. Determining planning applications does not appear to have become easier or indeed swifter since 1991, and planning appeals can still be long drawn out (Cronin, 1993). If achieving greater certainty was the intention behind the legislation, the reality was otherwise. The far more telling impact has been on plan preparation where since 1991 the weight of objections has increased immeasurably as landowners and developers have realized that making sure the plan is right for them may have a rather greater significance now than before.

The Use and Abuse of Discretionary Power

While at first sight the Planning and Compensation Act looked as though it had given the development control system a new lease of life, in fact none of the old tensions had been resolved. For one thing, simply asserting the primacy of the development plan said little or nothing about the relationship between the plan and the development control decision. Debates on two issues during the 1980s and 1990s also reveal the depth of the confusions that remained. The first of these concerns the role of elected representatives in planning control decisions. The second, which is linked to it, has to do with planning agreements.

The question of the role of elected representatives is of course as old as local government and worries about whether councillors would behave responsibly in carrying out the duties imposed upon them have surfaced regularly. At the beginning of the century, we have already noted a certain distrust in the Local Government Board of the way that local authorities might use planning powers. Since 1947 there have been two related issues about the abuse of power. First, has been the worry about corruption. Given that decisions affecting land use and development may entail very considerable profits, the fact that corruption occurs is hardly surprising, and probably unavoidable. Really major scandals have been rare. But in the 1990s three local authorities have been investigated for corrupt practices which have involved both members and officers. Not all of these have necessarily involved the taking of bribes. In North Cornwall, the problem was that members were taking decisions which breached planning policy in order to favour friends and relatives. In a way this was behaviour almost more insidious than taking bribes because councillors did not stand to benefit directly. It presented a world of local government in which a circle of committed interests was being favoured above those of the electorate at large (Lees, 1993).

A second perceived abuse of local authority power has been the use of statutory decision-making to advance 'political' ends. The image of 'loony left' local authorities motivated entirely by extreme political ideology was regularly paraded in the tabloid press in the 1980s and served to spread a general mistrust of local government. The accusation that local authorities' development control decisions were often politically motivated had surfaced in the Environment Sub-Committee's investigations, when representatives for the development industry emphasized that their legitimate requests for permission were refused on spurious grounds. The idea was taking root that local councillors could be suborned from the proper exercise of their duties not only by money and influence, but also by inappropriate politics.

Two attempts have been made over the past 20 years to address this problem. The first was the Widdicombe Report of 1986 (Widdicombe, 1986) which was not confined to the planning powers of local authorities but looked at the role of councillors and officers in general. Widdicombe's conclusion was that the system did not require fundamental change. What was needed in his view was a series of modifications to the existing system that could ensure that there was greater transparency in the decision-making and that decision-makers could be made more readily accountable for the decisions they took. So Widdicombe proposed a series of procedural changes which would ensure that greater accountability and transparency could be achieved.

The Nolan Report on standards in public life (Committee on Standards in Public Life, 1997) was the direct result of public disquiet about allegations of 'sleaze' in central government rather than in local authorities. However, given the level of interest in cases such as North Cornwall, Nolan also addressed the question of ethical behaviour in local government and in particular within local authority planning. Nolan's analysis was in many ways helpful. He identified four areas in which public concern about the propriety of decision-making centred. These included the roles of members and officers in the process, the question of best practice and procedure, planning gain and the independent scrutiny of decisions.

Nolan rejected outright the idea of limiting councillors' involvement in development control. Control decisions were not quasi-judicial and planning was not an exact science. Moreover in his view excluding councillors from decision-making would be 'unlikely to succeed' and implied a mistrust of elected representatives which was inappropriate.

It should be fairly stated that there is nothing intrinsically wrong if planning committees do not invariably follow the advice of officers. (p. 73)

This was an important endorsement of the negotiated nature of planning by consent and an important corrective to one strand of thinking behind the Planning and Compensation Act: the desire to limit local authorities' discretion by binding their development control decisions more closely to an approved plan.

Nolan's solutions to the perceived potential for improper behaviour were more limited. He considered, but rejected, the idea of third party appeals as a means of scrutinizing local authority decisions, because of the risk that this would bring the system to a standstill. However, he did advocate the greater use of the Secretary of State's call-in powers, and recommended that local authorities should always notify central government of applications in which they had an interest. On the question of agreement to secure planning gain, Nolan argued for a tightening of the legislation and the adoption of rules to allow greater openness in the discussion of agreements. These solutions were probably rather less significant than the way in which the report affirmed the characteristics of development control in the British planning system.

Over the past 25 years, the question of planning agreements, or obligations as they have become since 1991, to secure planning gain has been a minefield of genuine apprehension and confused thinking. Much has been written about the recent practice of agreements, but it is as well to remember their origin. We have already seen how the 1909 Act allowed local authorities to enter into agreements with developers, and that these agreements were sometimes used to overcome the hiatus between a declaration to prepare a plan and its final approval. These agreements expressed a mutual interest and were conducted as between equal players. They were a direct successor to the private agreements of the previous 200 years.

The 1947 Act did not abandon the possibility of making agreements, and indeed the power was drawn more widely than it had been in previous legislation. Pre-war legislation emphasized the use of agreements to restrict land use; by 1947 local authorities were empowered to enter agreements for any purpose connected with the use or development of land. There was a crucial limitation, however: agreements needed the consent of the Minister. As a result, little use appears to have been made of agreements between 1947 and 1968. It was the 1967 *Management Study on Development Control* (Ministry of Housing and Local Government, 1967) that recommended that planning agreements should no longer require ministerial approval. The argument was that agreements were an invaluable tool in facilitating development, an argument given greater force by the succession of judgements which restricted the way in which conditions might be used.

The law was changed in 1968, and thereafter agreements were used more widely, although a study in the early 1990s suggested that agreements were less common than popular opinion supposed (Grimley J.R. Eve, 1992). Already by the end of the 1970s, the use of agreements was giving cause for considerable concern. In general terms, their use was criticized on three counts: that they were applied to inappropriate ends; that the process by which agreements were reached was at best opaque and at worst corrupt; and that local authorities were in a position to exert undue leverage on developers. None of these criticisms was entirely without foundation. Desmond Heap argued against what he described as a taxation on development unsanctioned by Parliament (Heap, 1980). This in turn reflected a belief that local authorities were extracting 'inappropriate' benefits from developers in exchange for giving planning permissions. Planning gain was inappropriate, so the argument ran, if the benefits were unrelated to the development for which permission was being sought. Community groups feared that deals were being stitched up behind closed doors in a way that excluded any possibility of a community input into the decision. Local authorities ran the risk of losing their objectivity in seeking planning gain. Finally, there was the fear that the relationship between local authority and developer was not an equal one, and the danger of councils exerting undue leverage on developers found a particular resonance with those who had argued that local authorities were too powerful.

In part, these criticisms were allayed by the Grimley J.R. Eve study. This found that agreements were entered into in a tiny minority of applications and that by far the most common use of agreements was to ensure that the necessary infrastructure was provided or to control the phasing of a project. The report concluded that there was no evidence that planning agreements were being misused. Rather less sanguine accounts of the use and abuse of planning agreements were given to the Nolan Committee, not only by those who might have been predicted to advance them such as the Housebuilders Federation, but also by councillors and local authority officers. Healey and her colleagues also found evidence of the distorting effects of negotiation over planning agreements (Healey et al., 1995). Significantly, these commentaries do not so much call into question the effects on developers as to raise issues about the integrity of local authority planning policy and about ethical behaviour in determining planning applications. This suggests that the proper use of agreements is still far from clear.

Certainly government policy since 1979 has not helped. An initial view of the Conservative government appears to have been that planning agreements were yet another means by which local authorities interfered with market processes. The Property Advisory Group which Heseltine had set up to advise him in 1979, reported on planning gain in 1981 (Property Advisory Group, 1981). Their view was a highly restrictive one which saw the idea of local authority seeking planning gain as fundamentally distasteful. They were prepared to concede that planning gain was acceptable in infrastructure provision where the criteria for imposing a condition were met but thwarted for 'technical legal reasons', and very reluctantly, in the case of mixed-use developments. This extraordinarily narrow approach contained an inherent illogicality: the terms of an agreement which met the criteria for a planning condition would avoid the need for an agreement. That apart, however, central government did not fully accept the Property Advisory Group's conclusion and a circular two years later was rather more liberal in its approach (Department of the Environment, 1983).

The government's attitude represents something of a dilemma in the application of neo-liberalism to planning. On the one hand, planning agreements clearly represented the worst of local authority meddling in the market-led development process. On the other, the value of agreements to facilitate development could not easily be ignored. In that light, agreements could clearly play a role in enabling the market to operate in the most effective way. The fact that the 1983 circular should have adopted a relatively muted approach is not entirely surprising. Rather more surprising, though consistent with the view that the agreements facilitated development, was the change brought in with the Planning and Compensation Act. This introduced the concept of the planning obligation. For the first time, developers were to be allowed to make unilateral declarations of the benefits that they would provide if granted planning permission. These benefits would then become a material consideration in determining the planning application.

The reaction to this clause was predictably one of unease. And indeed it was paradoxical that a government which had accused local authorities of selling planning permissions should now apparently be encouraging developers to buy them. In the face of such criticism the government hastened to say that it expected the use of unilateral obligations to be limited to appeals after a local authority had refused planning permission. A further government circular tried to spell out in more detail the limits of acceptability (Department of the Environment, 1991). Five tests of the reasonableness of obligations were incorporated and the government reiterated the need for obligations to be reasonably related to the scale of development. The circular did nothing to remove the ambiguities of policy and further, contained a new, tacit acceptance that private subsidy for public expenditure was acceptable (Healey *et al.*, 1995). But an early case, *R. v Plymouth City Council* ex parte *Plymouth & South Devon Cooperative Wholesale Society, Ltd.,* 1993, did everything to confirm the critics' worst fears.

In 1991–92, Plymouth City Council received three planning applications for superstores. One of these, by the Co-operative Wholesale Society, was in a district centre and was in accordance with the Local Plan. The other two, by Sainsbury and Tesco, were on adjacent sites next to a new roundabout on the main approach road to Plymouth from the east at Marsh Mills. The City's view was that there was room for only one superstore at Marsh Mills but was persuaded by Sainsbury to run what in effect was a competition: both applications would be granted subject to an obligation to carry out a range of benefits. The developer judged to have produced the better range of benefits would be allowed to proceed. Sainsbury won this competition with an obligation to provide, among other things, road and environmental improvements, contributions to a crèche and a park-and-ride scheme, and an art gallery and bird-watching hide. The Co-op meanwhile was asked to scale down its proposal, although in the end it was granted planning permission. The Co-op, understandably angered by this procedure, took Plymouth City Council to court on the grounds that the benefits proposed by Sainsbury and Tesco had been immaterial to the development proposed and should not have been a consideration. The Court of Appeal ruled otherwise, however, and in doing so exposed the weaknesses in government policy and, perhaps, the process as a whole. The courts could rule on whether a consideration was material but, whether or not it was necessary, was a matter of policy. It was for the City Council to decide what weight to attach to the benefits proposed by the developers. As it was not a case being determined at appeal, the policy tests of Circular 16/91 did not necessarily have a role (Gilbart, 1993; Ashworth, 1993; Crow, 1998).

The Plymouth case was not the last word on planning obligations. A second case in the Oxfordshire town of Witney (*Tesco Stores v. Secretary of State for the Environment and Others*, 1995) put a rather different complexion on the way in which obligations might be used. As at Plymouth, there were three retail developers competing for superstores on three different sites outside the town centre. Once again there was general agreement that only one superstore could be justified. At an inquiry into alterations to the Local Plan, the inspector expressed a preference for the site chosen by Tesco. There was an added complication at Witney. The town had a single bridge crossing of the River Windrush which became badly congested at rush hours and a new relief road had been proposed. At the inquiry into the alterations to the Local Plan, the inspector recommended that the District Council should, as a matter of policy, negotiate with developers for contributions to the construction of the road.

Tesco's application to develop a superstore was rejected on the grounds of traffic congestion. The County Council argued that without the relief road, the extra traffic generated by the superstore would be unacceptable. But the Tesco site already had permission for office use. When Tesco appealed against its refusal the inspector upheld the appeal arguing that the increase in traffic would not be much greater than that generated by offices. The inspector also argued that it would be unreasonable to require Tesco to contribute to the full cost of constructing the relief road. Nevertheless, at the very end of the inquiry, Tesco signed an obligation to provide £6.6 million for the construction of the road if permission were granted for the superstore.

The Secretary of State rejected the inspector's recommendation, noting among other things that the contribution to the building of the relief road was not a good reason for granting planning permission. Tesco challenged the Secretary of State's decision arguing on the basis of the Plymouth case, that the obligation to fund the relief road was properly related to planning and to the development, and was in consequence a material consideration. For the Secretary of State to argue on the basis of Circular 16/91 that the road was unnecessary to the development was tantamount to declaring that the obligation was not material. In the end the courts upheld the Secretary of State's decision. Applying a test of necessity was not the same they argued as declaring an obligation as immaterial to the decision: the issue was about the weight that should be given to such obligations when determining a planning application. A test of necessity was something for the Secretary of State or a local planning authority to apply as a matter of policy (*Journal of Planning and Environment Law*, 1995).

The Tesco case set an important limitation on the use of obligations and allayed at least some of the fears that planning permission could now be bought by the judicious offer of a package of benefits. It further served to emphasize the distinction between what, as a matter of law could be a material consideration, and the weight that as a matter of policy should be attached to such a consideration. So much is reasonably comforting. The Department of the Environment issued a new circular in which a series of policy tests for obligations was set out and these included necessity, relationship to the proposed development, and the question of the scale and the kind of benefits proposed (Department of the Environment, 1997).

Yet the Tesco case did not go very far in addressing the fundamental problems in the use of obligations. Even the distinction between law and policy was not necessarily clarified. As Purdue remarked in his commentary on the case,

. . . there does not appear to be much difference in practice between giving no weight to an obligation and completely disregarding the obligation as immaterial. *(Planning and Environment Law,* 1995, p. 603)

The more intractable problems remained as intractable as ever. The Tesco case did not, for example, resolve the question of whether planning obligations represented an unacceptable tax on development nor, if they were acceptable as a form of tax, whether there might not be better ways of collecting it. It did not resolve the ethical issues or the balance of power between local authorities and developers. It did not question the effect of negotiation on the process of development control. Significantly, however, Lord Keith in his judgement rejected the idea that a system of impact fees on the American model would be preferable to planning obligations, because of the way that the test of rational nexus between the impact of development and the fee demanded had led to judicial involvement in planning decision:

My Lords, no English court would countenance having the merits of a planning decision judicially examined in this way. The result may be some lack of transparency, but that is the price which the English planning system, based upon central and local political responsibility, has been willing to pay for its relative freedom from judicial interference. (*Journal of Planning and Environment Law*, 1995, p. 599)

Quite apart from the character of decision-making in British administration, planning gain and planning obligations throw into relief the idea that local planning authorities have an interest in the development of land which ensures that they cannot be aloof and impartial arbitrators. For some commentators (e.g. Crow, 1998) the potential for corruption and unethical behaviour that lurks behind the negotiation of planning gain outweighs its benefits. The most recent analysis finds objections to the use of planning obligations that go beyond the relatively simple question of corrupt practice. Campbell and her colleagues (2000) argue that obligations are regressive and have a profoundly negative effect on the planning system as a whole. The provision of benefits is wholly dependent on the type of development and its location. Far from being a benign instrument, obligations are having an adverse effect on land-use patterns and are leading to a marketization of planning. They would appear to be making the question of what the development control system should be and do ever more urgent.

A Radical Change?

The history of the period from 1979 to 1997 is not one of a relentless progression from one idea of planning to something that was radically different. Nevertheless, the conclusion that the development control system did undergo a profound change, for all that the legislation remained largely intact, is hard to resist. It is not merely that the discourse on delay whose foundation had been laid in the 1970s now came to occupy a central place in government thinking. Far more important is the implicit view that if development control had any legitimacy it was as an enabling activity that would facilitate the work of developers and so ultimately contribute to the economic development of the country. Such a view is not without its attractions. It counters the inherent negativity of a system whose ultimate sanction is only ever to say 'no'. It sits, we may argue, squarely within the intentions of the very first planning legislation at the beginning of the twentieth century.

The beguilingly positive quality of the language of enabling should not obscure the differences between the values of the early 1900s and those of the 1980s and 1990s. The 1909 Housing, Town Planning etc. Act was certainly designed to promote rather than restrict development. But its purpose was to ensure the orderly release of land, to facilitate the application of appropriate standards, and to allow the local authority to initiate the development process. No longer would the development of cities be left entirely to the decision-making of landlords and private housebuilders, with the local authority left to prevent the worst abuses of private development. The idea of civic involvement in development, if not couched in terms of public participation as it was to be from the late 1960s, was nevertheless inescapable. Conservative policy of the 1980s had no such vision for local authority involvement in the development process. The enabling that local authorities would do would be essentially a technical exercise that would help the market to operate efficiently. If the market identified a site for development which had not been allocated in a statutory plan, the local authority was nevertheless to help the development to proceed. The telling use of the word *'amateur'* by Heseltine to describe local councillors on planning committees in the speech quoted by Circular 22/80 (Department of the Environment, 1980) is symptomatic of the way in which local councils were to be sidelined. Transferring development control powers to the Urban Development Corporations tended in exactly the same direction.

Such a view clearly narrowed the purpose of development control to seeking outcomes which aided market-led prosperity. It also failed to recognize the value of the system as a means of regulating conflict and articulating community preferences. This failure was ruthlessly exposed, as we saw, in the inquiries into the developments of Tillingham Hall and at Bramshill Plantation. The modification introduced by the 1991 Planning and Compensation Act which made development plans the first consideration in determining planning applications apparently righted the failure. It certainly will have satisfied those who argued at the Tillingham Hall and Bramshill Plantation inquiries that the resolution of the conflicts that both developments gave rise to should have taken place in the context of the 'more democratic' process of plan preparation. But although there is an issue to be debated here, we may argue that the change to the legislation was as much about facilitating development and constraining public involvement as it was about trying to improve dispute resolution. If local authorities were committed to policies in their Local Plans, there would be less scope for public objection to specific development proposals. There would be no repetition of the embarrassments in Essex and Hampshire.

The government, the development industry, the planning profession and community groups all set some store by the modifications of the Planning and Compensation Act. It could be said that all four were disappointed. Plan preparation became bogged down in the innumerable objections made by landowners and developers in order to protect their own development strategies. Local authorities were left struggling to find a basis for policy that went further than simply assisting development that would be useful to the economy. Community groups found it no easier to have their voices heard at the stage of plan preparation than they did in public inquiries. The development industry still complained about delays. Neither the policy shifts of the 1980s nor the legislative change of 1991 had apparently resolved the issues that were raised in the 1970s.

Notes

1. The competition for what is now the Sainsbury Wing of the National Gallery was a protracted affair which had the competition assessors selecting a scheme which the Gallery's trustees did not like. The competition winners, Ahrends, Burton and Koralek, were then asked to rethink their winning design which was finally rejected in favour of the trustees' preferred scheme by the American architects, SOM, after the Prince of Wales had referred to the Ahrends scheme as 'a monstrous carbuncle on a much-loved and elegant friend' (Jencks, 1988, p. 43; *Architects' Journal*, 1983). The case did not involve the use of a Special Development Order but it did cast a blight on architectural competitions generally.
2. Where not otherwise referenced material on Tillingham Hall and Bramshill Plantation (Foxley Wood) is taken from planning application files held by Thurrock Borough Council and Hart District Council respectively.
3. Hart District Council, Planning application files 15478 and 15488, fiches 110–112.

Chapter Seven

Towards the New Millennium

The hope was strong that the return of a Labour administration to power with a massive majority in 1997 would have a largely beneficial impact on planning. Development control itself did not appear to be high on the government's agenda, but the emphasis on community participation and the need for a regional tier of government which would have a responsibility for strategic policy, in both economic development and land-use planning, seemed to augur well for the future. And yet there were from the beginning worrying signs that 1997 might not see the hoped for revolution in attitudes. In 1992, the Party's election manifesto had included a commitment to introduce third party rights of appeal against 'developments which fly in the face of their local plan' (Dale, 2000, p. 332). The introduction of third party rights continued to be Labour policy after the election (Crow, 1995). But the Labour Party was moving away from the idea. Although the 1997 manifesto promised that the European Convention on Human Rights would be incorporated into British law, the reference to a third party right of appeal on planning decisions had disappeared. Then, too, the commitment to directly elected regional assemblies evaporated immediately after the election, not be revived until 2002. On the other hand, the introduction of an examination in public for Regional Planning Guidance in the same way as for Structure Plans suggested that the Labour government did intend to honour its pledge to involve the public to a greater degree in public policy-making.

Within a year of taking office, the new government began to issue a series of consultation papers entitled *Modernising Planning* (Department of the Environment, Transport and the Regions, 1998). These were not intended to introduce fundamental reform but rather to guide the process as it existed and to introduce the new vision for regional strategy. Only one of the *Modernising Planning* series dealt with development control and appeared to offer nothing new. Indeed its one main contribution was to set a target of 80 per cent of all planning applications to be dealt with in the 8-week period set down by the General Development Order. As the processing rate had remained constant at about 63 per cent in the previous decade, the targets looked ambitious. But whether or not the target could be achieved, the fundamental problem of this requirement was the way in which it once again confirmed a managerialist approach to development control, in which efficiency and performance were the key attributes to be nurtured.

A rather different approach appeared at first sight to be offered by the Best Value programme. Under the Conservatives, local authorities had been required to submit their services to competition from outside organizations. Compulsory Competitive Tendering was a device to ensure that ratepayers got value for money, and that services managed by the local authority were subject to the bracing environment of private enterprise. Some services lent themselves well to such an approach and waste collection and building management were frequently contracted out. Planning was largely unaffected by this change, however, and remained almost entirely a local authority function. The purpose of the Best Value Programme introduced in 1997 seems to have been two-fold. It was designed to assess the quality of the service offered as well as the value for money paid. It was also designed to enable assessment of those services, such as planning, which had not been exposed to the financial rigour of Compulsory Competitive Tendering. Though this emphasis on the quality of service and not just on economy was an improvement, the way in which the quality of service was to be measured in development control suggested an unwelcome trend. Describing the applicant for planning permission as a 'customer' – in the same way that railway passengers had been re-baptised some years earlier – put a very different complexion on development control from one that stressed community involvement or the resolution of conflict. In Best Value, development control would be essentially a two-way process between the local authority and the applicant-customer who would be buying the service with a fee that he or she paid for the planning application. Within this framework, speed of delivery would once again be an important criterion, although not the only one. But the overall effect, once again, was to reduce the debate on development control to a discussion of effective management of a procedure.

At the same time that the *Modernising Planning* series and the Best Value Programme were being introduced, the Blair government also set about tackling the problem of cities with the appointment of the Urban Task Force. Again the essential thrust of the Urban Task Force went well beyond the question of development control and was intended to re-invigorate government urban policy. The Urban Task Force was given an open ended remit to consider how cities might be changed for the better. Chaired by the architect Richard Rogers, the resulting report, *Towards an Urban Renaissance* (Department of the Environment, Transport and the Regions, 1999) laid heavy emphasis on urban design and the use of 'master plans' to achieve quality in the built environment. The report also carried a three-fold critique of existing planning procedures:

◆ The system does not adequately recognise the special needs of urban areas; it is not attuned to the inherent complexity of assembling and bringing forward urban sites for redevelopment;

◆ The system has become stultified; it generally takes too long to plan and make planning decisions;

◆ The system is reactive; it has become too focused on 'controlling' development. (p. 191)

These criticisms were of course as much aimed at plan making as development control, but there was no doubt that the development control system was also well within the Urban Task Force's sights. 'Streamlining planning decisions' was an essential part of the reform being advocated and though 'some of the delay and inflexibility can be laid at the door of the planning system itself, and the lack of resources . . . much is down to the attitude and approach of local planning authorities, and a lack of priority status within some local authority decision making structures' (p. 197). The remedies offered took two forms. One was to take punitive action against local authorities whose 'performance is not good enough by any reasonable combination of measures' (p. 198). Such measures would include increased use of the Secretary of State's call-in powers, enabling developers to recover fees paid for planning applications if the local authority 'is responsible for unnecessary delays' and 'as a last resort, appointing a statutory agent with the relevant statutory planning powers'. The other form of action was to reduce 'regulatory guidance of standards [which] might unnecessarily restrict development' (p. 198). Here the accent was on flexibility to achieve urban regeneration with a relaxation on the control of design as an undercurrent.

The depressing aspect of both the analysis and the remedies offered by the Urban Task Force is that they had developed hardly at all from the thinking of the Dobry and Environment Sub-Committee reports of the 1970s. The critique was wearisomely familiar, as was the absence of any measure of what a reasonable period for taking planning decisions might be. Moreover there is an inherent contradiction between the desire for speed and the insistence on flexibility. If plans were to become simpler and more flexible (another recommendation of the Urban Task Force), the need for negotiation and therefore the time taken to determine the final form of the development might if anything be greater than under the present system.

Towards an Urban Renaissance was followed in 2000 by a government White Paper (Department of the Environment, Transport and the Regions, 2000) which responded to the Urban Task Force's recommendations. The White Paper was both welcomed as the first coherent statement of government policy for cities for more than 20 years and criticized by at least one member of the Urban Task Force for failing to tackle all the proposals (Hall, 2001). On development control it did little more than reaffirm the government's intention to use the Best Value programme to ensure the improvement of standards and it noted the improvement that had already been introduced to streamline the planning appeals procedure. The most significant change was to recommend the introduction of Urban Regeneration Companies in Liverpool, East Manchester and Sheffield, each of which was to prepare master plans for the 'renaissance' of their areas. But this change, already in place by the time the White Paper was published, did not directly affect development control. The Labour government's first term of office was therefore characterized by external pressure to reform and by marginal changes. But land-use planning was evidently not yet at the centre of the government's concerns.

The relative lack of interest changed after the 2001 elections. A political figure with a much higher profile than either of his predecessors, Lord Falconer, was appointed as Minister for Planning and given a clear remit to reform the planning system. The appointment of Lord Falconer, whose previous ministerial task had been to implement the Millennium Dome project at Greenwich, was widely seen as a concerted attempt to get to grips with the system. Certainly Falconer's own pronouncements left no doubt in anyone's mind as to his intended approach. Within a month of his appointment he was launching his first onslaught on delay (*Planning*, 2001a) and by November he was telling the Confederation of British Industry that he would '"sort out" the planning quagmire' (*Planning*, 2001b). By the end of the year he had published the *Planning Green Paper* (Department of Transport, Local Government and the Regions, 2001a) which was heralded as proposing the biggest reform for 50 years.

The fact that planning should have moved from the sidelines to the forefront of the government's agenda needs explanation and two factors seem to be important. The first was the inquiry into the proposal for a fifth terminal at Heathrow Airport. The inquiry which had lasted 4 years and was reported to have cost some £70m was finally determined in November 2001. For the government, the time taken to reach the required decision was inordinate for a project of national significance; for those who had objected to the scheme, the inquiry was vitally necessary to ensure that their voice was heard. The Terminal 5 case was a classic confrontation of national need and local impact. The British Airports Authority and the government were convinced that the competivity of Heathrow within Europe could only be maintained by building the new terminal. The surrounding London Boroughs, amenity groups and individuals were all fearful of the possibility of increased aircraft noise, and of the impact on an already congested corner of Greater London. The frustration with the slowness of the process to take a vital decision and with the supposedly flagrant self-interest of those who opposed unpalatable development too close to their own homes suggested that radical reform was necessary.

The second factor is more in the realm of gossip than of ascertainable fact. Developers were said to have expressed their disquiet to the Prime Minister himself that cumbersome planning procedures were delaying development vitally necessary for the economy. If the rumour is true, it reads remarkably like a re-run of the 1970s and early 1980s with the difference that it was industrial entrepreneurs and not housebuilders who were making complaints. But the essence of the complaints – to judge from the tenor of the proposals in the *Planning Green Paper* – was the same. It took too long to obtain planning permission. Planning policy was too complicated. There was no certainty of outcome and local authorities could be obstructive of new development. Whether the picture of industrialists tramping a path to No. 10 Downing Street, to voice their concerns to a receptive Tony Blair, is credible or not, it is the case that the Treasury embarked on a study of town planning in 2000 whose intention was to assess the economic impact of the British planning system. The report was never made public and is believed to have been less damaging to the planning system than rumour had initially suggested. But the fact that the Treasury should have become involved at all is a remarkable indication of the way in which government was thinking.

The Green Paper was published in December 2001 and covered the whole of the planning system, not just development control. It therefore contained a great deal of detail that need not concern us here. Nevertheless its fundamental premises were important because they were relevant also to the proposals on development control. The first concern was with the complexity of planning. There were too many different types of plan and the rules for different types of development were 'often unclear'. Planning appeals:

can seem obscure. People find it hard to understand the way in which the system works.

Both applicants and others with an interest in a proposed development can find it hard to understand the basis on which decisions are taken. (para 2.3)

The second concern was with speed and predictability: 'the planning process is too often perceived to be a set of rules aimed at preventing development rather than making sure that good development goes ahead' (para 2.4). Planning applications were taking too long to determine. The outcomes of planning applications were uncertain. Preparing and revising plans was slow and expensive. Appeals took too long to be dealt with. The final concern was for greater community involvement. Here the basic premise was that although the present system was, as the paper puts it, 'very "consultative"' the community often 'feels disempowered' (para 2.5). There was another aspect to this concern. Planning was not 'customer focused' so that people found it hard to get information and advice.

Although other parts of the Green Paper could claim to be announcing radical change, Chapter 5 which dealt with reforms to the development control system did not in fact break new ground. As Lock (2002) puts it, 'the fundamental change for development control . . . is a collection of ideas old and new, big and little. The DTLR's accumulated list of loose ends and bright ideas is here' (p. 44). There were proposals for improving 'customer service', which included the creation of a 'user-friendly' checklist to aid applicants, for greater use of information technology to make information available to the public and for a single regime for all consents necessary for new development (paras. 5.6, 5.7, 5.12, 5.15). New targets were set for the processing of planning applications which recognized that larger developments might take longer than minor applications. Sixty per cent of major commercial and industrial buildings were to be determined in 13 weeks; 65 per cent of minor commercial and industrial buildings and 80 per cent of all other applications were to be determined in 8 weeks. A review of statutory and non-statutory consultees would be undertaken as yet another way in which the processing of applications might be speeded up. The target for the proportion of planning applications to be delegated to officers for decision-making was to be set at 90 per cent. Developers would be able to enter delivery contracts for larger commercial and industrial development which would ensure a greater predictability of process (para 5.25) in return for which developers would waive their right of appeal. A final proposal was for the introduction of local development orders. These would work in the same way as the national General Permitted Development Order and would confer planning permission on certain kinds of development. Unlike the General Permitted Development Order, however, the local authority itself would identify the development to which the local order gave permission (para 5.48).

In addition to these minor proposals for improved management and incremental change, the Green Paper made three recommendations which had rather wider import. The first of these was the introduction of what are called Business Planning Zones in which 'no consent will be necessary for development [particularly of leading edge technology companies], if it is in accordance with tightly defined parameters'. The principle was identical to that of the Simplified Planning Zones of the 1980s whose use, as we have seen, was strictly limited. The idea of zones in which permission is granted in advance for certain types of development is seducing in its apparent simplicity and in its potential for the swift implementation of projects. But there is a dual flaw in this argument. It assumes that all conditions for new development within the zone can be accurately predicted. It also assumes that complying with a generalized set of criteria will be simple: in practice the scope for dispute is great and the need for some means by which proposals can be checked is inescapable. It is all the more likely to be true if high quality development is the aim and tightly defined parameters are the means of achieving that aim.

The second recommendation stemmed directly from the experience of the Terminal 5 inquiry. The proposal was that in future all national infrastructure projects should no longer be dealt with by ministerial call-in followed by a public inquiry and transferred instead to a parliamentary procedure. Inevitably, it was this proposal which attracted most attention from the public at large and from the national media. Apart from the question of how national infrastructure projects would be defined, the proposals have been widely criticized because they would limit the possibility of opposing projects whose import would be environmentally problematic. Such was the argument of organizations like the Council for the Protection of Rural England. In a colourful analogy, Hall (2002) suggested that the proposal was like a solution to the Königsberg theorem (demonstrating the impossibility of reaching every part of the city of Königsberg while only crossing each of its seven bridges once) which involved blowing up the bridges. Moreover the Green Paper proposals were singularly lacking in detail as to the nature of the procedure envisaged. In his replies to the House of Commons Select Committee on Transport, Local Government and the Regions, Lord Falconer seemed to imply that the decisions on national infrastructure projects would not, or would not always, be put to a free vote.[1] The result would be that national projects could be forced through in the face of local opposition. Nevertheless, the problem conceals a real dilemma. We can argue that the 1947 development control system has been largely successful through the inquiry process in reaching decisions on projects of local and regional significance in the light of all the facts. It has been very much less successful in balancing national policy and priorities with local impacts. The problem had already surfaced in the 1970s with projects like the Sizewell B Nuclear Power Station and the inquiry into a third London airport (Barker and Couper, 1984). The difficulty is that the local impact of a proposal may well have a bearing on national policy, such that taking a decision at national level on approximate location may not be optimal once local factors have been taken into account.

The third recommendation was a negative one. The Green Paper dismissed the idea of introducing third party rights of appeal even when limited to certain kinds of decision. The dismissal was summary. Having rehearsed four potential cases for third party rights – departures from the development plan, major projects, projects in which officers' recommendations are overturned by councillors and local authorities' own development – it concluded: 'None of these approaches add up, in our view, to a case for third party rights of appeal. It could add to the costs and uncertainties of planning. We cannot accept that prospect' (para 6.22). This was a far cry from the 1992 Labour Manifesto; and there was no reflection on the question of human rights to which we will turn below.

The government issued two other consultation papers immediately following the publication of the Green Paper. One dealt with amendments to the Use Classes Order (Department of Transport, Local Government and the Regions, 2002). The changes proposed did not amount to a major restructuring of land use and its control within the planning system. In general terms, however, the paper stressed the deregulatory character of Use Classes Order – in that it excludes certain changes of use from the need for planning permission if they are within the scope of a single Use Class – and sought to increase the number of changes between Use Classes which could be permitted development because they have no significant impact. In detail, the paper presented as an option the division of the B1 Business Class, the measure that had resulted from the push to deregulation in the early 1980s (see above p. 138), to separate out offices and 'clean production processes' and so answer some of the criticisms levelled at the B1 Class when it was introduced.

The other consultation paper was potentially more important and dealt with planning obligations (Department of Transport, Local Government and the Regions, 2001b). The paper argued that the use of planning obligations was unpredictable, that negotiations were time consuming and inherently lacking in transparency, and that there was a lack of accountability in the way in which contributions were used. The paper rejected three possible approaches. The first, tightening the policy constraints current imposed by Circular 1/97 (Department of the Environment, 1997) by introducing a 'necessity' test, was seen as being too restrictive. A second option, to *reduce* policy constraints to allow local authorities free rein in their negotiations was rejected for potentially increasing the differences between local authorities and adding to delays in development control. The final option rejected was the imposition of impact fees, on the American model, to replace planning obligations. The argument against impact fees was that fixing an appropriate fee scale would be difficult and that flexibility to consider site-specific problems would be lost. There was no reference to the litigiousness that impact fees gives rise to in the USA and the judicial interference in planning which, as we saw, Lord Keith had criticized at the time of the Tesco case at Witney (see above pp. 165–166). The government's preferred option was to set tariffs for planning obliga-tions calculated as a function of the size or the value of the development. The government would fix a national scale of tariffs, but local authorities would have some discretion about how the tariffs would be applied locally and could set down the criteria by which tariffs would be reduced. Differential tariffs could apply to greenfield and brownfield development. The intention was that the national scale would not preclude negotiation about site-specific problems such as access. These proposals for planning obligations went some way to addressing the problems with obligations that the paper itself acknowledges. But they did not deal adequately with the inherently regressive character of negotiation over planning gain that Campbell and her colleagues (2000) noted. Moreover, setting a scale of tariffs for planning obligations presents the same difficulty as would the introduction of impact fees.

Some of the proposals discussed above represent commendable improvements to good management of the process. Others may yet do so after consultation and amendment has refined the initial thinking. But discussion of detail and of marginal improvements obscures the more fundamental issues. The first is that these proposals are not for the most part radical and do not suggest real reform. Commentators like Bennett (2002), while commending proposals which related to good management practice, simply noted that there was no fundamental change. Steeley (2002) in rationalist mode went further and criticized the Green Paper as a whole as having 'no objectives matched with mechanisms', although his major concern appeared to be with the 'NIMBY's and marauders who will still be able to abuse the system'. And Delafons (2002), a former chief planner at the Department of the Environment, taking a longer view saw the Green Paper as neither the first nor the last of the reforms of the planning system. Indeed the proposals for development control fell firmly into the tradition of tinkering with the mechanisms that characterized all the proposed and implemented reforms since 1947. The Dobry review of development control in the 1970s (see above, pp. 122–125) was in many ways more comprehensive and more genuinely reformist.

The second point is that the Green Paper perpetuated the managerialist approach of all previous attempted reforms of development control. It used the language of management most obviously in terms such as 'customer care' and 'user friendliness'. This, we may argue, is a subtle distortion of the development control process. It assumes that development control is primarily about delivering a service which a customer is 'purchasing' by paying a planning application fee. It casts development control into the mould of a bi-lateral exchange in which goods are delivered by the local planning authority (the right land, in the right place, at the right time?). It fails to acknowledge the multiplicity of interests that are represented in the development of land and the use of buildings or the complexity of resulting conflicts between those interests.

The third point is that there were a number of contradictions throughout the Green Paper and the consultation papers which had clearly not been thought through. For development control (as in fact for the plan-making parts of British planning) there is an inherent conflict between the desire for increased speed and efficiency and the intention to improve community involvement. Reducing the time taken to process applications, limiting the number of consultees and increasing the proportion of decisions delegated to officers all seemed to restrict rather than increase community involvement. These fears were not allayed by the fact that changes proposed to the preparation of plans and policies also appeared to limit rather than develop community involvement. Beneath this conflict is an even more difficult problem: what constitutes 'good' participation in the planning process? When does public involvement empower and when does it simply obstruct? When does self interest become public interest? There are no simple answers to these questions but we do need to reflect on what price we wish to pay for the right to be involved, and if needs be object, and what value we place on the local impacts of development. Real reform will have to deal with these questions. A second contradiction is evident in the desire for simplification. As all too frequently occurs when simplicity and clarity are the aim, the proposals designed to meet that aim may have the opposite effect. Though this tendency is most apparent in the proposed hierarchy of plans, some of the proposals for development control also seem to suggest complexity, not simplicity. This is particularly true of the idea for local development orders.

Lord Falconer was committed to achieving legislative change by 2004, but was transferred to the Home Office in a government re-shuffle in May 2002. And it seems likely that the government was embarrassed by the enormous response to the Green Paper and a highly critical report by the parliamentary Select Committee on Transport, Local Government and the Regions. Nevertheless, the process did not lose momentum and a Bill was placed before Parliament at the beginning of December, 2002. The Planning and Compulsory Purchase Bill is at least as important for what it did not contain as for what it proposed to enact, at any rate as far as the development control system is concerned. Perhaps most significantly, the proposal for a parliamentary procedure for major infrastructure projects has been abandoned in face of the considerable opposition to the proposal from all quarters. And the proposal for tariffs for planning obligations has also been quietly dropped.

On the other hand, the government has introduced, as the result of pressure from, among others, the Royal Town Planning Institute, a statement of statutory purpose for town planning, the first time that such a purpose has been identified in the legislation since 1947. Yet in the form in which it was presented to Parliament, the statement – to exercise the plan-making functions of the Bill 'with a view to contributing to the achievement of sustainable development' (Clause 38) – is so general as to contribute little. Nor does it say anything directly about the purpose of development control.

None of this looks like a radical change to the planning system. It is doubtful that the Green Paper or the Act itself once it receives royal assent will become the point of reference for the planning system in the years to come. Perhaps as with the House of Commons Environment Sub-Committee report of the 1970s its significance will be in the mobilization of opinion that it gave rise to, not for its own recommendations. The least attractive outcome would be if the failure to address fundamental issues led to a further weakening of the system.

Procedural Justice and the Human Rights Act

Quite apart from the government's proposals for reform, development control has received a challenge from a very different quarter. Britain had been a signatory to the European Convention for the Protection of Human Rights in the 1950s. Only since 1998 has the Convention been incorporated into British law in the Human Rights Act which came into force in October 2000. Rather belatedly, the planning profession awoke to the realization that the Act (and the Convention) might have a considerable impact on the way in which the planning system works. Two major issues emerged from the debate, both of which have to do with Article 6 of the Convention which guarantees the right to a fair trial.

The first issue has to do with third party rights within the system. Article 6 makes reference to 'civil rights and obligations' which must be protected by the right to a fair trial. Such rights clearly include those of the landowner but might equally be said to include those who are affected by decisions taken by landowners and local authorities. Yet third parties have traditionally had few rights in the planning system and no right to appeal against decisions taken by the local authority. As Grant (2000) puts it:

In terms of legal rights, the British planning system is wholly one-sided. This reflects its historical roots in a closed regulatory system, rather than the contemporary realities of a modern participative democracy. In taking decisions on planning applications, the primary relationship is still that between the applicant and the decision-maker. Third parties have the right to make representations, and local authorities have a correlative duty to take such representations, if properly made, into account. But such third parties have no right of appeal against the grant of a planning permission. They may participate in an appeal brought by the applicant against a refusal of permission, or conditions imposed, by the local authority, but have no power to initiate a merits appeal themselves. They are restricted to making a claim for judicial review. (p. 1216)

We have already noted that the Labour government had explicitly excluded the possibility of third party rights in the Planning Green Paper. As yet the question of third party rights has not been tested in the courts in the light of the Human Rights Act, but that moment may come.

The second issue has to do with the role of public inquiries, in particular when an application is called in by the Secretary of State. The question is whether a public inquiry can ever be both independent and impartial as required by Article 6 of the Convention. Even before 1998 there were straws in the wind indicating the likely need for change. In 1996, for example, the case of an enforcement appeal, *Bryan v. United Kingdom*, was brought before the European Court of Human Rights. In it, the plaintiff argued that his civil rights were at stake, because the Secretary of State, to whom the appeal was addressed, had the right to recover the final decision. In these circumstances could an inquiry be described as impartial and independent? The European Court argued that, though the inquiry could not be so described, in general the system did comply with the Convention because there was a further right of appeal to the High Court (Johnston, 2000). But as Grant (2000) remarks, this was a patently unsatisfactory argument because in the British system the courts do not reconsider matters of policy on which inquiry is the last word.

A second case, this time brought before the Scottish courts under the Human Rights legislation, demonstrates the difficulty more clearly. The case of *County Properties Ltd. v. Scottish Ministers*, 2000, concerned the suitability of a replacement for a historic building and the application had been called in by the Minister. Historic Scotland, the government's historic buildings agency, was a key witness at the inquiry. The judge ruled that the inquiry could not be impartial and independent if a government appointed reporter (as inspectors are called in the Scottish system) was, partly on the basis of evidence from a government agency, to advise a Minister on an appropriate determination. The upshot of this case seemed to be that the Secretary of State would have to abandon his or her role as the authority of last resort and new ways of ensuring the independence of the inspectorate would have to be found. A possible solution is the creation of an environmental court within which a fully independent inspectorate would be given the formal existence by statute that it currently lacks (see Grant, 2000).

However, the case which it was widely believed at the time would be crucial was the redevelopment of the Alconbury airfield in Cambridgeshire. The outcome hinged on whether the Secretary of State's call-in power under Section 77 of the 1990 Town and Country Planning Act was in fact compatible with the 1998 Human Rights Act. It was the first time, therefore, that the general call-in power had been tested against the human rights legislation. Although the Divisional Court had ruled that the manner in which the Alconbury cases had been dealt with – there were four cases heard by the Divisional Court – was in fact in breach of Article 6, the House of Lords disagreed. The fact that the Secretary of State held an inquiry into the cases, presided by an inspector, and the fact that there was the potential for judicial review of the decision-making were enough to ensure that the right to a fair hearing was respected. The conclusion that Lindblom (2001) reached was that the Alconbury cases demonstrated that the British town planning system is not incompatible with the Human Rights Act.[2]

It was a nasty moment all the same. As Grant observes, there is an irony in the fact that the impact of the Convention, so much concerned with substantive rights, should in the British planning system have posed its greatest threat to procedures. Yet this is entirely consistent with the way in which the system emphasizes procedural fairness as a means of ensuring just outcomes. It was, after all, a system which was moulded by the relationship between lessees and landlords, whom the local authorities sought to replace, and which was forged by a system of common law that placed great emphasis on due process. Procedures that were open and fair – and followed scrupulously – would be the guarantee of the rights of individuals.

It is worth noting, by way of conclusion, how very characteristically British is this concern for the reform of development control. Reform of planning systems is much in the air within Europe and quite apart from the proposals in the Green Paper, major reform has been put into effect in France and Norway within the recent past and reform is under discussion in the Netherlands. In none of them has the reform of the process of determining applications for development projects been an objective, however. In France, the *Loi relative à la solidarité et renouvellement urbains* (*loi SRU*; urban solidarity and renewal law) of 2000, introduced by a Communist minister in the government of Lionel Jospin, aimed to integrate land-use planning with an urban policy designed to combat social exclusion (Barbé, 2001). It was also concerned to loosen the perceived rigidity of the old *plans d'occupation des sols* (see above, pp. 5–7) with their regulations which, so it was thought, tended to freeze existing land uses rather than taking a deliberately prospective view of the way in which an area might develop. But nothing in the new law altered the fundamental relationship between the plan and the decision on individual development proposals, nor was there any change to the process of granting and refusing applications. Indeed, there is reason to doubt whether the new plans under the *loi SRU* will differ greatly from their predecessors. The one change that does get close to what we would think of as development control is the requirement that any intention to undertake major development or renewal by using the discrete zoning mechanism, the *zone d'aménagement concerté* (*ZAC*; action area plan), must now be clearly announced in the local plan itself. Hitherto, it had been possible for local authorities to use *ZAC* in ways which implied considerable discretionary leeway to depart from committed policy, which was thought to be highly undesirable (Booth and Stafford, 1994). The intention, and perhaps the effect, was to constrain the decision-making process yet further and by so doing, to ensure the certainty and legality of the process were upheld.

The explanation for this preoccupation with development control in Britain and an absence of debate in other parts of Europe is of course in part a direct reflection of the differences between discretionary and regulatory systems of planning. If the plan itself is the sole source of authority for decisions on individual proposals, the process of applying for and determining applications for development is immediately downgraded: it becomes, as we noted in Chapter 1, an administrative procedure in which in theory the respect for the regulations in force is the prime concern. The discretionary nature of the British system transforms the process and makes it highly political. Or put another way, introducing the wild card of 'other material considerations' introduces the possibility of a whole set of implied values, professional judgements and choices. It is at once the system's inherent weakness and its greatest strength. It is a weakness when the values and interests that inform decisions are hidden in a fog of corporatism. It is a strength when the process allows preferences and conflicts to be articulated and choices made in a deliberate, open and reasoned way.

The debate on the effects of the Human Rights Act certainly went beyond the discussion of managerial efficiency that has dogged the past 25 years. Yet it does not go to the heart of the problem. Development control has undoubtedly changed since universal control was introduced in 1947. The belief in an over-arching public interest which would inform the decision to grant or refuse planning permission has been eroded. In its place has come the dual ethos of development control as the enabler of development, and negotiation as the means by which local authorities could achieve the facilities that they no longer had the money to pay for. For a profession that still adheres to the principle of public interest, the change is demoralizing and has contributed to a loss of direction. But though the policy confusions of the 1980s, generated by a particular political philosophy, have played an important part in present uncertainty, the seeds of that uncertainty predate 1979. The failure to treat development control as anything other than a bureaucratic exercise in the past 50 years has obscured both its strengths and its weaknesses and has allowed the debate to be dominated by a concern for efficiency.

Notes

1. House of Commons Select Committee on Transport, Local Government and the Regions. Minutes of Evidence taken 18 December 2001, HC 476-i, 22 February 2002.
2. There were three conjoined appeals heard by the House of Lords: *R. (Alconbury Developments Ltd. and others) v. Secretary of State for the Environment, Transport and the Regions; R. (Holding and Barnes) v. Secretary of State for the Environment, Transport and the Regions; Secretary of State for the Environment, Transport and the Regions v. Legal and General Assurance Society Ltd (Alconbury).*

Chapter Eight

Future Glory?

It is perhaps not too far fetched to compare the structure plan with the dignified parts and development control with the efficient parts of planning . . . and it is in this sense that development control comes into its own, not as the means of implementing some 'dignified' plan, but as an 'efficient' means of legitimating change in the environment.

(Davies, 1980, pp. 14–15)

Davies's surprisingly upbeat description of development control was written when the system had been under sustained attack for nearly a decade. Like Haar, whose quotation opened the book, he was praising the process of development control for precisely the reasons that the creators of the system in the 1940s had proposed it: planning by consent is, at least potentially, flexible and responsive to local needs and efficient in handling the process of change. Yet these virtues have been consistently down-played both within and outside the profession in the face of the inflexibility and the time wasting that has been seen as the system's major weaknesses. The fact that the final report of the Urban Task Force could repeat in very much the same form criticisms of development control which had already been current more than a quarter of a century before suggests that there is a crisis in development control which has not been fully addressed. The strengths of the development control system are not in doubt, but simply rehearsing those strengths is clearly not enough to offset the problem. While development control will always fail to satisfy at least some of those who are users of the system, we need to look further to be able to understand why the system is seen as problematic.

Perhaps the heart of the matter is to be found in the concept of interest in land which lay at the centre of the attempt to define private property rights within a feudal system of tenure. We argued that the ability to conceptualize over-lapping and concurrent interests in land, and to divide current from future interest was a potent force in the promotion of urban development and came in time to inform thinking about the land-use planning system. It was conceptually possible to divide current enjoyment of land from future development rights and therefore to nationalize the future development rights even while allowing the continued private ownership of the rights to current enjoyment. The question that such a formula gives rise to, however, is what kind of interest the state has actually acquired by legislating to prevent development taking place without a valid permission. Is it in practice equivalent to the interest of others with title to the land? Does the State simply become a landowner like any other?

The questions are worth asking because there has been one strand of thinking which implies that there is a direct relationship between the State ownership of development rights and the private property interest of owners. Much better, the argument might go, to mediate those interests through classic contractual relationships than to leave it to cumbersome bureaucracy and the exigencies of possibly arbitrary political control. Pearce (1981), for example, has argued that there might be a case for contractual relationships between developers and those affected by development which would allow for the settlement of disputes and financial redress. Such a contractual relationship depends for its effect on the application and extension of the common law of nuisance and requires the courts to act as the guarantors of the rights of both developers and individuals. There have, too, been advocates of the Hong Kong system, in which government is both planning authority and, for much of the territory, ground landlord. Again, the advantages of the contractual relationship between developer and controlling authority are cited. Developers are given clearer instructions about the kind of development they may undertake and the potential for enforcement through the courts is greater. Payment of lease premiums expresses the mutual advantage to both sides (Lai, 1998). Such a system not only facilitates development, it is fairer to all those affected by it. Finally, within Britain there have been occasional calls for a return to the leasehold system with large landowners acting both to promote development and then to maintain it thereafter.

Pearce recognized that the control by contract that he explored has significant problems. It would exclude those unable to afford to arrange the process of litigation. It would also exclude those whose property rights (as shorthold tenants, for example) were limited, in rather the same way that the Assize of Nuisance in the thirteenth century only applied to freeholders. Pearce also noted that judges would be forced into the role of policy-makers which they probably were not well able to fulfil. Finally, the point made by McLaren (1983) about the application of the law of nuisance in the nineteenth century is also relevant: establishing to what extent an individual suffers from a development might be hard to establish. Pearce argued that though the theory might be sound the practice would almost certainly be problematic.

The case argued by Lai and by those who advocate a return to an era of great landlords is in some ways harder to refute. In the Hong Kong case, the government exercises the statutory land-use control as well as acting as landlord. The contract entered into with the developer is a contract which binds the developer to the conditions of a statutory plan. The contract provides a far surer way of upholding long-term planning strategy than traditional enforcement mechanisms, while at the same time ensuring the development goes ahead. The argument in favour of a return to the leasehold estate follows similar lines. The landowner enables the initial development and controls its form and layout, while at the same time ensuring the long-term management of the area. As with Hong Kong, there is a belief that enforcement is easier where there is a direct contractual relationship between controller and developer. Neither the history of the great estates in the eighteenth and nineteenth century nor that of Hong Kong necessarily offer wholehearted support to such an analysis. As we have seen, the great estates were far from uniformly successful in carrying out and then maintaining development. And in Hong Kong, successful though the promotion of development has been, controlling the activities of developers has not always been easy. But there is a more fundamental objection than simply the difficulty of implementation.

In the Middle Ages, we saw that the earliest form of regulatory control was simply concerned with resolving disputes between neighbours. The role of the mayor and alderman of London was effectively an adjudicatory one and there was no sense of a common purpose or interest other than in maintaining a general social cohesion. Already in the Middle Ages, there was an indication of something that went further than private disputes in the sporadic control over infringements of the street line. And slowly, as we saw, there arose a doctrine of common nuisance and general interest that did not merely affect adjoining owners but had a wider impact. The Tudors and Stuarts developed that doctrine in the series of royal proclamations that both forbade and controlled new building. But the Stuarts in particular muddled general and personal interest in a way that was to be their undoing. They wanted to control urban development in the interests of the greater good of society as a whole, but were notoriously happy to collect fines from those who infringed the proclamations, as a way of replenishing the royal exchequer.

In this respect, the privatization of control from the late seventeenth century onwards, with private landlords exercising control for the leasehold system, should have been even more nakedly self-interested than the monarchy had been. And indeed landowners had a short-term interest in raising revenue from their estates that could lead them to be as oblivious of any common purpose as Charles I. But the aristocratic estates at least had the distinguishing characteristic of concern for future generations. Landownership was a definer of status, and protecting the interests of future generations meant taking a long-term as well as short-term view of land development. Moreover, entailing an estate on future generations limited the ability of the present incumbent to act wilfully in disposing of his inheritance. At its best, the long-term interests of the family coincided with the more general interests of society at large. There was an important trustee relationship between the current occupier and unborn generations of the family which gradually extended to a benign if paternalistic relationship between a landlord and his lessee. But this kind of relationship was fragile, and Seven Dials and Somers Town (see pp. 44–47) are object lessons of what could go wrong if for whatever reason the long-term interests in maintaining dynastic succession broke down. The trustee role in land development gradually came to be played by municipal council and not with powers conferred by contract or by the common law of nuisance, but by statute.

The question of the nature of the interest in land comes to a head in the 1947 Town and Country Planning Act with the nationalization of future development rights. Medieval lawyers had striven to give the abstract motion of future interests in land a concrete existence, and to ensure legal protection for future rights in the present. This was the kind of understanding that underlay the drafting of post-World War II planning legislation. But was the interest nationalized in 1947 akin to that of the interests of any other kind of landowner? The answer has to be no. First of all, it establishes very clearly the nature of the trustee relationship between the controlling authority and the land to be developed. Unlike the successor in title to the freehold of a great estate, the State never comes into occupation of the land in which it holds the future development rights. It acts as a guardian of those rights in the interests of the common purpose. Secondly, this future interest subsumed the idea of common nuisance and general protection from the abuse of land-use rights that common law had struggled with over several centuries. Statute would be a surer guarantor of protection than ever the law of nuisance could be.

The drafting of the 1947 Act also recognized the ambiguous nature of that interest which is represented by the nationalization of future development rights. The fact that local authorities are required to consider other material considerations in fulfilling their trusteeship suggests the negotiated nature of that interest. It is not something necessarily to be determined in advance of the application to develop nor can it be wholly expressed in the plan. It needs to be worked out afresh on each occasion. This is one reason why so much emphasis is placed on the process of development control, because there is a need to be certain that the interests at stake can indeed be correctly identified. Public inquiries have a pivotal role in exposing the rationale for decision-making and in defining the nature of the interests in a given development. But to concentrate only on the process begins to obscure the search for the nature of the common interest itself. What has gone wrong in the past 30 years is that we have lost sight of what it is that the 1947 Act has nationalized.

One of the major difficulties is that the attempts to articulate what we want to achieve in disposing of the nationalized interest in future development have been weak. Formulations such as Lewis Keeble's reference to 'sightliness and convenience' (Keeble, 1952, p. 411) do not take the argument very far. However, what Keeble's views begin to suggest is that development control decision-making is informed by a professional value system which provides a defence for the profession but is never fully explicit. Other values are at work, too. Aspects of planning policy enjoy considerable popular support which suggests that not only professional values are brought to bear on the definition of material considerations in the disposal of future development rights. The ambiguities are captured in two ways. One is to use a catch-all word like 'amenity' as the justification for interference in the development of land. It proved remarkably useful in its imprecision in concealing the reasons for the control being exercised. The other way is to use measurable standards of one kind or another which serve as proxies for underlying values. This was how the public health system worked. Outlawing back-to-back housing or ensuring minimum street widths were not ends in themselves, they were intended to deliver a healthy environment, which in turn was designed to promote the moral welfare of society. The reaction to these bylaws was of course to ask for more elasticity. Raymond Unwin, who in the early years of the last century was advocating an alternative vision for new development, clearly had a social objective as much as an aesthetic one. But in the end, this objective, translated first by the subtle layouts for New Earswick, Letchworth and Hampstead Garden Suburb, was distilled into the crude measures of density and the spacing of dwellings which could be applied in town planning schemes.

Of these proxy measures, perhaps the green belt has been the most perplexing. It has the very considerable merit of combining great precision – its limits are fixed and the prohibition on development is clear – with an essential vagueness of intent. Is it intended simply to keep towns apart or does it have some kind of intrinsic merit? Why is stopping the spread of urban areas such a significant objective? The answers to these questions are bound up with a vision of the good life which has widespread popular appeal. It is popular with judges, according to McAuslan (1980), because its limits are well defined and its prohibitions are unequivocal. Professional values intersect with popular concern in a way which does nothing to illuminate the search for the true nature of public interest in the control of development.

If green belt policy stands for the ambiguities of the values that underpin the control of future development rights, Section 106 agreements have led to a more distorting effect on the understanding of the public interest in the control of future development rights. On the face of it, the Section 106 agreement represents no more than a useful extension of the general principle of negotiating the nature of the material considerations that will affect the determination of planning applications. Negotiation is healthy because it helps to resolve the potential for conflict between private short-term interests and public long-term ones. It enables development to go ahead by allowing for the correction of adverse affects. However, in doing so it begins to equate the nationalized interest in the future development of land, achieved through the universal control of development by the State, with the interest of anyone else with a title. Above all, it suggests that each is tradable. This has the effect of replacing the trustee obligation with a contractual relationship which pre-supposes a mutual advantage. It stresses the short-term gain at the expense of long-term strategy. It places a money price on the gain to the local authority. Finally, the process by which planning gain is negotiated is firmly protected from public gaze. Section 106 agreements are forged typically between planning officers and the developer and even elected representatives have little insight into the nature of the negotiation. The public at large is excluded. Development control procedures within local authorities are not necessarily very transparent, but the negotiation on planning gain is decidedly covert in a potentially damaging way.

The fear in all this is that by internalizing its values for too long development control is losing the plot. Worse, procedural remedies that have been suggested for reducing delay and increasing performance serve only to emphasize this loss of direction. The only reasonable way forward is to enquire how we might in practice rediscover the nature of the nationalized right to future development. There seem to be four significant areas in which we need to ask questions about what we want the system to deliver. The first is about the boundary between public and private interest. The second centres on the process of control. The third concerns the policy base for decision-making in the public interest. The fourth has to do with the role of development control in dispute resolution.

At the outset we argued that the maturing of a system of public control needed to go hand-in-hand with the development of private property rights. And at the beginning of this history we saw how control was about resolving the infringement of the limited rights that freeholders had to properties that they occupied. On the face of it, so limited an objective is at odds with a loftier conception of public interest. Government policy has in the 50 years since the 1947 Act been at pains to distinguish between planning's true role and the inappropriate use of development control in dealing with quarrels between neighbours. In fact this adjudicatory role has a long tradition and to some extent has taken over from the common law of nuisance in dispute resolution. The fact that it has done so almost certainly reflects the 'efficiency', in Davies's terms, of the system, as against the much more cumbersome legal process, with its restricted access (Davies, 1980). There is a case for saying that there is also a common interest in solving disputes which apparently only concern the disputants.

There is a more general problem with the boundaries between control of a public interest and private property rights. At least part of the argument in favour of making control a question of contract between the developer and those affected by development is that it does not infringe the rights of property owners. The contract allows free negotiation of rights and benefits without the involvement of a meddling bureaucracy. In practice, public attitudes have been mixed. Much criticism has been levelled at development controllers interfering in matters which did not concern them. But the public at large has also looked at the planning system to protect its interests and has criticized the development control system for not being stringent enough. This has been true at both large and small scales. For every case like Tillingham Hall and Bramshill Plantation there are the unsung cases of enforcement action against vehicle repair workshops in residential roads where people have felt that their right to enjoyment has been infringed by the activities of others. The boundary between the public and private domains and public and private interest are by no means as clearly defined as popular imagination or government advice would have us believe. We willingly accept the limitation of others' freedoms in order to protect our own. Davies concluded that if 'development control did not exist it would be necessary to invent something like it' (1980, p. 15), and even if the assertion is contestable, it nevertheless points to a very considerable service that development control provides for the public at large in balancing private advantage and private loss.

The second significant area has to do with the process of control. The trusteeship of the interest in land that has been nationalized since 1947 has traditionally been with local authorities that were constituted in the late nineteenth century. Changes to local government in the twenty-first century may have a considerable impact on the ability of local authorities to guarantee that role. The election of mayors and the introduction of cabinet government in local authorities in particular could be retrograde. If the development plan becomes a matter for the local authority cabinet as a strategic policy but development control is handled administratively at a lower level, then there is a risk of rupture between the development plan and development control, and a potential downgrading of development control into a kind of licensing function. This would limit the scope of development control and serve once again to ensure that the other important issues were not properly debated. Another important aspect of the process has to do with the rights of third parties. One of the impacts of nationalizing development rights was to place a particular emphasis on the right of redress for those whose property interests were affected. It left interested third parties in an ambiguous position: invited to comment on applications but with few formal rights of redress if their comment was improperly ignored. Debate of both these issues goes beyond the scope of this book but they, too, need to be addressed if development control is to retain its legitimacy.

The third significant area is that of the policy base for development control decision-making. One aspect of the problem is the vexed relationship between the development plan and development control which, as we know, is a direct result of the way in which the 1947 Act and its successors have been drafted. We have already seen how, over the past 50 years, and particularly in the last 20, attitudes to that relationship have fluctuated wildly, from the heavy emphasis placed on the discretionary freedom to approve useful development in the early 1980s to the 'plan-led system' inaugurated by the 1991 Planning and Compensation Act. Neither formulation has proved very useful. If development control is simply an enabling activity which smoothes out the wrinkles to enable development to go ahead when and where it is proposed, then the development plan has little or no function. But the Planning and Compensation Act has opened up another equally damaging possibility. The impact on development control decision-making is not clear, but as we saw, the impact on plan-making has been dramatic. In an effort to ensure that development control decisions can be justified by the plan, some authorities have produced plans which are minutely prescriptive. There is an argument for saying that this slows the process of plan preparation bly increasing the potential for objection and reduces the prospective quality of plans. Larger issues may become lost in a welter of minor detail and plans become out of date by the time they are formally approved.

The development plan is not, of course, the only source of policy. We have already touched on the question of implicit values which inform development control decisions, whether these values are those of the planning profession or the public at large. As we have seen, these values are somehow concealed in references to policies whose prescriptions are clear but whose underlying rationale is not; such has been the case with green belts. Sometimes these values are implicit in references to good order, prosperity, seemliness, and above all, amenity. We are now so far removed from the sources of some of these ideas and policies that the time has come to explore them again. This suggests a return to the roots of the planning system in the kind of debate that has not really taken place since the 1940s.

Publicly held values in land-use planning are even more problematic. Much play has been made in the past 20 years of nimbyism, the naked protection of self-interest by communities well able to defend themselves by virtue of their money and expertise. Green belts are popular with the public because they are a good way of ensuring that views are maintained and new development in adjoining fields is held at bay. Of rather longer standing have been the attempts to use building and land-use control to maintain social exclusiveness. The Earl of Bedford wanted to attract the gentry and the aristocracy to the new development at Covent Garden. His successors strove to build for a genteel clientele north of Oxford Street and struggled to maintain the gentility thereafter. The Calthorpes, the Devonshires and George Wostenholm tried to do the same in the nineteenth century and were aided and abetted in that end by their lessees themselves. 'Maintaining the character of the area' has a strong overtone of social protectionism as well as aesthetic preference and has regularly been used in the late twentieth century to prevent new development. American zoning ordinances have been used to exactly the same effect in the USA, by prescribing a form of development which will of itself exclude the socially undesirable. Exploring the values that underwrite these sorts of decision takes us into distinctly murky water. What this approach to development does do is to highlight the blurred boundary between physical and aesthetic objectives and the social and intangible values for which they stand proxy.

Both the role of the development plan and the reference to implicit value systems raise important questions about how policy should be expressed. Yet policy-makers have always had the greatest difficulty in formulating criteria except in terms of measurable standards. In the end, there was not a great deal of difference between the way that constraints on residential development were expressed in planning schemes after 1909 and their expression in the bylaws before the passing of the Housing, Town Planning etc. Act. The motives had changed and with them the form of development, but the idea of prescribing fixed limits persisted. Much the same was true after 1947. Where we might have expected central government to define criteria for judging the material considerations that local authorities would need to take into account in reaching decisions on planning applications, instead there was a return, once again, to prescriptive, measurable standards. Something of the same kind has happened since 1991 in the plan-led system, with local authorities trying to fix limits in plans. A desire for fixed limits is of course fuelled by developers themselves. Not infrequently they have argued that they will follow limits providing they know what these limits are. The accusation levelled at local authorities is that they do not specify clearly the constraints that they wish to impose and the constraints vary over time. Yet a flexible system of development control requires a maturity of thinking about the criteria it uses if the full value of the system is to be realized.

The final significant area for debate has to do with conflict resolution. Of its very nature the control of development is about conflicting values, classically between public interest and private gain, but as we have seen, also between different levels of private interest. Some of the resolution of these conflicts must take place at the level of plan-making where general strategies need to be debated and indeed as far as possible determined. The trouble has always been that the acceptability of strategy is only really tested in its application in detail. The Conservative government found that out to its cost in the defeat of its policy to encourage new development in the Tillingham Hall and Bramshill Plantation cases. The Planning and Compensation Act has had the tendency to shift the place of dispute resolution about detail to the plan preparation stage when in fact that detail might have been reasonably left to the development control process. Objectors at the Bramshill Plantation inquiry argued that the inquiry was the wrong place in which to be determining a policy of a new settlement, and that it was less democratic than participation in the plan-making process in which future locations could be identified upstream of proposals. In fact, of course, the inquiry allowed for a very thorough airing not only of the arguments in favour of and against a particular development on a particular site, but also the more general questions of alternative locations for new development in a wider area. In part, of course, the success in dispute resolution depends on the process as much as on the level at which it takes place. Though public inquiries into appeals are not without limitations, they have nevertheless proved remarkably robust in their handling of disputes over future land use. Better that the detailed application of policy is hammered out at this level than it be allowed to obscure the process of plan preparation.

These four areas represent questions to be addressed rather than solutions. They lack the exalted certainty of the 'heroic' years of the 1940s and earlier when the need for controlling development became an established principle. Then, the good life that would be achieved by development control combined aesthetic harmony with social order and would see the replacement of the chaos of incompatible uses with clarity and convenience. These are no longer exactly the values of the twenty-first century. But the fact that they are no longer present values does not mean that people care any less passionately about their environment, nor that the appearance and the location of new development impinge any less on their perception of the way things should be. What is clearly not acceptable is that decisions should be imposed by a paternalistic government, by rapacious developers, or by the wilfulness of neighbours.

Development control has a value, therefore, not as a means of imposing an aesthetic canon nor of promoting a vision of an ordered environment. What it does offer is the place where such questions may be debated; it is in the process that so much of its worth resides. None of this should obscure the fact that it is a process that may all too easily be hijacked – whether by the nimbies or by society's real power brokers – nor that cosy consensus building is at best difficult and at worst impossible. But even those tortuous medieval discussions of leaky privies and dripping gutters point to the way in which the right to good living conditions might be explored. There are perhaps three things to say by way of conclusion. The first is to assert that the desire to influence the form and appearance of the built environment remains a reasonable object of a development control system. The second is to note the necessity for having a way of translating general policies and principles of the kind that are to be found in development plans into the specifics of a particular place or a particular site. The development control system has demonstrated its capacity to achieve this kind of translation. The third is to note the multiplicity of potential interests in the development process that the development control must mediate. Any attempt to reduce development control to a two-way relationship – between controller and controlled or neighbour and neighbour – without recognizing that others have a stake in the outcome impoverishes development control.

These are the key issues that must be faced if development control is to survive in the twenty-first century. The British development control system is a strange and unique creature whose potential is not always fully recognized. This book is written in the belief that development control matters and that it deserves better than it has generally received. The task ahead is one we shirk at our peril.

Bibliography

Acland, A.H.D. (1914) *Report of the Land Enquiry Committee*, Vol. 2. *Urban*. London: Hodder and Stoughton.

Adler, M. and Asquith, S. (eds.) (1981) *Discretion and Welfare*. London: Heinemann.

Aldridge, H.R. (1915) *The Case for Town Planning*. London: National Housing and Town Planning Council.

Ambrose, P. (1986) *Whatever Happened to Planning?* London: Methuen.

Ambrose, P. and Colenutt, R. (1975) *The Property Machine*. Harmondsworth, Middx.: Penguin.

Allmendinger, P. and Thomas, H. (1998) Planning and the new right, in Allmendinger, P. and Thomas, H. (eds.) *Urban Planning and the British New Right*. London, Routledge, pp. 1–20.

Architects' Journal (1983) The last picture show? *Architects' Journal*, **179**(50), pp. 16–17.

Ashworth, S. (1993) Plymouth and after (II). *Journal of Planning and Environment Law*, December, pp. 1105–1110.

Ashworth, W. (1954) *The Genesis of Mordern Town Planning: A Study in the Economic and Social History of the Nineteenth and Twentieth Centuries*. London: Routledge and Kegan Paul.

Babcock, R.F. (1966) *The Zoning Game*. Madison: University of Wisconsin Press.

Babcock, R.F. and Siemon, C.L. (1990) *The Zoning Game Revisited*. Cambridge, Mass.: Lincoln Institute of Land Policy.

Barbé, C. (2002) La genèse de la loi, *Droit de l'Aménagement, de l'Urbanisme et de l'Habitat*, Annuaire 2001. Paris: Dalloz, pp. 25–36.

Barker, A. and Couper, M. (1984) The art of quasi-judicial administration: the planning appeal and inquiry systems in England. *Urban Law and Policy*, **6**, pp. 363–476.

Barlow, M. (1940) *Report of the Royal Commission on the Distribution of Industrial Population*, Cmd. 6153. London: HMSO.

Barnes, T.G. (1971) The prerogative and environmental control of London building in the early 17th century: the lost opportunity. *Ecology Law Review*, **VI**, pp. 62–93.

Baron, T. (1980) Planning's biggest and least satisfied customer. *Proceedings of the Town and Country Planning Summer School*, 6–17 September, pp. 34–40 [Supplement to *The Planner*].

Bell, S. (1992) *Out of Order! The 1987 Use Classes Order: Problems and Proposals*. London: London Boroughs Association.

Bennett, B. (2002) Ups and downs for development control. *Town and Country Planning*, **71**(2), p. 49.

Bexfield, H. (1945*) A Short History of Sheffield Cutlery and the House of Wostenholm*. Sheffield: The author.

Booth, P. (1980) Speculative housing and the land market in London 1660-1730: four case studies. *Town Planning Review*, **51**(4), pp. 379–398.

Booth, P. (1996) *Controlling Development: Certainty and Discretion in Europe, the USA and Hong Kong*. London: UCL Press.

Booth, P. (2002) Nationalising development rights: the feudal origins of the British planning system. *Environment and Planning B: Planning and Design*, **29**, pp 129–139.

Booth, P. and Stafford, T. (1994) Revisions and modifications: the effect of change in French *plans d'occupation des sols, Environment and Planning B: Planning and Design*, **21**, pp. 305–322.

Brett-James, N.G. (1935) *The Growth of Stuart London*. London: George Allen and Unwin.

Brindley, T., Rydin, Y. and Stoker, G. (1996) *Remaking Planning: the Politics of Urban Change*, 2nd edition. London: Routledge.

Bristow, M.R. (1984) *Land-use Planning in Hong Kong: History, Policy and Procedures*. Oxford: Oxford University Press

Cabinet Office (1985) *Lifting the Burden*, White Paper, Cmd. 9571. London: HMSO.

Cameron, W.S. (1937) Problems arising under interim development control and during administration of operative planning schemes. *Journal of the Town Planning Institute*, **23**(2), pp. 38–46.

Campbell, H., Ellis, H., Gladwell, C. and Henneberry, J. (2000) Planning obligations, planning practice and land use. *Environment and Planning B: Planning and Design*, **27**, pp. 759–775.

Cannadine, D. (1980) *Lords and landlords: the aristocracy and the towns 1774–1967*. Leicester: Leicester University Press.

Cangi, E.C. (1993) Civilizing the people of Southeast Asia: Sir Thomas Raffles' town plan for Singapore. *Planning Perspectives*, **8**, pp. 166–187.

Cherry, G.E. (1974) *The Evolution of British Town Planning*. Leighton Buzzard, Bucks: Leonard Hill.

Cherry, G.E. (1996) *Town Planning in Britain since 1900*. Oxford: Blackwell.

Chew, H.M. and Kellaway, W. (eds.) (1973) *London Assize of Nuisance 1301–1431: a Calendar*. London Record Society, Vol. 10. Leicester: London Record Society.

Chew, H.M. and Weinbaum, M. (1970) *The London Eyre of 1244*. London Record Society Vol. 6. Leicester: London Record Society.

Clarke, L. (1992) *Building Capitalism: Historical Change and the Labour Process in the Production of the Built Environment*. London: Routledge.

Committee on Administrative Tribunals and Enquiries (Franks Committee) (1957) *Report*, Cmnd. 218. London: HMSO.

Committee on Standards in Public Life (1997) *Standards of Conduct in Local government in England, Scotland and Wales*, 3rd Report, Vol. 1 Report, Cmd. 3702–1. London: HMSO.

Committee on the Qualifications of Planners (Schuster Committee) (1950) *Report*, Cmd. 8059. London: HMSO.

Conseil d'Etat (1992) *L'urbanisme: pour un droit plus efficace*. Paris: La Documentation Française.

Consortium Developments (1984) *The Plan for New Country Towns*. London: Consortium Developments.

Cox, A. (1984) *Adversary Land and Politics*. Cambridge: Cambridge University Press.

Cronin, A. (1993) The elusive quality of certainty. *Planning Week*, **1**(4), pp. 16–17.

Crow, S. (1995) Third party appeals: will they work? Do we need them? *Journal of Planning and Environment Law*, pp. 376–387.

Crow, S. (1996) Development control: the child that grew up in the cold. *Planning Perspective*, **11**, pp. 399–411.

Crow, S. (1998) Planning gain: there must be a better way. *Planning Perspectives*, **13**, pp. 357–372.

Cruickshank, D. and Burton, N. (1990) *Life in the Georgian City*. London: Penguin.

Cullingworth, J.B. (1975) *Environmental Planning 1939–1969*, Vol. 1: *Reconstruction and Land Use Planning 1939-1947*. London: HMSO.

Cullingworth, J.B. (1980) *Environmental planning 1939-1969*, Vol. 4: *Land Values, Compensation and Betterment*. London: HMSO.

Cullingworth, J.B. (1993) *The Political Culture of Planning: American Land-use Planning in a Comparative Perspective*. New York: Routledge.

Cullingworth, J.B. and Nadin, V. (1997) *Town and Country planning in the U.K.*, 12th ed. London: Routledge.

Culpin, E.G. (ed.) (1909). *The Practical Application of Town Planning Powers*, Report of the National Town Planning Conference. London: King.

Dale, I. (ed.) (2000) *Labour Party General Election Manifestos 1900–1997*. London: Routledge.

Davies, H.W.E. (1980) The relevance of development control. *Town Planning Review*, **51**, pp. 5–17.

Davies, H.W.E., Edwards, D. and Rowley, A.R. (1986) The relationship between development plans, development control and appeals. *The Planner*, **72**(10), pp. 11–15.

Delafons, J. (2002) A short history of reform. *Town and Country Planning*, **71**(2), pp. 46–47.

Department of Employment (1986) *Building Businesses . . . Not Barriers*, White Paper, Cmd. 9794. London: HMSO.

Department of the Environment (1975) *Review of the Development Control System: Final Report by Mr. George Dobry, Q.C.*, Circular 113/75. London: HMSO.

Department of the Environment (1980) *Development Control: Policy and Practice*, Circular 22/80. London: HMSO.

Department of the Environment (1983) *Town and Country Planning Act 1971: Planning Gain*, Circular 22/83. London: HMSO.

Department of the Environment (1984*a*) *Land for Housing*, Circular 15/84. London: HMSO.

Department of the Environment (1984*b*) *Industrial Development*, Circular 16/84. London: HMSO.

Department of the Environment (1985) *Development and Employment*, Circular 14/85. London: HMSO.

Department of the Environment (1986) *The Future of Development Plans*. London: Department of the Environment.

Department of the Environment (1987) *Changes of Use of Buildings and Other Land: the Town and Country Planning (Use Classes) Order 1987*, Circular 13/87. London: HMSO.

Department of the Environment (1989) *The Future of Development Plans*, White Paper, Cmd. 569. London: HMSO.

Department of the Environment (1991) *Planning Obligations*, Circular 16/91. London: HMSO.

Department of the Environment (1992) *Housing*, Planning Policy Guidance Note 3. London: HMSO.

Department of the Environment (1997) *General Policy and Principles*. Planning Policy Guidance Note 1. London: HMSO.

Department of the Environment (1997) *Planning Obligations*, Circular 1/97. London: HMSO.

Department of the Environment, Transport and the Regions (1998) *Modernising Planning: Development Control and Development Plan Preparation*. London: HMSO.

Department of the Environment, Transport and the Regions (1999) *Towards an Urban Renaissance*, Final report of the Urban Task Force. London: E&FN Spon.

Department of the Environment, Transport and the Regions (2000) *Our Towns and Cities: the Future: Delivering the Urban Renaissance*, White Paper, Cmd 4911. London: The Stationery Office.

Department of Trade and Industry (1988) *Releasing Enterprise*, White Paper, Cmd. 512. London: HMSO.

Department of Transport, Local Government and the Regions (2001*a*) *Planning: Delivering a Fundamental Change*, Green Paper. London: The Stationery Office.

Department of Transport, Local Government and the Regions (2001*b*) *Planning Obligations: Delivering a Fundamental Change*, Consultation Paper. London: The Stationery Office.

Department of Transport, Local Government and the Regions (2002) *Consultation on Possible Changes to the Use Classes Order and Temporary Uses Provisions*. London: The Stationery Office.

Dobry, G. (1974a) *Review of the Development Control System: Interim Report*. London: HMSO.

Dobry, G. (1974b) *Control of Demolition*. London: HMSO.

Dobry, G. (1975) *Review of the Development Control System: Final Report*. London: HMSO.

Dyos, H.J. (1961) *Victorian Suburb: a Study of the Growth of Camberwell*. Leicester: Leicester University Press.

Encyclopaedia of Planning Law (1991) *Monthly Bulletin*, July 1991. London: Butterworth.

Essex County Council (1973) *A Design Guide for Residential Areas*. Chelmsford: Essex County Council.

Evenson, N. (1980) *Paris: a Century of Change, 1878–1978*. New Haven, Conn.: Yale University Press.

Gaskell, S.M. (1983) *Building Control: National Legislation and the Introduction of Local Bye-laws in Victorian England*. London: Bedford Square Press.

Gaudemet, J. (1995) *Dominium-imperium*: les deux pouvoirs dans la Rome ancienne. *Droits*, **22**, pp. 3–17.

George, M.D. (1925) *London Life in the 18th Century*. London: Kegan, Paul, Trench, Trubner.

Gibbon, I.G. (1922) Zoning, in Heath, P.M. (ed.) *A Record of the Town Planning Exhibition held in the Town Hall, Manchester, 9–14 October 1922*, Manchester: The Manchester and District Joint Planning Advisory Committee, pp. 154–178.

Gilbart, A. (1993). Plymouth and after (I). *Journal of Planning and Environment Law*, December, pp. 1099–1104.

Grant, M. (1982) *Urban Planning Law*. London: Sweet and Maxwell.

Grant, M. (2000) Human rights and due process in planning. *Journal of Planning and Environment Law*, pp. 1215–1225.

Gray, K.J. and Symes, P.D. (1981) *Real Property and Real People: Principles of Land Law*. London: Butterworth.

Grimley J.R. Eve (1992) *The Use of Planning Agreements*. London: HMSO.

Haar, C.M. (ed.) (1984) *Cities, Law and Social Policy: Learning from the British*. Lexington, Mass: Lexington Books.

Haar, C.M. (1989) Reflections on *Euclid*: social contract and private purpose, in Haar, C.M. and Kayden, J.R. (eds.) *Zoning and the American Dream: Promises still to keep*. Chicago: The Planners Press, pp. 333–354.

Hall, P. (2001) How much better than no bread? *Town and Country Planning*, **70**(1), pp. 2, 3.

Hall, P. (2002) Blowing up bridges. *Town and Country Planning*, **71**(2), p. 51.

Harper, R.H. (1985) *Victorian Building Regulations*. London: Mansell.

Harris, J. and Higgott, G. (eds.) (1989) *Inigo Jones: Complete Architectural Drawings*. New York: Drawing Centre.

Harrison, J. (1984) Planning fees – right third time? *Journal of Planning and Environment Law*, July, pp. 472–484.

Harrison, M. (1972) Development control: the influence of political, legal and ideological factors. *Town Planning Review*, **43**(4), pp. 254–274.

Harrison, M. (1975) Dobry and social policy, *The Planner*, **61**, pp. 236–237.

Healey, P., Purdue, M. and Ennis, F. (1995) *Negotiating Development: Rationales and Practice for Development Obligations and Planning Gain*. London: E&FN Spon.

Heap, D. (1980) Planning bargaining – the pros and cons: or how much can we stand? *Journal of Planning and Environment Law*, October, pp. 632–637.

Hennock, E.P. (1973) *Fit and Proper Persons: Ideal and Reality in 19th Century Local Government*. London: Edward Arnold.

Herbert-Young, N. (1998) Central government and statutory planning under the Town Planning Act 1909. *Planning Perspectives*, **13**, pp. 341–358.

Hill, H.A. and Nicholls, A.W. (1937) *The Complete Law of Town and Country Planning and the Restriction of Ribbon Development Act*. London: Butterworth and Shaw.

Holdsworth, Sir W. (1927) *An Historical Introduction to the Land Law*. London: Oxford University Press.

Home, R. (1992) The evolution of the use classes order *Town Planning Review*, **63**(2), pp.187–201.

House of Commons (1977) *Planning Procedures*, 8th Report of the Expenditure Committee, Session 1976–77, 3 vols. London: HMSO.

House of Commons (1978) *Planning Procedures*, 11th Report of the Expenditure Committee, Session 1977–78. London: HMSO.

Humber, R. (1990) Prospects and problems. *Proceedings of the Town and Country Planning Summer School*, 23 February, pp. 15–19.

Jencks, C. (1988) *The Prince, the Architects and New Wave Monarchy*. London: Academy Editions.

Johnson, B.H. (1952) *Berkeley Square to Bond Street*. London: John Murray.

Johnston, B. (2000) Planners ready to tackle rights issue. *Planning*, 29 September, pp. 12–13.

Journal of Planning and Environment Law (1978) Current topics: the General Development Order – amendments withdrawn. *Journal of Planning and Environment Law*, pp. 2–4.

Journal of Planning and Environment Law (1984) Notes of cases: Grampian Regional Council vs. City of Aberdeen District Council. *Journal of Planning and Environment Law*, pp. 590–592.

Journal of Planning and Environment Law (1995) Notes of cases: Tesco Stores Ltd. vs. Secretary of State for the Environment and others. *Journal of Planning and Environment Law*, pp. 581–604.

Journal of the Town Planning Institute (1937) Debates. *Journal of the Town Planning Institute*, **24**, p. 303.

Journal of the Town Planning Institute (1959) Report of conference: Stocktaking: 10 years of development control. *Journal of the Town Planning Institute*, **45**(2), p. 49.

Journal of the Town Planning Institute (1960) Report of S.E. Branch meeting. *Journal of the Town Planning Institute*, **46**(5), p. 124.

Julian, J. (1914) *An Introduction to Town Planning*. London: Charles Griffin.

Keeble, L. (1952) *Principles and Practice of Town and Country Planning*. London: Estates Gazette.

Keeble, L. (1957) The planning situation. *Journal of the Town Planning Institute*, **43**(7), pp. 174–177.

Keeble, L. (1983) *Town Planning made plain*. London: Construction Press.

Lai, Lawrence W-C. (1998) The leasehold system as a means of planning by contract. *Town Planning Review*, **69**(3), pp. 249–275.

Lambert, R. (1962) Central and local relations in mid-Victorian England: the Local Government Act Office 1858–1871. *Victorian Studies*, **6**(2), pp. 128–150.

Larkin, J.F. and Hughes, P.L. (eds.) (1973) *Stuart Royal Proclamations*, Vol. I, *Royal Proclamations of King James I 1603–1625*. Oxford: Oxford University Press.

Larkin, J.F. and Hughes, P.L. (eds.) (1983) *Stuart Royal Proclamations*, Vol. II, *Royal proclamations of King Charles I 1625–1644*. Oxford: Clarendon Press.

Lees, A. (1993) *Enquiry into the Planning System in North Cornwall*. London: HMSO.

Lindblom, K. (2001) Development and democracy: the place of human rights in our planning system after Alconbury. *Journal of Planning and Environment Law: Planning Law: the cappuccino years*. pp. 3–23.

Lock, D. (2002) Reality check required. *Town and Country Planning*, **71**(2), pp. 42–45.

Loengard, J.S. (1989) *London Viewers and their Certificates*, London Record Society Vol. 26. London: London Record Society.

Marshall, R.J. (1993) Town planning in Sheffield, in Binfield, C., Childs, R., Harper, R., Hey, D., Martin, D. and Tweedale, G. (eds.) *A History of the City of Sheffield Society 1843–1993*, Vol. 2. Sheffield Society: Sheffield Academic Press, pp. 17–32.

McAuslan, P. (1975) *Land Law and Planning: Cases, Materials and Text*. London: Weidenfeld and Nicolson.

McAuslan, P. (1980) *The Ideologies of Planning Law*. Oxford: Pergamon.

McKellar, E. (1999) *The Birth of Modern London; the Development and Design of the City 1660–1720*. Manchester: Manchester University Press.

McLaren, J.P.S. (1983) Nuisance law and the industrial revolution: some lessons from social history *Oxford Journal of Legal Studies*, **3**, pp. 155–221.

McLoughlin, J.B. (1973) *Control and Urban Planning*. London: Faber and Faber.

McLoughlin, J.B. and Webster, J.N. (*c*.1970) *Development Control in Britain*. Manchester: University of Manchester, Centre for Urban and Regional Research.

Miller, M. (1989) *Letchworth: the First Garden City*. Chichester: Phillimore.

Miller, M. (1992) *Raymond Unwin: Garden Cities and Town Planning*. Leicester: Leicester University Press.

Minett, J. (1974) The Housing, Town Planning etc. Act 1909. *The Planner*, **60**, pp. 676–680.

Mingay, G.E. (1963) *English Landed Society in the 18th Century*. London: Routledge and Kegan, Paul.

Ministry of Health (1922) *Memorandum 70/D*. London: The Ministry of Health.

Ministry of Health (1933) *Town and Country Planning Act*, Circular 1305. London: HMSO.

Ministry of Housing and Local Government (1953) *Planning Appeals*, Circular 61/53. London: HMSO.

Ministry of Housing and Local Government (1955) *Green Belts*, Circular 42/55. London: HMSO.

Ministry of Housing and Local Government (1967) *Management Study on Development Control*. London: HMSO.

Ministry of Housing and Local Government (1968) *The Use of Conditions in Planning Permissions*, Circular 5/68. London: HMSO.

Ministry of Housing and Local Government/Department of the Environment (1969–1977) *Development Control Policy Notes 1–15*. London: HMSO.

Ministry of Local Government and Planning (1951a) *Drafting of Planning Permissions*, Circular 58/51. London: HMSO.

Ministry of Local Government and Planning (1951b) *Town and Country Planning 1943–1951: a Progress Report*. London: HMSO.

Ministry of Town and Country Planning (1947) *Notation for Survey Maps*, Circular 29. London: HMSO.

Ministry of Town and Country Planning (1948a) *Survey for Development Plans*, Circular 40. London: HMSO.

Ministry of Town and Country Planning (1948b) *Town and Country Planning (Development Plans) Regulations*, Circular 59. London: HMSO.

Ministry of Town and Country Planning (1949a) *Report of the Survey*, Circular 63. London: HMSO.

Ministry of Town and Country Planning (1949b) *Town and Country Planning (General Development) Amendment Order*, Circular 67. London: HMSO.

Morrill, J. (1993) *The Nature of the English Revolution*. Harlow: Longman.

Moss, B.A. (1935) Is town planning a failure? *Journal of the Town Planning Institute*, **22**(4/5), pp. 157–159.

Muthesius, S. (1982) *The English Terraced House*. New Haven, Conn: Yale University Press.

Neale, R.S. (1975) The bourgeoisie, historically, has played the most revolutionary part, in Kamenka, E. and Neale, R.S. (eds.) *Feudalism, Capitalism and Beyond*. London: Edward Arnold, pp. 84–102.

Nettlefold, J.G. (1914) *Practical Town Planning*. London: St. Catherine Press.

Offer, A. (1981) *Property and politics 1870–1914: Landownership, Law and Urban Development in England*. London: Cambridge University Press.

Olsen, D.J. (1973) House upon house: estate development in London and Sheffield, in Dyos, H.J. and Wolff, M. (eds.) *The Victorian City: Images and Realities*, 2 vols. London: Routledge and Kegan Paul.

Olsen, D.J. (1982) *Town planning in London: the 18th and 19th Centuries*, 2nd ed. New Haven, Conn.: Yale University Press.

PA Cambridge Economic Consultants (1995) *Final Evaluation of Enterprise Zones*. London: HMSO.

Pearce, B.J. (1981) Property rights versus development control. *Town Planning Review*, **52**(1), pp. 41–60.

Pearl, V. (1961) *London and the Outbreak of the Puritan Revolution; City Government and National Politics*. Oxford: Oxford University Press.

Perkin, H. (1989). *The rise of professional society: England since 1880*. London: Routledge.

Planner (1989*a*) Green light for Foxley Wood. *The Planner*, **75**(12), 14 July.

Planner (1989*b*) Final flurry for Foxley Wood. *The Planner*, **75**(24), 6 October.

Planning (1978) Planning complaints still rising. *Planning*, no. 265, 28 April.

Planning (1980) Giant offices felled along with local plan. *Planning*, no. 378, 25 July.

Planning (1981*a*) Special orders from Marsham Street. *Planning*, no. 423, 19 June.

Planning (1981*b*) Uncertainty over policy on orders. *Planning*, no. 444, 13 November.

Planning (1983) Development order beats eight week limit. *Planning*, no. 527, 15 July.

Planning (1990) County plans likely to retain statutory force. *Planning*, no. 887, 21 September.

Planning (1991) Young reinforces plan lead in control system. *Planning*, no. 919, 24 May.

Planning (2001*a*) Falconer launches first speed attack. *Planning*, no. 1426, 6 July.

Planning (2001*b*) Falconer vows to 'sort out' planning quagmire. *Planning*, no. 1444, 9 November.

Planning Advisory Group (1965) *The Future of Development Plans*. London: HMSO.

Potter, S. (1986) New towns in the real world. *Town and Country Planning*, **55**(11), pp. 304–308.

Price, C. (1975) *Islington and the Planning Acts: a Critical Enquiry*. London: CIP Development Securities Ltd.

Property Advisory Group (1981) *Planning Gain*. London: HMSO.

Punter, J.V. (1986) A history of aesthetic control, Part 1. *Town Planning Review*, **57**(4), pp. 351–358.

Purdue, M. (1994) The impact of section 54a. *Journal of Planning and Environmental Law*, May, pp. 399–407.

Rasmussen, S.E. (1967) *London the Unique City*, reprint ed. Cambridge, Mass: MIT Press.

Reade, E.J. (1982) Section 52 and corporatism in planning. *Journal of Planning and Environment Law*, January, pp.8–16.

Reeder, D.A. (1960) The politics of urban leaseholds in late Victorian England, *International Review of Social History*, **6**, pp. 413–430.

Robinson, H. (1936) The work of the planning officer. *Journal of the Town Planning Institute*, **22**(4/5), pp. 77–87.

Royal Institute of British Architects (ed.) (1911) *Transactions of the Town Planning Conference, London 10–15 October 1910*. London: Royal Institute of British Architects.

Schaffer, F. (1974) The Town and Country Planning Act 1947. *The Planner*, **60**(5), pp. 690–695.

Sharp, T. (1940) *Town Planning*. Harmondsworth: Penguin.

Sheppard, F.H.W. (ed.) (1970) *The Parish of St. Paul, Covent Garden*, Survey of London, Vol. 36. London: Athlone Press.

Sheppard, F.H.W. (ed.) (1977) *The Grosvenor Estate in Mayfair, Part I, General History*, Survey of London, Vol. 39. London: Athlone Press.

Slough Estates (1979) *Industrial Development: a Case Study in Factory Building*. Slough: Slough Estates.

Stainton, J.H. (1924) *The Making of Sheffield 1865–1914*. Sheffield: E Weston & Sons.

Steele, R. (ed.) (1910) *A Bibliography of Royal Proclamations of the Tudor and Stuart Sovereigns 1485–1714*, Vol. I, *England and Wales*. Oxford: Oxford University Press.

Steeley, G. (2002) Green light? *Town and Country Planning*, **71**(3), pp. 90–91.

Summerson, J. (1945) *Georgian London*. London: Pleiades Books.

Summerson, J. (1966) *Inigo Jones*. Harmondsworth: Penguin Books.

Sutcliffe, A.R. (1981) *Towards the Planned City: Germany, Britain, the United States and France 1780–1914*. Oxford: Basil Blackwell.

Thornley, A. (1993) *Urban planning under Thatcherism: the Challenge of the Market*, 2nd edition. London: Routledge.

Town and Country Planning Association (1980) Charges for planning applications. *Town and Country Planning*, **49**(9), p. 307.

Town Planning Institute (1916) *Papers and Discussions Vol. 3, Memorial to Right Hon. Lord Rhondda*, following p. 41.

Underwood, J. (1981) Development control: a case study of discretion in action, in Barrett, S. and Fudge, C. (eds.) *Policy and Action*. London: Methuen, pp. 143–162.

Unwin, R. (1909) *Town planning in practice*. London: T. Fisher Unwin.

Uthwatt, A.A. (1941) *Expert Committee on Compensation and Betterment: Interim Report*. Cmd. 6291. London: HMSO.

Uthwatt, A.A. (1942) *Expert Committee on Compensation and Betterment: Final Report*, Cmd. 6386. London: HMSO.

Viner, C. (1791) *A General Abridgement of Law and Equity*, 2nd ed. London: Robinson, Payne and Brooke.

Wakeford, R. (1990) *American Development Control: Parallels and Paradoxes from an English Perspective*. London: HMSO.

Waldron, J. (1990) *The Law*. London: Routledge.

Westergaard, J. (1964) Land use planning since 1951. *Town Planning Review*, **35**(3), pp. 219–237.

Widdicombe, D. (1986) *The Conduct of Local Authority Business*, Report of the Committee of Inquiry into Local Authority Business. London: HMSO.

Wike, C.F. (1913) *Development of Town Planning and Housing in Sheffield,* Conference of the Institution of Municipal and County Engineers, Gt. Yarmouth, 16–17 July, p. 113.

Wraith, R.E. and Lamb, G.B. (1971) *Public Inquiries as an Instrument of Government.* London: Allen and Unwin.

Index